Praise for
A People's History of the Peculiar

"*A People's History of the Peculiar* is the perfect desk reference for ordinary insane people. Nick Belardes is a force of nature."
—Brad Listi, author of *Attention. Deficit. Disorder.*

"And I thought my friends were weird. Reading *A People's History of the Peculiar* is like wandering around the Epcot Center on hallucinogens—colorful, crazy, occasionally terrifying, and always exciting. If you're a trivia buff with a penchant for the madcap, do yourself a favor and buy this book."
—Matthew Shaer, *Christian Science Monitor*

"Nick Belardes is an imaginative writer with a truly new and unique voice—he will both startle and thrill you with his stories that pop out from the dark, like the teasing dangers in Mr. Toad's Wild Ride."

—Jessica Anya Blau,
author of *The Summer of Naked Swim Parties*

"For the reader who needs to know why the characters in *Dilbert* don't have mouths, your oracle has arrived. *A People's History of the Peculiar* is every bit as silly as it is informative. Belardes has ransacked the useless information files and uncovered some gems."
—Jonathan Evison, author of *All About Lulu*

A PEOPLE'S HISTORY OF THE PECULIAR

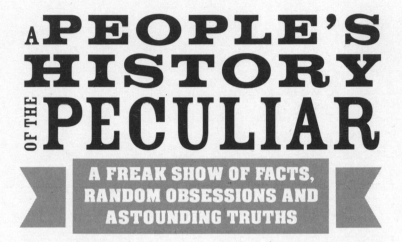

A PEOPLE'S HISTORY OF THE PECULIAR

A FREAK SHOW OF FACTS, RANDOM OBSESSIONS AND ASTOUNDING TRUTHS

BY NICK BELARDES
FOREWORD BY CAROLINE LEAVITT

ViVa
EDITIONS

Published in the United States by Viva Editions,
an imprint of Cleis Press, Inc., 2246 Sixth Street, Berkeley CA 94710.

Printed in the United States.
Cover design: Scott Idleman/Blink
Cover photo: iStockphoto
Text design: Frank Wiedemann

10 9 8 7 6 5 4 3 2 1

Trade paper ISBN: 978-1-936740-83-3
E-book ISBN: 978-1-936740-92-5

Library of Congress Cataloging-in-Publication Data

Belardes, Nick.
 A people's history of the peculiar : a freak show of facts, random obsessions & astounding truths / Nick Belardes.
    pages cm
  ISBN 978-1-936740-83-3 (pbk.)
1. Curiosities and wonders. I. Title.
AG243.B416 2014
001.9--dc23
                                    2013043799

CONTENTS

IX FOREWORD
by Caroline Leavitt

XII RANDOM THOUGHTS
by Brad Listi

XIV INTRODUCTION
BOYHOOD MAPS, MODERN-DAY TRIVIA

1 CHAPTER 1
AMASSED FROM THE PAST:
Curious and Fantastic Facts from the Archives of History

40 CHAPTER 2
UNNATURAL SCIENCES:
Bizarre Discoveries from Biology to Outer Space

67 CHAPTER 3
PUZZLING AILMENTS:
Most Mysterious Maladies

95 CHAPTER 4
IDIOSYNCRATIC INVENTIONS:
Technologies We Depend On Every Day
and Some Useless Contraptions

118 CHAPTER 5
ODD OCCUPATIONS:
Some of the Dirtiest, Weirdest Jobs That
You Never Wanted but Have to Know About

135 CHAPTER 6
SATURDAY NIGHT FEVER:
Popular Films for Obsessive Fans

163 CHAPTER 7
ECCENTRIC AUTHORS AND FANTASTIC ART:
Great and Little-Known Works by the
Wildly (and Weirdly) Creative

193 CHAPTER 8
MYSTERIOUS PLACES:
Exploring Some of the World's Most
Mystifying Nooks and Crannies

245 BIBILIOGRAPHY

257 ACKNOWLEDGMENTS

258 ABOUT THE AUTHOR

FOREWORD

When I was 10, I read a story in an old, pulpy *Weird Tales* magazine of my father's about how there were invisible holes in the atmosphere, portals that would lead to another dimension, and you could slip through them without warning. "No one who ever went through has ever come back," the text warned, but I took this as a fabulous invitation. Who knew if those people even wanted to come back? What if what those people discovered in their new environment was a thousand times better than in their old? I immediately went outside to try to find that hole, and it wasn't until I disrupted a party my parents were having by repeatedly walking with my arms outstretched through the rooms that my father got to the bottom of my obsession and told me you couldn't believe a story that crazy, that the magazine had made it up. That, of course, escalated my love for make-believe. I saw its power! I began writing novels, making things up that seemed so real I believed in them the same way I did in those portals. But that didn't stop me from still looking for those holes, and it certainly didn't stop my love for the weird, the unusual, the outrageous. The world, I knew, was stunningly full of real-life marvels if we could just stop to look for them.

Which brings us to Nick Belardes.

Like all wonderful things, Nick came as a surprise to me. He was a voice on Facebook who was funny, smart, deep with feeling, and surprising. We were both writers drawn to the bizarre. We quickly became friends. But Nick has many layers, and that includes thinking about life and people and planets and everything else with or without mass in a brand new way. I mean, truly, what's more crucial than a sense of wonder? This book is a compendium of blisteringly funny facts, outrageous anecdotes, and all kinds of zany information you really need to know.

Come on, don't you really want to know that when viewed from above, the Capitol dome actually resembles the Egyptian symbol for eternal life? Don't you want to be the life of the party by telling Nick's story of how Jefferson's grandson was an ax murderer? If you hate your job and wish you could do anything else, Nick gives you oddball choices of how your working life could be weirder, wilder—or perhaps worse. Want to be a dog treat taster? What about a fortune cookie writer? (I want this job, and so did Lisa Yang, who wrote 20 fortunes a week.)

This book is just plain equal opportunity out-there. Nick ponders whether or not Hello Kitty haters really hate. He doles out delectable tales about exploding pythons that you are not going to be able to wait to share with friends. And admit it, don't you really want to know the right table manners for a cannibal feast? (Which fork is for the eyes, again?) There are vampire fish swimming through the pages and discussions of robot faces—a riotous compendium of everything any smart, curious, or bordering-on-the-insane person would want to know about and explore.

But what's best about Nick's book is his voice—the "come on a journey with me" delight, the infectious zoom, the Wile E. Coyote smarts—are all here. Nick makes you look at things differently, with a kind of awe—and isn't that what life is really about? To tell you the truth, this is the book—the crazy diamond oracle—that I'm leaving out on the coffee table as a kind of litmus test for guests. If they pick it up, they've won a place in my heart. If they read it they can be my friend forever, and if they start quoting from it, why, we're kindred souls. And who knows, maybe there are holes in the universe leading to other dimensions. If anyone can tease out that fact, I know it's going to be Nick.

Caroline Leavitt
USA Today and *New York Times* bestselling author of *Is This Tomorrow* and *Pictures of You*

RANDOM THOUGHTS

Imagine: You're walking through an open green field in springtime. Beautiful day. Perfect weather: slight breeze.
But all is not right. Something dreadful is weighing on you. It is a time of flux and crisis. You move through the tall grasses oblivious to the surrounding beauty. And for a while, you forget that you're even walking. For a while, you forget that you're even *alive*.

And yet you have come to these pasturelands seeking relief. You have come to these fertile grasses in search of perspective and levity.

And eventually—after, say, 30 minutes or so—you wake up. You remember your original purpose. You catch yourself and separate yourself from the incessant stream of thought. You stop, take a deep breath, and gaze upward, to the sky. And I mean you *really* look at it. You really take a moment to ponder it.

And you feel better.

There is something very primal about this simple act—something deeply profound and totally ordinary. Human beings have been doing it since the beginning of time. It might be the easiest and most effective way to forget ourselves, to remember how utterly small we are, and how utterly connected we are to the greater cosmic machinery.

We are utterly connected to the greater cosmic machinery.

This is very natural. It is also very weird.

Right now, for better or worse, we are situated on a giant sphere of whirling matter in an ocean of infinite blackness.

It is important to remember this fact.

Another good thing to remember: Dinosaurs lived here once. Reptiles. Millions of them. They dominated this place. Millions of years ago. Some of them were as small as hens.

Nick Belardes is a writer who remembers these kinds of things. He is a man with a deep appreciation for the epic, fundamental strangeness of our existence. And now he has written a book that is, in its own unique way, a heartfelt testimony to our timeless cosmic plight.

A People's History of the Peculiar is designed to keep you rooted in an appropriate sense of disbelief. It might function well as a desk reference or as night reading on a bedside table. It could also be useful in a bathroom, or on an airplane, or in a hospital bed, or in a prison cell. Take it to the desert and read it around the campfire. It will serve as a pleasant reminder that no one really knows what the hell is going on around here.

Brad Listi
Los Angeles

BOYHOOD MAPS, MODERN-DAY TRIVIA

When I was a boy I got my first taste of trivia through maps. I'd lock myself in my room and gaze at big drawings of America or theme park foldouts. I looked for all the little things: the most hidden place names and most secluded park rides. They were like the mazes you get in grade school. Trace from point A to point B. Find your way out. The dead ends were always the most mysterious because you had to lose yourself to get there. And then there was all the trivia that went along with those attractions: when the rides were built, the length of the roller coaster tracks, what kind of technology was involved, and what was unique about each ride.

My favorite map wasn't that of Six Flags Magic Mountain, Great America, or Disneyland (which came in at a close second—who couldn't love a map of Adventureland?). No, as a boy, my favorite was the oddest map I'd ever seen. Created in 1981 by Sergio Aragones, "A MAD Pictorial Map of the United States" was tucked into a copy of *MAD* magazine that I bought at a grocery store. Okay, my mother bought it. I threw it in the grocery cart when she wasn't looking. Anyway, I ripped the map out and plastered it to my wall, studying it for all the smallest yet most imaginative reasons.

Its intricate drawings depicted smoggy California, mad oilmen, cliff dwellings, dinosaur bones, and annoying tourists—yes, even travelers are a mystery. Even the map's guilty-looking cartoony hot dog cart guy slopping relish on a New York dog was filled with tiny bits of information. It's amazing how many books filled with trivia I read as a child just from looking at that map.

Little did I realize as I later worked on a master's degree in history and dug through 16th- and 17th-century maps of the early Americas—any historical maps, really—that I was so interested because of the trivial aspects. Unknown mountain ranges, unexplored regions, mythical lakes and rivers. Such mysterious places!

Naturally I became interested in odd facts. After scribbling pen and inks and paintings for several years, I fell back into the trivia-related part of my life: history. It's truly the discipline of odditics and trivia. I gobbled it up, studying explorations, events, cultures, and shared tragedies for all their unique little details. I encountered biohistory and dug in to uncover many puzzling ailments from Earth's afflicted past. And then I peered into American literary history in the mid-20th century for all the bizarre details that so often mark the journeys of writers.

Later, after college and teaching history, I would draw maps: high-tech maps detailing wireless connectivity in factories, between radio towers, even on farmland. The world had gone wireless and these people needed maps!

And then there were more maps as I drew an entire series for Jonathan Evison's novel *West of Here*. They were odd, cartoonish maps of the American Northwest, not unlike old Sergio Aragones maps whose pop-culture drawings and witty sarcasm brought the most trivial aspects of geography, people, history, news, culture, and even invention into picturesque form.

As I think back, Aragones's work was one of my most random obsessions. I couldn't get enough of the cartoons he drew in the margins and that great big colorful map of his that I can still envision in boyhood reflections. When I think about it, I truly became his map: an artist and a historian attracted to the weird and unusual in people and culture. I'm really just a reflection of society's love for such oddities. Just read the news. There's always a bizarre story up near the front-page headlines that feeds all the souls out there hungry for such weird information.

I'll take what Listi says about being connected to something greater than ourselves just one step further: We are utterly connected to searching for *meaning* within the greater cosmic machinery. Sure, we recognize that connection. But the meaning we hunger for is like the muse Clio—ever elusive yet revealing glimpses in the oddest ways. We can't help but continue grasping. She can't help but continue taunting.

It's so funny to think about the routes we can trace, and where they take us. That's often what people do, you know— follow their obsessions. I dare you to trace your own and jot them down or realize new random obsessions from reading this book. Write them in the margins if you must.

It makes me smile to think readers might be like that boy who opened all those maps years ago. Maybe *A People's History of the Peculiar* is a book of maps after all. Unfolded, it becomes a doorway. Walk through into a book of knowledge, places, and journeys, like all those great little Aragones drawings from my childhood that were so telling about history, ideas, people, and mysterious places.

Nick Belardes

CHAPTER 1

AMASSED FROM THE PAST: CURIOUS AND FANTASTIC FACTS FROM THE ARCHIVES OF HISTORY

E xamining the past, one must understand whether history comprises "everything that happened," as philosopher R.G. Collingwood once wrote, or just whatever the written record illuminates. Dr. Oliver Rink, a professor of early Dutch America, once explained history as a drunk man searching for his lost keys under a lamppost. When the man was asked why he was searching near the lamppost while his car was a block away, in the dark, Rink imagined the drunkard saying, "Because there's light over here." If history is the light cast by that streetlamp, how much of the past is left to be illuminated and discovered?

The ever-changing prism of perspectives that defines our present also transforms long-discovered details of the past. That's because historians are always experimenting with new approaches to reinterpret wars, peoples, culture, economics, and politics. History is under constant pressure in the present to shake the dustrags of past interpretations and reexamine what's underneath. But, of course, that only leads to more questions and further mystery.

In "Amassed from the Past" you will get a look at many topics, including a peek at witchcraft in early America ("To Burn or Not to Burn"). Don't even begin to think historians are done examining the Puritan obsession with the idea of Satanic people in their midst. You will read an account of a bizarre sighting by the maidservant Tituba. In "Did Napoleon's Gastric Secret Cost Him Waterloo?" I examine the idea that an ailment affecting one man could have a great impact on the outcome of history. In "Why Obama Was Sworn In as President in Washington, D.C." I look at the how yellow fever epidemics in the 1790s could have prevented the construction of the capital in the most enlightened city in America. Perhaps you didn't know that Philadelphia was once called the federal city? Many wanted the capital there.

One of the greatest American mysteries revolves around what happened to the lost colony of Roanoke Island in North Carolina in the late 1500s. Did the colony perish at the hands of hostile natives? What were the cryptic tree carvings found at the site? We'll look at an original source document that reveals more in "The Strange Fires of Roanoke." In "September 11, 1775" I reveal a connection between tragic historical events and the idea of government betrayal. You'll find even more enigmatic history in sections on Christopher Columbus's ship's log, Thomas Jefferson's mental state and ax murderer grandson, the apocalypse of 2012, a note from the Kennedy assassination hearings, and a letter doubting President Abraham Lincoln. In reading this chapter you'll find that while history constantly presents itself as fact, it really may be only a fuzzy glimpse of time past and just an elusive grab at the idea of truth.

TO BURN OR NOT TO BURN

Historian John Putnam Demos points out in his 1982 book *Entertaining Satan* that so-called witches of 17th-century America were in reality men and women, like Rachel Clinton and John Godfrey, who were different, troublesome, and perhaps a bit insane. Of course, you can go right to source material and open up the *Records of Salem Witchcraft*, a collection of 17th-century documents gathered in 1864. And while historians examine such documents and come up with theory upon theory for whether there really were witches in Salem or it was all a mass hysteria caused by oppression and accusations between genders and classes, one can't help but get a chill when reading some of the maidservant Tituba's words as she was examined in 1691:

THE EXAMINATION OF TITIBE

(H) Titibe, whan evil spirit have you familiarity with?
(T) None.
(H) Why do you hurt these children?
(T) I do not hurt them.
(H) Who is it, then?
(T) The Devil for ought I know.
(H) Did you never see the devil?
(T) The devil came to me and bid me serve him.
(H) Who have you seen?
(T) Four women sometimes hurt the children.
(H) Who were they?
(T) Goode Osburne and Sarah Good and I doe know who the other were. Sarah Good and Osburne would have me hurt the children but I would not. She further saith there was a tale man of Boston that she did see.
(H) When did you see them?
(T) Last night at Boston.

(H) What did they say to you?

(T) They said, hurt the children.

(H) And did you hurt them?

(T) No there is 4 women and one man they hurt the children and they lay all upon me and they tell me if I will not hurt the children they will hurt me.

(H) But did you not hurt them?

(T) Yes, but I will hurt them no more.

(H) Are you not sorry you did hurt them?

(T) Yes.

(H) And then doe you hurt them?

(T) They say hurt the children or wee will doe worse to you.

(H) What have you seen?

(T) A man come to me and say serve me.

(H) What service?

(T) Hurt the children, and last night there was an appearance that said kill the children and if I would no go on hurting the children they would do worse to me.

(H) What is the appearance you see?

(T) Sometimes it is like a hog and sometimes like a great dog, this appearance shee saith shee did see 4 times.

THE 45 DEATHS OF TECUMSEH

Born in 1768 and dead in 1812, the mystical Shawnee, Tecumseh, rallied Native American tribes during a crucial time in U.S. history. Strangely, there are more than 45 accounts of his death. No one can seem to agree on who killed him or under what circumstances.

IS THERE AN IRAQ WAR SYNDROME?

Historian Howard Zinn, author of *A People's History of the United States*, writes, "The 'disease' has shown up again," suggesting that the fragging of officers during the Vietnam War and the symptoms of "Vietnam Syndrome" are reappearing in Iraq with soldiers in revolt. Zinn claims it is because the war in Iraq is steeped in deceptions such as supposed "weapons of mass destruction" and 9/11 connections. He adds that as many as 5,000 U.S. deserters have fled to Canada yet they are rarely discussed in the U.S. media. Reasons for desertion have included sexual harassment, harassment from officers, and war atrocities. Zinn's discussion of desertions leads to this paradox pervading the American military in Iraq: It was wrong to invade but right to remain.

RANDOM DESERTION TALES

ROBIN LONG: In 2005, this war deserter fled to Canada. He was later deported to America, which sent a message to U.S. servicemen that Canada wasn't the option it once was for war deserters seeking refugee status.

HIDING FOR 60 YEARS: Two Japanese military men, 87-year-old Yoshio Yamakawa and 83-year-old Sudzuki Nakauti, were found deep in the jungles of the Philippines island of Mindanao. They had deserted the Imperial Japanese Army more than 60 years earlier during World War II.

THE CRACKDOWN: In 2007, the *New York Times* reported that the number of deserters and those with unauthorized absences rose sharply, resulting in thousands of negative discharges and prison for even combat-tested soldiers.

THE FRENCH WOODS: Lt. Glenn Gray was on counterintelligence duty in November 1944 when he found a Pennsylvanian deserter in some French woods. The deserter was accustomed to camping out and intended to stay until the war's end. All of the soldiers the man had trained with had been killed.

306 COWARDS: During World War I the British government executed 306 men for cowardice or desertion. More than 80 years later, John Reid, the Armed Forces Minister, stated that the men should be regarded as victims of war. None of the men were pardoned even though some were likely as young as 14.

MONUMENT TO DESERTERS: In Ypres, Belgium, 85 years after the Great War, a monument was built to honor those executed for refusing to fight. The steel plaque is engraved with a verse from Rudyard Kipling: "I could not look on death, which being known, men led me to him, blindfold and alone."

DESERTERS WHO MURDER: In 2002, two Russian paratroopers shot and killed nine people during a two-day escape from a Volga River base. They were eventually tracked down and killed.

WAR OF 1812: During this war the rate of desertion for American soldiers was 12.7 percent.

HARPER'S WEEKLY: On September 26, 1863, *Harper's Weekly* wrote that Civil War deserters were forced to march to their own funeral behind their coffins. All died instantly except for one man who sat upright nearly a minute after the firings.

SOLDIER'S SPELL

There are mysteries in what makes a soldier and how soldiers cope with what they do. Here's a quote to ponder from historians Fred Anderson and Andrew Cayton in their book *The Dominion of War*: "Soldiers always die in war, and those who survive must somehow make sense of those deaths and of their own survival." If they have to make sense of it, why do they do it? Military historian John Keegan has mentioned a soldier's spell that many military personnel seem to fall under: "the spell of an entirely different world."

MYSTERIOUS CONVICTIONS OF SACCO AND VANZETTI

Did a belief in an anarchist strain of humanism doom two men to death? Thousands upon thousands of people protested in American streets in 1927 when Italian immigrants Bartolomeo Vanzetti and Ferdinando Nicola Sacco were convicted without evidence and executed for the 1920 murder of a pay-clerk and a security guard in Braintree, Massachusetts. It's one of the greatest American controversies. Both men held a belief in a full democracy where neither poverty nor foreignness might exist. But they also followed Italian anarchist Luigi Galleani, who advocated revolutionary violence. Both men were considered anarchist immigrant workers at a time just after the 1919 Red Scare when union workers were often jailed for protesting harsh working conditions. Decades later, the convictions of Sacco and Vanzetti continue to befuddle historians and politicians alike. Many historians consider the trial and its aftermath a blatant disregard for the civil liberties of the men, as their guilt was implied by related events like dodging the draft. In 1977,

Massachusetts Governor Michael Dukakis refused to pardon the men, but he did say that American justice had failed.

THE BOSTON MASSACRE

An unruly crowd of Bostonians on March 5, 1770. Thousands marching in the streets. Riots under way. A few British soldiers, quite possibly fearing for their safety, fire their weapons into a surrounding mob. If *massacre* means "wholesale slaughter," then shouldn't the bombings of Hiroshima and Nagasaki also be considered such? Howard Zinn, in his 2007 book *A Power Governments Cannot Suppress*, writes that there are far more numerous and far larger massacres in American history, yet the Boston Massacre is still taught as if it was one of the worst.

DID NAPOLEON'S GASTRIC SECRET COST HIM WATERLOO?

Napoleon Bonaparte is said to have suffered from twitches, migraines, blackouts, hemorrhoids, rages, and weeping. He is also said to have scratched his face and legs until they bled because of dermal stress. But did hemorrhoids cause the general of the French Army to lose the battle of Waterloo? Psychohistorian Arno Karlen has said that Napoleon had hemorrhoid fits from his late twenties onward. It was an agony, a walking torment; even lying down was an occasion for misery. After escaping Elba in 1815, Napoleon had a fit on June 13 and rode on horseback all day, in what one can only conclude was an uncomfortable, mad state. By June 17 the French had won a battle at Ligny. But instead of capitalizing on the victory and speedily issuing orders, Napoleon lay awake in pain throughout the night. He awoke sluggish and exhausted and throughout the day was in a ghost-white, painful fog filled with indecision, which cost his army a crucial advantage.

OBSESSIVE BITE: Napoleon is said to have taken long baths, possibly the only relief he could find from his secret hemorrhoid affliction.

WHY OBAMA WAS SWORN IN AS PRESIDENT IN WASHINGTON, D.C.

Philadelphia, the American city of enlightenment, had been the meeting place for Congress during a 10-year run and was one of the proposed sites for the nation's new capital. Why didn't Philadelphia make the final cut? Historian Kenneth R. Bowling writes, in his 1991 book *The Creation of Washington, D.C.: The Idea and Location of the American Capital*, that by 1789 there were Americans who expected their capital to be a new Rome or Byzantium, where freedom, justice, and peace would reign in a seat of science, manufacturing, and commerce for the world.

THE FIRST FEDERAL CITY

Having a section of land set aside outside the states as an area solely for federal jurisdiction was a new idea that grew on American culture slowly. People were already used to calling Philadelphia by names relating to its affiliation with the federal government. Philadelphia's Congress area was known as "federal town" and "Residence of Congress." Those names paved the way for the emergence of new, more dominant terms such as "federal city" and "imperial seat." But questions arose regarding where the capital should be located. Some government officials and citizens said that the capital should be set inland—as Paris was situated away from the French coastline—yet not too far west, toward the American wilderness. Others argued that the capital should be built next to an existing, large urban center as well as near a port or on the coast. That way, more people and more newspapers could observe the government and keep the young republic in check.

A FOUNDING FATHER'S FEUD

By 1790, according to Bowling, Vice President John Adams believed that only a great city would be appropriate as the location of the capital, which had to be close to information sources, commerce, and strong media outlets. Richard G. Miller writes, in *The Federal City: 1783–1800*: "Among the reasons for Philadelphia's hearty support of the federal Constitution was the hope that a new start in government would provide the occasion to bring the national capital back to where it belonged, to the largest, wealthiest, and most centrally located city in the Union." And why not? Philadelphia and Bucks County were willing to offer a tract of land close to the city for a new federal district. For Philadelphians, the city regarded as the most enlightened city in the world would prosper even further. At the time, it was a hip and cool urban center with the latest fashions and trends. Even the most enlightened doctor of the Revolutionary era, Benjamin Rush, agreed. But a bill soon failed to pass. In 1790, another attempt was made to transform a portion of Philadelphia into the capital. Alexander Hamilton, confronted by certain political movers and shakers within the city, wasn't convinced Philadelphia was a good choice and so the idea dragged on unresolved. Petitions flooded in to Philadelphia newspapers to help rally a public outcry to keep the nation's capital there, but even those seemed to fall on deaf ears.

Between 1782 and 1790, Philadelphia had grown from 38,798 to 42,520 people. During that era, more Greek and Roman designs emulating the ancient Roman Republic were erected by officials still hoping Philadelphia would continue its reputation as the early seat of republican power. Miller writes, "But for whatever the reason—disdain for a grog-shop contest, or Philadelphian self-doubt—their hearts were not quite into the effort." Bowling points out that during the enlightened city's tenure as the seat of Congress, many members of Congress considered Philadelphia a city of dirt, mud, salty water, and weather-related illnesses.

THE YELLOW FEVER PLAGUE OF 1793

Philadelphia was certainly known for its seasonal ailments. But could the idea of disease have kept the nation's capital away from Philadelphia? Perhaps clues lie within a series of yellow fever epidemics that struck Philadelphia beginning in 1793.

Yellow fever is a devastating coastal disease spread by mosquitoes that feed off infected hosts. The bugs become carriers of the disease and spread the infection when feeding off other humans. Without the mosquito abatement found in cities of the modern era, severe mosquito populations easily harbored the infection and, breeding in stagnant waters, grew to untold numbers. Another disadvantage was that people didn't know that yellow fever was spread by mosquitoes. When the epidemic struck Philadelphia in 1793, some doctors simply thought it was a miasma caused by piles of rotting coffee dumped on docks. Doctors couldn't explain why those with the disease didn't cause it to spread when traveling to other areas. It was in the *Aedes aegypti* mosquitoes that were breeding and feeding in Philadelphia, possibly originating with an infected person on a ship arriving from Africa or the West Indies.

Alexander Hamilton, along with his wife, also fell ill in September 1793, presumably of yellow fever. That likely didn't help the cause of Philadelphia becoming the nation's capital, as Hamilton, like George Washington, was already a proponent of building the nation's capital elsewhere.

Yellow fever is mentioned several times in Alexander Hamilton's papers. A letter from George Washington to Hamilton of September 6, 1793, states: "With extreme concern I receive the expression of your apprehensions, that you are in first stages of the prevailing fever. I hope they are groundless, notwithstanding the malignancy of the disorder is so much abated, as with proper & timely applications not much is to be dreaded."

ARCHITECTURAL MYSTERIES OF WASHINGTON, D.C.

Pentagram city: A look at early maps or even satellite images of the street grid of Washington reveals what resembles the inverted five-point broken pattern of a pentagram. Some people say that early Masonic developers of Washington purposely incorporated the broken pentagram, honoring Sirius the Dog Star and related esoteric beliefs. The erratic astronomical path of Venus as viewed from Earth is said to resemble a broken pentagram just like the street grid and is also referred to as a five-pointed flower. A question remains whether these geometric celestial designs and the street grid symbolize Satan or the perfection of man.

CAPITOL BUILDING ANKH: It's suggested that when viewed from the air, the dome of the Capitol building, along with portions of nearby streets, forms the shape of the Egyptian symbol of eternal life.

WASHINGTON MONUMENT OBELISK: The Washington Monument's design is that of a common obelisk with Egyptian origins. Ramses II had 14 such obelisks raised at Tanis alone. The original purpose of an obelisk was to proclaim a king's power. Imaginary lines drawn upward from the sloping sides of obelisks are meant to meet in Heaven. Egyptian obelisks are also interpreted as Baal's (the Devil's) shaft.

WHITE HOUSE GLYPH: The White House grounds

and driveway possibly form a sun disk. Could it be part of a scaled-down Crown of Hathor, such as Isis once wore?

SIRIUS DOME STARS: The star Sirius, also called the Dog Star, is symbolized by images of the Egyptian god Anubis guarding the gates of Hell. Such symbols are associated with the Devil in the form of the pentagram—a five-pointed star. Not only are five-pointed stars on the American flag, they also adorn the helmet of the bronze Statue of Freedom which stands atop the Capitol dome. In 1993, the statue was removed by a helicopter for repairs after $790,000 had been raised to fix corrosion, cracks, and rusting.

CORNERSTONES: Many prominent buildings in Washington had their cornerstones laid by a society of freemasons who used corn, oil, and wine during their ceremonies. The buildings include the White House, the Washington Monument, and the Capitol. Anti-masons say that the true god worshipped by Masons is Baal.

CORN AND BAAL: One common theme in Washington's architecture is corn. The Hebrew word for corn is *dagan*. A derivative of dagan is Dagon, who was worshipped as a fish god and god of corn. His son was Baal, interpreted by some religious experts to be Satan. Baal could be the model for the bearded male figure carvings that can be seen throughout the Capitol. One park even has a bearded giant awakening from a grave.

ATHENA ARTWORK: While many believe America was built on Christian principles, there are some who believe otherwise. Goddess images of Athena in sculptures and paintings throughout the U.S. Capitol suggest ties to Rosicrucianism. One painting of Athena can be found in the Library of Congress. Satyr carvings can also be found in the library.

DANTE ALIGHIERI STATUES: There are statues of the writer of *Divine Comedy* throughout Washington. At least one statue commemorating the 600th anniversary of Dante's death can be found at Meridian Hill Park, which is located on the 77th meridian. Dante was a Rosicrucian, a member of a secret society of mystics that inspired freemasonry.

REFLECTING POOLS AND STAR ALIGNMENT: In architecture, Hermetic principles such as the mystic idea "As above, so below" were incorporated into the triangle imagery of the Masonic square and compasses, as well as in the many reflecting pools that can be found at the Washington Monument, the Capitol, the Lincoln Memorial, and the Supreme Court. In keeping with the principle "As above, so below," some buildings in Washington are aligned to stars, including Sirius.

DID THOMAS JEFFERSON HAVE A MENTAL CONDITION? AND WAS HIS GRANDSON AN AX MURDERER?

That anyone could consider Parisian life dreary is almost numbing to ponder. But there, in Paris, sat Thomas Jefferson in 1787, dreary, dull-minded, and in a lethargic state. He was practically an invalid. Truly, the pursuit of happiness was often just that for America's often-dejected ideological architect. But then, it's sometimes said a touch of insanity can come with brilliance or genius. Perhaps that was the case for the author of the Declaration of Independence.

In Michael Knox Beran's *Jefferson's Demons: Portrait of a Restless Mind*, Jefferson is described as having fits of laziness, where every object around him appeared loathsome. Beran writes, "His creative activity was rooted in the peculiarities of his nervous organization." He adds that Jefferson's anxiety led to bouts of apathy and dejection as he fell into sluggish moods, fought violent headaches, and had breakdowns that preceded periods of intense creativity.

But was Jefferson mad? Beran doesn't come out and say that Jefferson had a mental condition, though there may have been some kind of cover-up regarding the mental health of the president.

As Beran points out, Virginians didn't need to wait for Darwin to believe that the Jeffersons could pass down the mental wreckage of their household from one generation to another. Beran tells of tales of child murder in the Jefferson family and alludes to something perhaps a bit off in the Jefferson bloodlines.

A member of the Daughters of the American Revolution has stated privately that there is political cover-up over a murderous act committed by Jefferson's grandson Lilburn. She claimed that Lilburn was a crazed and troublesome relative.

According to our source, as the story goes, Thomas Jefferson bought a plantation north of Cincinnati from George Washington for Lilburn. "The grandson was troublesome, so [Jefferson] wanted to get him out to the wild West," she said. Lilburn was shipped to Ohio along with a young wife and slaves. The reason? "He was crazy, psychotic, had fits of anger, and terrorized people. He had a favorite water pitcher his mother poured water from. A young male slave dropped the pitcher and he freaked out and hacked the slave to death with an ax. Then there was a big cover-up."

When our source asked the Daughters of the American Revolution if the rumor was true, she said, "They wouldn't show me the documents, but they said, 'Yes, it's true.'"

If the story is true, did Lilburn inherit some kind of mental condition through the bloodlines of the Jeffersons? Could there be hidden medical documents that discuss not only the state of Lilburn Jefferson's mind, but the state of Thomas Jefferson's as well?

Our source also claims that Lilburn's story is told in Robert Penn Warren's epic poem *Brother to Dragons*. "It seems greatly fictionalized. But where did he come up with the story?"

While the tale of Lilburn may be mere rumor, clues about Thomas Jefferson's mental condition can be found in his biography. For example, though Jefferson suffered long periods as a near invalid, he also believed in taking two hours of exercise, especially walking, every day. Was he just trying to keep up his physical health? Or was that his way of also fending off something he knew deeply about himself? Jefferson believed that people could slip into a lazy, melancholy fit that could lead to madness if they didn't walk each day. Now why would he say that?

BLENNERHASSETT ISLAND AND BURR'S CONSPIRACY

Another historical mystery centers on an island on the Ohio River that is proposed to have been the meeting place for conspirator Aaron Burr and his cronies, whose aims were idiosyncratic at best. Some historians suggest that Burr's aims were never truly known, as much evidence against him was discounted during a trial for treason in 1807. Burr's alleged conspiracies include seeking to overthrow Thomas Jefferson's presidency, pushing for war with Mexico, and seceding from the Union in a territory of his own with armed farmers where he could fight off the U.S. government.

One of the conspirators' meeting places was the quasi-feudal Blennerhassett Island on the Ohio River, where Anglo-Irishman Harman Blennerhassett (who married his own niece Margaret Agnew) built a villa and science lab. Blennerhassett was an aristocrat of great fortune, who, along with Burr, wanted to separate the Western states from the Union. While the conspiracy failed and Blennerhassett was run off, his West Virginia island villa became a historic park and place of great mystery. The home burned down in 1811, but its foundation was rediscovered in 1973 and the mansion rebuilt. Reports of ancient Native American burial grounds and easily spooked horses add to the island's mystery. A hotel on the island is said to be haunted by the "Four O'clock Knocker," who pounds on doors at 4:00 A.M. The website WVGhosts.com claims that apparitions have been seen and that a curse was brought back along with the coffins of Mrs. Blennerhassett and one of her sons.

WAS OPPENHEIMER AN IDIOT?

Physicist J. Robert Oppenheimer had a unique role in the building and use of the atomic bomb, and as an overseer in the use of atomic energy long after the Manhattan Project. Sure, Oppenheimer later said, "I was an idiot" while on the hot seat for lying to Manhattan Project security officers in 1943. But that didn't mean he was an intellectual moron. There remains an enigma about the man and the history in which he played an integral part. In the aftermath of World War II, historian Charles Thorpe, in his 2006 book *The Tragic Intellect*, said that Oppenheimer utilized a considerable behind-the-scenes influence over atomic energy policy that eventually was stripped away. Thorpe writes about Oppenheimer, "He frequently employed overtly moral, and sometimes even religious language to talk about the implications of the atomic bomb and the role of the scientist." Did scientists involved with the atomic bomb see themselves as having some sort of messianic role, as well as being harbingers of doom? Could Oppenheimer really have held high morals and at the same time help create the most destructive weapon ever designed and used by mankind? What do you think? Grab a double mocha, a group of friends, and ponder.

THE STRANGE FIRES OF ROANOKE

One of early America's enduring mysteries is what became of a lost 16th-century colony on Roanoke Island in present-day North Carolina. What happened to these colonists from England? Were they abandoned? What do early historical records tell us? Digging into the original narratives reveals first-hand accounts of the mystery of Roanoke Island. Original records, some compiled from Richard Hakluyt, well known for gathering many of the seafaring accounts of early exploration of the Americas, can be found in *Early English and French Voyages: 1534–1608*.

DANGEROUS NATIVES, SUPPLY FAILURES, AND STRANGE SMOKE

In 1584, Captain Arthur Barlowe described native peoples on the island. Could they have wiped out the colony and what had been a peaceful cohabitation? Does this sound like a peaceful people? Or perhaps a sign of being surrounded by non-peace-loving natives? Barlowe writes:

> ... and on the evening following, wee came to an Island which they call Raonoak ... and at the north end thereof was a village of nine houses, built of

Cedar and fortified round about with sharpe trees to keepe out their enemies, and the entrance into it made like a turne pike very artificially.

The natives happily greeted and fed the explorer and his men. But around 1586 a colony was left on the island. After attempts to bring supplies to the colony failed, an exploration to find the colony in 1590 also provided fruitless, but not without shades of mystery. John White set out to explore the coast that year and saw smoke in two separate places above Roanoke Island. His words leave more mystery to the enigmatic disappearance of the colony than strange carvings found on a tree on the island. On August 15, White writes:

At our first comming to anker on this shore we saw a great smoke rise in the Ile Roanoak neere the place where I left the Colony in the yeere 1587, which smoake put us in good hope that some of the Colony were there expecting my returne out of England.

The next day, White writes about his team's further exploration:

… our 2 boates went a shore, and Captaine Cooke, and Cap. Spicer, and their company with me, with intent to passe to the place at Roanoak where our countrymen were left … out twoe boats put off unto the shore, in the Admirals boat we sounded all the way … we were very sore tired before wee came to the smoke. But that which grieved us more was that when we came to the smoke, we found no man nor signe that any had been there lately, nor any fresh water in all this waye to drink.

DROWNINGS, MYSTERIOUS FIRES, AND TREE CARVINGS

As White and his men tried to reach the original colony, one of their boats sank. Seven out of 11 sailors on the boat drowned. Four were good swimmers and were saved by Captain Cooke's sailors. Distraught from such a setback, White and his men redoubled their efforts and seemed ever more willing to find the missing colony, which by now was devoid of much-needed supplies from the motherland.

The account of what White and his men found goes down as one of America's greatest mysteries. The men called out, sang songs, and made their way toward a fire they thought was that of the Roanoke colony. What were the mysterious fires and the strange footprints they found? Some historians suggest that the colony moved peacefully to nearby Croatoan Island (present-day Hatteras Island). Others suggest that they were massacred upon reaching their new destination by the order of Chief Powhatan before the arrival of the Jamestown colonists. But that could have just been boasting among tribes who wanted to appear more powerful to other tribes in the area. The reality is, the colony's boats were gone and many of their stores left dug up, as the colony had tried to hide many of their wares underground. And, besides, no evidence of the colony was ever found on Croatoan.

Read carefully as White clearly explains the mysterious day of August 17, 1590, then try to think of what could have happened to the missing colony on Roanoke:

> "… it was so exceeding darke, that we overshot the place a quarter of a mile: there we espied towards the North ende of the Island the light of a great fire thorow the woods, to which we presently rowed: when wee came right over against it, we let fall our Grapnel neere the shore and sounded with a trumpet a Call,

and afterwardes many familiar English tunes of Songs, and called to them friendly; but we had no answere, we therefore landed at day-breake, and comming to the fire, we found the grasse and sundry rotten trees burning about the place ... we came to the place where I left our Colony in the yeere 1586. In all this way we saw in the sand the print of the Salvages feet of 2 or 3 sorts troaden in the night, and as we entred up the sandy banke upon a tree, in the very browe thereof were curiously carved these faire Romane letters C R O ... at my departure from them in An. 1587 I willed them, that if they should happen to be distressed in any of those places, that they should carve over the letters of name, a Crosse ... but we found no such sign of distresse ... and 5 foote from the ground in fayre Capitall letters was graven CROATOAN without any crosse or signe of distresse ... "

THE MISSING SHIP'S LOG OF CHRISTOPHER COLUMBUS

Luis Marden writes, in the forward to Robert H. Fuson's translation of Christopher Columbus's log, that the winds and currents of the globe could not have changed all that much in 500 years. A sailboat is a sailboat, and the winds and currents would propel a vessel across the great Atlantic Ocean at roughly the same speeds then as now. Marden points out that no one really knows the exact winds and currents that guided Columbus's voyage in 1492. Marden says that whereas Columbus traveled a distance of 3,200 miles in just over 33 days, he himself sailed from the Canary Islands to the Little Bahama Bank and Florida, around 3,700 miles, in 36 days. It's a difficult feat and one that individuals and teams often seek to duplicate.

THE MOST ENIGMATIC OF EXPLORERS

You wouldn't think there would be much mystery shrouding such a great part of American and world history. Yet Fuson, paraphrasing Winston Churchill, says that "Columbus is a riddle wrapped in a mystery inside an enigma." Where was Columbus born? Unknown. When was Columbus born? Unknown. Family background? More mystery, with possible political implications, as Columbus himself hid his past. What of Christopher Columbus's log, written between August 3, 1492, and March 15, 1493? Because Columbus's impact on history is so great, Fuson writes that this single ship's log is a document with no historical parallel and is a "singular documentary link between the Middle Ages and the Renaissance." That's a bold statement for a document that is questionable.

THE BARCELONA COPY AND THE DOMINICAN FRIAR

The log itself is a mystery. Where the original lies nobody knows. But a crafty Dominican friar named Fray Bortolome de Las Casas, a personal friend of Columbus's family who had an obsession with Columbus's voyages, somehow got access to the Barcelona copy of the ship's log between 1544 and 1552 at the San Pablo monastery. There de Las Casas prepared a handwritten copy. While historians would love to believe that his copying of Columbus's ship's log is entirely accurate, honest, and forthright, the simple fact is, historians can't prove the validity of the document. Did de Las Casas simply excerpt as much of the original as he could before having to return the document to the owner? Did he embellish any of the document? In the end, de Las Casas is taken at his word because his is the only copy of Columbus's ship's log.

That said, historians and readers must decide for themselves whether the log is accurate, and determine from it the nature of the man Columbus, his behaviors, his obsessions, his loves, his ability to navigate, his religious practices, and so forth. Was Columbus a greedy villain? A seafaring hero? A madman? Read a bit and decide for yourself as Columbus writes on Tuesday, December 18, 1492, not long after his discovery of Española:

> Today I traded for only a small quantity of gold, but I learned from an old man that there were many islands in the vicinity—at a distance of 300 miles or more, according to what I was able to make out—in which a lot of gold is found. I was told that on some of these islands there is so much gold that the whole island is gold. On others they gather it and sift it with sieves and melt it to make bars, and work it in a thousand ways. I was shown, by signs, how this is done. The old man indicated to me the course to take to get to those islands and the place where they may be found. I decided to go there, and if the old man had not been one of the principal persons belonging to the king, I would have taken him along. If I had known the language, I would have begged him to accompany me, and I believe we are on such good terms that he would have gone along of his own free will. But since I already consider that these people belong to the Sovereigns of the Castile, it is not right to offend them. So I decided to leave him alone.

OBSESSIVE BITE: Had Columbus not been so obsessed and had he listened to experts, he might have learned the true circumference of the Earth without having to cross thousands of miles of open ocean.

ON THE CONDUCT OF WAR, 1865

It is always interesting to look at history through the kaleidoscope of the present. For instance, what is the proper conduct of war, and to what great lengths do governments that commit atrocities go to convince themselves and their peoples that they are justified in their wartime behavior? War is death, destruction, submittal, conquest. Finding something right in it at times seems banal. It's sometimes hard to digest the idea that war can be conducted in any civil fashion. The American Civil War was a bloody and tragic series of battles and atrocities that revolved around states' rights, secession, and a union that wouldn't stand for what it called treason. Take a look at this passage regarding the U.S. Civil War from the *Report of the Joint Committee on the Conduct of the War at the Second Session Thirty-Eighth Congress*, written on May 22, 1865, by B.F. Wade, Chairman of the Committee. The document is the opening report of a voluminous collection of reports on government–military relations. As a reader, you might not be able to resist judging the document harshly. Taken out of context and subjected to present perspectives, the events of history can always be made to seem mysterious. But be careful. The Civil War was its own dangerous time in an America with vast cultural differences to today. This particular document preceded hundreds of pages of testimony regarding the Army of the Potomac, the Battle of Petersburg, the Red River Expedition, and more. The book itself was yellowed, aged, and dusty. Consider carefully the words of B.F. Wade:

> Your committee at the close of the labors in which the most of them have been engaged for nearly four years past, take occasion to submit a few general observations in regard to their investigations. They

commenced them at a time when the government was still engaged in organizing its first great armies, and before any important victory had given token of its ability to crush out the rebellion by the strong hand of physical power. They have continued them until the rebellion has been overthrown, the so-called confedcrate government been made a thing of the past, and the chief of the treasonable organization is a proclaimed felon in the hands of our authorities. And soon the military and naval forces, whose deeds have been the subjects of our inquiry, will return to the ways of peace and the pursuits of civil life, from which they have been called for a time by the danger which threatened their country. Yet while we welcome those brave veterans on their return from the fields made historical by their gallant achievements, our joy is saddened as we view their thinned ranks and reflect that tens of thousands, as brave as they, have fallen victims to that savage and infernal spirit which actuated those who spared not the prisoners at their mercy, who sought by midnight arson to destroy hundreds of defenceless women and children, and who hesitated not to resort to means and commit acts so horrible that the nations of the earth stand aghast as they are told what has been done. It is a matter for congratulation that, notwithstanding the greatest provocations to pursue a different course ... have ever treated their prisoners humanely and generously, and have in all respects conducted this contest according to the rules of the most civilized warfare ...

SEPTEMBER 11, 1775

September 11, 2001, for many marks a moment of betrayal. Whether that betrayal lies in suspicions of conspiracy against the American government, hatred against fanatical Muslims, or otherwise, sentiment rings strong across ethnicities, classes, and regions.

But what about through time?

Could history be so mysterious, so filled with synchronicities? Regarding September 11, some people are reported to have had premonitions. Others simply relate to that date or to numbers related to 9/11. Some stare at clocks at precisely 9:11 or get weird feelings on the anniversary. What such feelings mean no one is sure of, other than that history may have a way of casting a web of synchronicities over the past, present, and future. It's unexplainable. It's flat-out bizarre.

September 11, 1775, marks an interesting time in American history. A nation was about to be born, on the cusp of change and transformation. The wheels of history were turning at full speed as the War for Independence was well under way. George Washington had become the commander of the Continental Army and would be for eight and a half years, until 1783.

The Papers of George Washington: Revolutionary War Series consists of military correspondence between Washington and military and civilian leaders, family, private individuals, and others. The synchronicity with modern-day atrocity, betrayal, and war on the American East Coast is not prophesied or hinted at in any way in the Washington papers written on September 11, 1775. But anyone who believes in synchronicity will feel a chill at the idea of betrayal. The excerpt below is just a glimpse of a greater story, in which a soldier, Levi Bowen, took absence without leave, he said, to take care of his sick family. A simple story can become a synchronistic symbol of betrayal in a land of citizens freshly embarked upon a world of war and change. Who is betraying whom? This is the government's response to Bowen's leave of absence:

> General Orders: Head Quarters, Cambridge, Sept. 11th, 1775. Parole Landcaster. Countersign Middleton. Col. Ebenezer Bridge of the 27th Regt of foot, in the service of the United Colonies; tried at a General Court martial, wherof Bridg. Genl Green was president, for "misbehaviour and neglect of duty, in the Action at Bunkers-hill, on the [1]7th of June last," The Court are of the opinion that Indisposition of body, render'd the prisoner incapable of action, and do therefore acquit him. Ensign Moses Howe of Col. David Brewers Regt tried by a General Court Martial, wherof Col. Alden was presdt—for "contempt of service["]; The Court after due examination of the Evidence, aquit the prisoner." Ensign Levi Bowen—of the same regiment, and tried by the same General Court martial for "absenting from his regiment without leave"—The Court find the prisoner guilty of the Crime laid to his Charge, and to therefore sentence him to be cashiered.

MYSTERY OF THE DEAD SEA SCROLLS

One was embossed on copper. The rest were engraved on leather. Some were torn to shreds. What were these mysterious scrolls? Perhaps the mystery is less about what the scrolls say and more about those who wrote them. And yet, part of the mystery is that, with the exception of the Nash papyrus, until the Dead Sea Scrolls were found, no Jewish text written on perishable material could be tracked to the pre-Christian period.

Geza Vermes might strike you as an obsessed man. His feelings are clear when he claims in the preface to his book, *The Complete Dead Sea Scrolls in English*, that "following the 'revolution' which 'liberated' all the manuscripts [Dead Sea Scrolls] in 1991—until that moment a large portion of them was kept away from the public gaze—every interested person gained free access to the entire Qumran library. I eagerly seized the chance and set out to explore the whole collection."

SCRIBAL CREATIVE FREEDOM IN AN ANCIENT JEWISH COMMUNITY

In the arid, hot wastelands of the Dead Sea's western shore just south of Jericho lies the ruins known as Khirbet Qumran. There, an ancient Jewish community crept up steep cliffs and hid their cultural and religious heart in 11 hidden caves. Between 1947 and 1956 the entire cave system was discovered, in part due to luck, bored soldiers, and the original Arab shepherd boy who stumbled onto the first bits of manuscript. The scrolls were speculated to have been hidden away for more than 2,000 years and are considered one of the greatest archaeological discoveries out of the Middle East.

While thousands of fragments were found in some caves, in Cave 4 was found the longest, which is referred to as the Temple Scroll. Yet, according to Vermes, the Dead Sea Scrolls don't reveal any new religious revelation. Vermes claims the primary novelty of the scrolls is that they show the scribal creative freedom of one ancient sect in rewriting its own literary/religious works. Creative freedom or poorly controlled copying? The Dead Sea Scrolls' biggest contribution may be to unraveling the history of Palestinian Judaism in the intertestamental period. That means revealing "new avenues of exploration in the shadowy era of the life of Jesus," according to Vermes.

DOOMSAYERS OF EARLY AMERICA

Was America filled with its own brand of self-made prophets and doomsayers during the Revolutionary War era? Historian Susan Juster wrote in her 2003 book, *Doomsayers*, that such lonely, ignored, and mocked characters were a sort of "company of prophets" in early America during the war-torn years of 1765 to 1815. Makes you wonder how such peculiar, lonely, religion-driven people could appear in the Age of Reason when intellectualism flourished in a newly enlightened world? Juster suggests that there were possibly thousands of prophets and prophetesses in North America in the late 1800s predicting plagues and tempests and wandering about teaching in the American wilderness and in towns and cities. Juster believes that many of these so-called seers were snickered at. There was Richard Brothers, the self-declared "nephew of Christ" who ended up in an insane asylum in the 1790s. Noah White in Massachusetts in January 1799 claimed to have dreams and visions of severe frosts, snow in summer, and trees covered in worms.

A COFFEEHOUSE CULTURE OF PROPHETS?

Part of what propelled these eccentric religious folks was an apocalyptic tradition in the public sphere of coffeehouses, newspapers, penny pamphlets, and volunteer societies. These societies rounded up their worshippers over tea and java and distributed their writings in such places. Knowing this might make you walk into a Starbucks or some other local coffeehouse and take a look around a time or two, especially if history really does repeat itself. But don't worry. Many of these folks were harmless and ended up locked away in insane asylums. Some people said they heard God's voice or were merely the deliverers and interpreters of His messages. Others became fortune tellers, visionists, and millenarians, or women of revelation like Jemima Wilkinson, who believed she had a special role in delivering people from the Devil. Wilkinson was a Quaker who grew ill in 1776 and when she recovered would only respond to the name of "Publick Universal Friend." She preached to many followers in the villages of New England as well as in Indian country, claiming to be the second coming of Christ.

DOUBTING LINCOLN

Without getting into the kind of argument that could last volumes, it's important to note that during the Civil War, Abraham Lincoln was not the greatest advocate for African Americans that America had ever seen. He was likely the right man in the right place who made the right choice. If war is a chess game, what other solution did Lincoln have but to free black slaves? His signing of the Emancipation Proclamation, which was an American decree of freedom, still left doubt in the minds of thousands. And in no way did such freedom mean equality or an easy life for black Americans. Many doubts were laid on the federal government—about the fair treatment of black soldiers, wartime atrocities, even about whether the Emancipation Proclamation could be reversed. Read this letter from Hannah Johnson, the mother of a Northern black soldier from Buffalo, to the U.S. president. She sent the letter on July 31, 1863, just half a year after Lincoln's proclamation. Keep in mind how few blacks could write and how many people this portion of Johnson's letter likely represented:

> Excellent Sir. My good friend says I must write to you and she will send it. My son went in the 54th regi-ment. I am a colored woman and my son was strong and able as any to fight for his country and the colored people have so much to fight for as any. My father was

a Slave and escaped from Louisiana before I was born morn forty years agone. I have but poor education but I never went to school, but I know it is right that a colored man should go and fight for his country, and so ought to a white man. I know that a colored man ought to run no greater risks than a white, his pay is no greater his obligation to fight is the same. So why should not our enemies be compelled to treat him the same, Made to do it.

My son fought at Fort Wagoner but thank God he was not taken prisoner, as many were. I thought of this thing before I let my boy go but then they said Mr. Lincoln will never let them sell our colored soldiers for slaves, if they do he will get them back quick. He will retaliate and stop it. Now Mr. Lincoln don't you think you ought to stop this thing and make them to the same by the colored men? They had lived in idleness all their lives on stolen labor and made savages of the colored people, but they now are so furious because they are proving themselves to be men, such as have come away and got some education. It must not be so. You must put the rebels to work in State prisons to making shoes and things, if they sell our colored soldiers, till they let them all go. And give their wounded the same treatment. It would seem cruel, but their no other way, and a just man must do hard things sometimes, that shew him to be a great man. They tell me some do you will take back the Proclamation. Don't do it. When you are dead and in Heaven, in a thousand years, that action of yours will make the Angels sing your praises I know it …

31

A CURIOUS NOTE FROM THE KENNEDY ASSASSINATION HEARINGS

John F. Kennedy, America's 35th president, was assassinated on Friday, November 22, 1963. One doesn't have to be a history buff to know there are mysteries surrounding Kennedy's murder, which was ruled to have been committed by Lee Harvey Oswald. A later ruling, in 1979, found serious flaws in the investigation and proposed that a conspiracy likely existed. While the mysteries and conspiracy talk regarding Kennedy's death seem limitless, I share here just one short, curious note among the many volumes that make up the U.S. government's official investigation released in print in 1964.

Dr. Olivier: Human skulls, we take these human skulls and they are imbedded and filled with 20 percent gelatin. As I mentioned before, 20 percent gelatin is a pretty good simulant for body tissues. They are in the moisture content. When I say 20 percent, it is 20 percent weight of the dry gelatin, 80 percent moisture. The skull, the cranial cavity, is filled with this and the surface is coated with a gelatin and then it is trimmed down to approximate the thickness of the tissues overlying the skull, the soft tissues of the head.

Mr. Specter: And at what distance are these tests performed?

Dr. Olivier: These tests were performed at a distance of 90 yards.

Mr. Specter: And what gun was used?

Dr. Olivier: It was the 6.5 millimeter Mannlicher-Carcano Western ammunition lot 6,000.

Mr. Specter: What did the examination or test, rather, disclose?

Dr. Olivier: It disclosed that the type of head wounds

the president received could be done with this type of bullet. This surprised me very much, because this type of a stable bullet I didn't think would cause a massive head wound, I thought it would go through making a small entrance and exit, but the bones of the skull are enough to deform the end of this bullet causing it to expend a lot of energy and blowing out the side of the skull or blowing out fragments of the skull.

FEBRUARY 20, 1978, LETTER FROM RONALD REAGAN TO CONGRESSMAN PHIL CRANE REGARDING MILITARY BUILDUP IN IRAQ

A lot can be said in a short letter, especially one from Ronald Reagan before he was elected president of the United States in 1980. A mysterious forewarning? What does this letter say about modern Republicanism, or about a modern view of Iraq and the political view of Democrats? This letter can be viewed in many different lights. For certain, it says a lot about Reagan's "wait and see" attitude, which kept America in the Cold War but out of any physical entanglement.

It was good to get your letter and I very much appreciate your words about the Middle East situation. I'll admit to wondering just where Begin and Sadat stand after that first round of spectaculars. I've had a feeling J.C. [Jimmy Carter] has been trying to look more involved than he really is—hoping perhaps that he might get some credit if a peaceful solution is achieved.

The military buildup in Iraq is alarming, and there has been no media mention of it to speak of. I hope I'll have a chance soon to talk with you about this ...

THE QUESTION OF THE 2012 APOCALYPSE

Could it be the Y2K Millennium bug all over again in 2012? Or will 2012, like "The War of the Worlds," the 1938 radio show by Orson Wells, influence mass hysteria? Some say that anxiety about a 2012 expiration date for planet Earth has been fueled by farcical websites with countdown clocks and books that make false claims about ancient timekeepers predicting the fall of mankind.

December 21, 2012, marks the end of the 5,126-year cycle of the Mayan Long Count calendar. The ancient Mayan civilization of the Yucatán region of present-day Mexico is known for its advanced understanding of astronomy and mathematics and for its great cities and architecture—including the Kukulcan Pyramid, which some perceive as a giant ancient Mayan clock built in cosmic alignment to the center of the Milky Way, the constellations, and the sun. Mainstream Mayan scholars do not agree with the doomsday theorists. David Stuart, director of the Mesoamerica Center at the University of Texas at Austin, told CNN, "There's going to be a whole generation of people who, when they think of the Maya, think of 2012, and to me that's just criminal." Some have said that 2012 is going to be a dramatic year for change. But that change could simply mean transformation and renewal. For all anyone knows, maybe a new technology will be discovered on the eve of a great galactic alignment. It is interesting, however, that the ancient Mayan culture would have arrived at such incredible cosmic calculations, as one scholar pointed out to CNN, centuries before the galactic center of the Milky Way was defined in the 1950s.

DYING LANGUAGE OF THE TUBATULABAL

California has several hundred languages, but most of them are endangered. One man is the future of an entire language. Jim

Andreas, 77, is the last willing speaker of Pakaanil, the native language of the Tubatulabal tribe. It's a language that has been spoken for at least hundreds of years in the mountainous regions of Central California. There are few who can utter the language, and only Andreas has been willing to share its secrets. A history of language suppression has caused languages like Pakaanil to die out or become endangered. Many native peoples were punished by Europeans for speaking native languages: they were made to feel ashamed, or the language was beaten out of them. It's unknown whether a lingering sense of shame prevents other elders from teaching their descendants. Hopes are that a Pakaanil dictionary will be completed as Andreas's voice is recorded and while students continue to learn the language.

FANNIE JONES AND THE MYSTERY OF SERVITUDE

Near the very end of the vast *Georgia Narratives*, accounts compiled in 1972 from ex-Georgia slaves, there is a short interview with then 85-year-old Fannie Jones from Augusta, Georgia. The book is filled with accounts taken post-slavery from those once in bondage. Each testimony offers a unique and mysterious glimpse into blended realities of servitude and freedom—two sides of a cultural coin. An interview with Jones at first reveals a typical story of slavery and freedom. But the reality is the description of a life that leads to more questions than answers.

THE TESTIMONY OF FANNIE JONES

I was born on Marse Jim Dubose's plantation 'bout de year 1853. My marster and Mistiss was de overseer and his wife. You see, honey, I was born in the over-seer's house. When my ma was 12 years old she was give to de overseer's wife, Miss Becky Ann, when she was married. My Marster was named Jesse Durden. I never did see Marse Jim Dubose's house nor none of de slave quarters, and I don't know nothin' 'bout dem or none of his Niggers. I jus' stayed in de house and waited on Marster and Mistiss. I cleaned up de house, made de beds, churned for Mistiss, and made fires for Marster. My Ma, she cooked for Marster and Mistiss, cleaned up de house, and waited on mistiss 'cause she was an invalid.

Marse Jim Dubose's plantation covered thousands of acres, and he owned hundreds of slaves. You see, my Marster was de man what handled all of dese here Niggers. Evvy Mornin, Marster Jesse would git up and go out and blow his horn, dat was de way he called de Niggers to de fields.

De overseer's house was a one-story buildin' and it was furnished in de old time stuff. De beds was teestered and had slats to hold de mattresses. When Marster would come in from de fields he would be so tired he never did go nowhar. Sometimes I would say to him, 'I'se cold,' and he would say, 'Nig, you jus' crawl up on the foot of my bed and git warm.' He would say 'Nig, what you want for supper?' and I would say, 'I wants some bread and milk and a little syrup.' He give me anything dat I wanted to eat, and us had good things to eat. Us had chickens, hogs, and good milk cows. I kin see de big bowls of milk now dat us used to have. Us made a heap of butter and sent it to Augusta onct a month and sold it for twenty-five cents a pound.

Atter freedom come, Marster said to me and Ma, 'You all is free now to go wherever you want to.' Ma, she wanted to go, but I jus' cried and cried 'cause

I didn't want to leave Marster and Mistiss; dey was too good to me. So Ma tuk me and us went to her grandma's down at Barnett. Us stayed dar awhile, den us lef' and went to Thomson. Us stayed at dat place a long time, and I was married dar to a man by de name of Claiborne Jones. Us had 'leven chillun, but dey is all daid now 'cept two. I lives here wid one of my daughters.

My husband belonged to Marse John Wilson. Durin' de war, Marse John wuz a captain, and he tuk my husband 'long to cook and to wait on him. He said one night de Yankees was atter 'em and him and Marse John jumped in a big ditch. Later in de night it rained and dey couldn't git out of de ditch, so de rest of Marse John's Company lef' 'em alone. De next morning when dey got out of de ditch, dey didn't know which way dey had went, but Marse John got a hoss and dey got on and rid 'til dey caught up wid dey company.

At Christmas dey give us anything dat us wanted. Dey give me dolls, candy, fruit, and evvything. Mistiss used to git a book and say, 'Nig, come here and let me larn you how to read.' I didn't pay no 'tention to her den, but now I sho wish I had. My Mistiss didn't have but one chile, Miss Cornelia.

RANDOM SLAVES IN HISTORY:

SPARTACUS: In A.D. 73, Spartacus was said to be one of 78 gladiators who escaped from the fighting school of Gnaeus Lentulus Batiatus at Capua. He was one of three elected leaders and was said to be not only strong, but cultured and intelligent.

AESOP: The writer of *Aesop's Fables*, possibly an African, was a slave in Samos around 550 B.C. According to Herodotus, Aesop was executed by people from Delphi and an ensuing pestilence was blamed on his death.

SAINT PATRICK: The patron saint of Ireland was born around 387 and was captured by raiders and enslaved for six years. Two letters from him survive. One of them, the *Declaration*, says that he was captured when he was 16 years old. While enslaved, he wrote that a voice told him he would soon go home. Legend states that Patrick later banned all snakes from Ireland, though the island likely never had any snakes.

FREDERICK DOUGLAS: The first African American nominated as a vice-presidential candidate, Frederick Douglas was born a slave and possibly had one white parent. His 1845 work, *Narrative of the Life of Frederick Douglass, an American Slave*, is one of the most important abolitionist writings of its time. He escaped slavery by dressing as a seaman and boarding a train.

ENRIQUE OF MALACCA: From the Moluccas Islands, Enrique of Malacca was probably the most well-traveled slave the world has ever known. He was the personal slave and interpreter of Ferdinand Magellan (1480–1521), the first man to circumnavigate the planet.

HARRIET TUBMAN: One of 11 children born into bondage, she was once hit on the head by an iron weight, which scarred her for life. In 1844, she married a free black man named John Tubman, but ran away, following the North Star. She later organized a secret group of safe houses called the Underground Railroad, which she used to lead hundreds of slaves to freedom.

HARK OLUFS: Son of the Danish nautical captain Oluf Jensen, Hark Olufs was captured in 1724 by Algerian pirates. His family could not afford his ransom, so he was sold as a slave and not released until 1735, when he commanded a cavalry and helped to conquer Tunis.

JOHN CASOR: Everyone wants a claim to fame, but John Casor's would not be coveted by anyone: He was the first man in Virginia Colony to be declared a slave for life.

KUNTA KINTE: A portion of Alex Haley's book *Roots* is based on a slave who was taken in 1767 from the Mandinka tribe and later brought to Annapolis, Maryland. Haley at first stated that Kunta Kinte was his forefather, but those claims have since been proven false. A memorial placed in Annapolis in 1981 was stolen by the Ku Klux Klan.

MIGUEL DE CERVANTES: Captured by Barbary pirates in 1575, the writer of *Don Quixote* (1605) spent five years in captivity. He once fought bravely on board a vessel and survived three gunshot wounds, two of which were to his chest.

CHAPTER 2

UNNATURAL SCIENCES: BIZARRE DISCOVERIES FROM BIOLOGY TO OUTER SPACE

The temperature at which water boils at varying elevations: that's science. Ancient trilobite fossils found in swarms on ancient seabeds—science again. Teddy bears floating on the edge of space because of scientists working with school-children? Believe it or not, that's science too. It's hard to know what to explore when science as a discipline is so broad and so amazingly rich in its spectrum of knowledge. It could mean how cells divide or how starlight shines from galactic centers. Gathering evidence, examining theories, and testing hypotheses are all part of the realm that helps us to further ourselves as human beings. But let's face it, science can get really far-out when you stop to think about it.

In "Unnatural Sciences" you'll get a glimpse of several branches of science, which I discuss in terms that I hope are easily understandable. You won't be left with grand equations and relentless statistics. But just as science both asks and answers questions, you'll probably be left wondering more about where information comes from and how science is proven.

"Fossil Hunters of the Ancient Dunkleosteus" jumps right into the realm of dinosaurs, where we are faced with the idea that some creatures from the past could easily chomp others to bits. And they didn't even have teeth, as you and I would imagine! In "Do Stars Watch Their Weight?" I examine findings that most stars push away galactic energy when they have their fill, though some stars are gluttons. "So Mars Has Methane, but Can You Live There?" takes a look at the idea that since methane has been found on Mars, life could exist in some form on the red planet. Haven't science fiction books and films been saying for years that there is life on Mars? Possibly my favorite slice of trivia in the entire book is "When U.K. Teddy Bears Invaded Space." Schoolchildren in England got to be a part of a project sending teddy bears to the edge of Earth's atmosphere. You'll read about whether the bears had a crash landing and how the kids got to help. Of course, you're also going to read about real Nessie lake monsters, frogs on the verge of extinction, vampire fish population control, and the enriching science of whale shark poo.

FOSSIL HUNTERS OF THE ANCIENT DUNKLEOSTEUS

There's an ancient 30-foot-long fish known as dunkleosteus that paleontologists affectionately call "dunks." But these aren't teddy bears of the sea. Their bite put them in league with the mighty *Tyrannosaurus rex*. Some experts say the armored fish could crunch down with as much as 22,000 pounds per square inch of pressure. Dunks didn't have traditional teeth, but rather plates that sliced their prey with the precision of modern-day paper factory chopping machines. Scientists say the way dunk teeth were organized allowed it to focus its bite in a tiny area called the fang tip. With a spring-loaded jaw, the dunks could also open their mouths incredibly fast: in one-fiftieth of a second. With that kind of speed, suction could have been created, causing victims to shoot into dunk mouths, accounting for so many partially digested remains found with dunk fossils. One thing is certain—these real-life dinosaurs with machinelike choppers sometimes chomped on each other. Evidence has been found in fossilized remains discovered in shale deposits with plate bite marks.

FOSSIL SMILES FOUND WITHIN CLIFF WALLS

Scientists say that in an ancient age of fishes known as the Devonian period, which occurred as long ago as 400 million years, *Dunkleosteus terreli* swam in an ancient sea. Interestingly, the sea is where the city of Cleveland, Ohio now exists. Paleontologists, using a 100-year-old method that employs ladders, rappelling gear, and pry bars, dig into shale cliffs that rise 50 feet above the ground. As recently as October 2008, Ohio researchers hunting ancient sharks also hunted the dunkleosteus, the remains of which settled at the bottom of ancient seas now known as Cleveland Shale. Millions of years ago, those areas had oxygen-deprived depressions, which meant little or no bacteria to eat dead dunk remains. The giant fish were then fossilized among what later became the shale cliff faces that rise above one of many nearby brooks. Experts say those depressions within the seabed were composed of a black muck that sometimes even preserved soft tissues of ancient fish.

Excavations have taken place in recent years at deposits in the Big Creek Reservation of the Cleveland Metroparks, while the Cleveland Shale has been offering up specimens of ancient fish since the mid-1800s. In the 1930s and 1940s, David Dunkle of the Cleveland Museum of Natural History, along with a colleague, wrote a research paper describing this armor-plated Devonian fish, which was named the dunkleosteus in his honor.

Experts who still dig within the shale beds search for oval dumplinglike mineral deposits called concretions, which are trapped between layers of shale. Their light-colored, rounded profiles hint of fossils inside. After a rain they may look like smiles in the cliff wall. Sometimes the hollow concretions are known to pop out and slide down the cliff on their own and splash into the water below. Researchers can be seen breaking open concretions with pickaxes, exposing the fossils hidden inside to sunlight for the first time in millions of years.

OBSESSIVE BITE: Dunkleosteus is a popular video-game dinosaur, having appeared in *Paraworld*, *Aquanaut's Holiday*, and *E.V.O.: Search for Eden.*

TWENTY-FIVE WEIRD DINOSAUR FACTS

FOSSIL FISH BRAIN: Using digital X-ray scans, in March 2009, experts revealed the discovery of the first fossil dinosaur brain. The 300-million-year old brain fossil found in Kansas was found in an iniopterygian, which is related to a ratfish. The palm-sized fish had a pea-sized brain, which strangely was much smaller than its braincase.

SEXY SPIKES: Related to a triceratops, the spiky-headed *Pachyrhinosaur lakustai* had a large bone on its nose that supported a huge central horn, two spiked bones over its eyes, and three forehead spikes. Experts believe other pachyrhinosaurs thought the spikes rather appealing. But that was 72 million years ago.

FROM MEAT TO VEGGIES: In 2005, a graveyard of birdlike feathered dinosaurs related to vicious velociraptors was discovered. Most unusual about the find was scientists' determination that *Falcarius utahensis* was likely in the early stages of changing its diet to meat. They made this discovery by examining the creatures' smaller leaf-shredding teeth.

AUSTRORAPTOR: Revealed in 2008, this relative of those infamous *Lost World* velociraptors is the largest so far found to have roamed the southern hemisphere. Found in the far-southern Patagonia region of South America, the 70-million-year-old *Austroraptor cabazai* changed thinking for paleontologists who previously had only found raptors as large as turkeys on the continent.

FEATHERED FREAK: Get in your time machine and turn the dial to 152 million years ago. Go to Inner Mongolia. Now, search for a rather fluffy feathered meat-eater named *Epidexipteryx hui*. You won't mistake it. It's supposed to be the only one around at the time that sported four ribbonlike tail feathers. In fact, the rest of its body was covered with short feathers. The creature was about the size of a pigeon. Handle with care.

NOT A *STAR WARS* HAIRDO: Jeanna Bryner, in a 2008 *USA Today* article, said that lambosaurs, with their duck bills and flattened snouts, also wore ornate headgear that looked like flashy flaps. She wrote that they "would have put to shame any 'Star Wars' hairdo." Experts suggest that their headgear was used for vocal communication. They also suggest that lambosaurs went through puberty and their voices changed.

VACUUM OF THE GODS: Around 65 million years ago, the nigersaurus slurped up plants with its vacuum-cleaner-shaped muzzle. Discovered in 1993, it was a true Mesozoic lawnmower, with a jaw of 600 teeth that regenerated if broken.

FOSSIL POO NABBED: One of the most infamous items stolen from London's Natural History Museum was a piece of 65-million-year-old fossilized titano-saurus poo taken in 2005. The museum also once lost live mosquitoes in the mail.

DINOSAUR MUMMY: In 2007, scientists announced the discovery of a perfectly preserved hadrosaur. The 67-million-year-old creature was found with skin intact around arms, legs, tail, and parts of the body.

SAHARAN T REX: Sadly, no tyrannosaur ever roam-ed Africa's largest desert. But a discovery in the Sahara Desert in 2008 revealed that the 110-million-year-old kryptops and eocarcharia were said to be fairly nasty 25-foot-long carnivorous beasts.

GIANT PERUVIAN DESERT PENGUINS: Human-sized penguins in South America? It's true, and contrary to popular belief, the fossil discovery of these waddling 35-million-year-old giants just proves that penguins aren't always at home on snow and ice.

THE RETURN OF THE WOOLLY MAMMOTH: Imagine going to the zoo and seeing a hairy beast that resembles an elephant. (No, not him—that's my brother-in-law, Artie. The one next to him.) Scientists believe they can retrieve DNA from ancient specimens. DNA can be put back together, experts say. But beware, German scientists are also doing the same with the Neanderthal.

LOVELY BABY MAMMOTH: In other giant hairy beast news, a perfectly intact baby mammoth was found in 2007 in northwest Siberia. Although she had been lying in frozen ground for 40,000 years, Alexei Tikhonov, deputy director of the Russian Academy of Science's Zoological Society, said, "She's a lovely little creature."

AMBER TREE FROG: In Chiapas, Mexico, an ancient tree frog was found encased in amber. The tree resin in which the frog was discovered is said to be around 25 million years old. One of the scientists studying the fossil wanted to attempt a DNA extraction. It's unknown if he was even allowed.

SEA SCORPION SURFBOARD: All that scientists found was a giant claw in western Germany. But that was enough to determine that the length of the giant 390-million-year-old sea scorpion, *Jaekelopterus rhenaniae*, was about the size of an eight-foot longboard.

GRANDPA TOPS: Found in Alberta, Canada, and hailed as the granddaddy of triceratops, *Albertacera-*

tops nesmoi showed off horns as long as a man's arm 78 million years ago. It's considered a missing link in the world of centrosaurs.

STICKY TAR PITS: The McKittrick Tar Pits outside Bakersfield, California, once bubbled with giant dragonflies, while the La Brea Tar Pits in Los Angeles is still coughing up specimens. Even areas around tar pits yield finds. An excavation in a parking garage in 2006 revealed prehistoric teeth, bones, animal remains, and a complete woolly mammoth skeleton.

FOSSIL LOGJAM: Petrified trees, dinosaurs, and other remains were all found jammed together in a Hanksville, Utah, dig. That's a lot of years of cramming. Or just one bad day 150 million years ago. A stegosaurus and four 130-foot-long sauropods were part of the amazing discovery in 2008.

ARCTIC SEA MONSTER: What's longer than a humpback whale, had cucumber-sized teeth, and the 200-million-year-old remains of which were found on a remote Arctic island? Experts call this monstrosity the tyrannosaur of the ocean. You can call it whatever you want. Just pray there's not a family of them in Loch Ness.

BEELZEBUFO: The fossil remains of this giant frog from Hell were discovered by scientists working in Madagascar. Thought to be 16 inches tall and weighing 10 pounds, the creature was very round and likely extremely aggressive. It may have eaten baby frogs for breakfast 70 million years ago.

DINOSAUR FIGHTS: If you've seen any dinosaur movie, you've witnessed dinosaur fights. And it's no great mystery that prehistoric creatures killed and ate each other. But rare evidence of scuffles between dinosaurs has been found in the battle scars on the skulls of triceratops. The find proves that the ancient horns of such creatures weren't just for looks.

GIGANTORAPTOR: There's not a parrot cage big enough for these 65-million-year-old birds. It had a beak that could cut a man in two. It walked on two legs, had feathers, was twice as tall as any human, and had knifelike claws. Gigantoraptor has been found in China's Gobi Desert, and thank the stars no one is trying to find ways to clone these monsters.

TINY AS HENS: The smallest dinosaurs ever discovered in North America were found in Red Deer, Alberta. Scientists believe *Albertonykus borealis* had tweezerlike jaws, huge claws, and were the size of hens. They were believed to have eaten Jurassic termites.

SIX-STORY PEEPER: Imagine taking a shower in your sixth-floor apartment and realizing that not only did you leave the curtains open but the entire building had gone back in time to the era of the sauroposeidon. This 60-foot-tall beast could easily see you soaping up, though presumably you would have heard the "earthquake god lizard" stomping your way. When it was first discovered in Oklahoma in 1994, experts thought they had found the trunks of prehistoric trees.

THE GREAT DINOSAUR BALL: Along the Arizona–Utah border more than 1,000 dinosaur footprints were discovered in 2008. Experts believe four different species made this prehistoric 190-million-year-old dance floor. The site has since been covered by sand dunes. In Yemen, tracks from a herd of 11 giant sauropods were once found in coastal mudflats.

DO STARS WATCH THEIR WEIGHT?

Get a little too much food at the table and you might just push it away. Forget that some experts say it's easier for men than women to resist being gluttons. Perhaps there's a sort of cosmic gluttony and weight-watching going on has nothing to do with the kind of food you and I might eat. That's because scientists believe baby stars are binge eaters that eat and eat, feeding off surrounding dust and gas from protostellar clouds as they form. Over time, a star munches on enough of the surrounding cosmic food to stoke the fires of its nuclear center. At that time, scientists say, the star begins emitting radiation.

BABY STARS DO GOBBLE THEIR COSMIC FOOD

Scientists from UC Berkeley, UC Santa Cruz, and Lawrence Livermore National Laboratory created 3-D supercomputer model simulations to test why stars don't continue growing and gobble up the very universe we live in. While those scientists say that stars produce so much light that the emanating radiation exerts more pressure on surrounding gas and dust than their gravitational forces pull in, they also suggest that baby stars don't necessarily stop chowing down on cosmic breakfasts, as previously thought. Could this be a cosmic diet program? Could such techniques be applied to nutritionist handbooks for obese children who need the latest version of Wii Fit? Probably not. But what's interesting is, scientists say that newborn stars are quite gluttonous, feeding on gas and dust, but they don't push all the cosmic food away from their midsections. They continuously feed.

CANNIBALS AMONG THE STARS

While stars aren't on the same diet as you, this theory also suggests that stars can feed off each other as cannibals. Scientists say that when stars are being born in protostellar clouds, they can create binary partners that eventually get munched on as well. A little more for the cosmic thighs. In 2000, research suggested that violent stellar mergers were more commonplace than most scientists thought. Perhaps the dense clusters of stars at the center of spinning galaxies inevitably feed off each other and produce catastrophic star-to-star collisions. Scientists say Earth dwellers should have little fear of rogue stars zooming into the path of the Sun, as they say our star, which resides in the cosmic backwaters of the Milky Way, will likely burn out long before any star comes floating by. Luckily, the universe is a big place after all.

THE UNNATURAL LAND OF TWINS

In Cândido Godói, Brazil, they believe there's something in the water that's producing blond, blue-eyed twins: within a one-and-a-half-square-mile area, about 80 families have 38 pairs of twins. This phenomenon has been occurring for decades. The expatriate Nazi physician Josef Mengele, strangely, was seen wandering the countryside and posing as a veterinarian at about the time the barrage of twin births began. Though there has been no proof of mad scientist experiments, some say Mengele could have used drugs and artificial insemination on rural folk. In fact, 80 percent of the inhabitants of Cândido Godói are of German descent. A former mayor of the town claims locals are withholding information about Mengele, who died in Brazil in 1979.

BODY PARTS CAN STAY INTACT IN WATER

A woman was walking her dogs along the Fraser River in a Vancouver suburb when she stumbled onto a dismembered foot. The foot, wearing a New Balance shoe, was that of a female. The woman who discovered it thought she'd found a leftover Halloween prank. Experts believe the foot could have drifted thousands of miles, because human body parts can remain intact in seawater for years when covered by shoes and strong clothes. But don't expect body parts to stay together. Experts believe that when bodies are submerged in the ocean, the parts—head, arms, legs, hands, and feet—naturally separate from one another.

> **OBSESSIVE BITE:** At least six feet in shoes have washed up on the coast of Canada between 2007 and 2008. One other shoe was found to have an animal's foot inside. A hoax?

SO MARS HAS METHANE, BUT CAN YOU LIVE THERE?

NASA says the red planet is a cold world of lonely red deserts. Don't tell that to the long-dead creator of *Tarzan*, Edgar Rice Burroughs. He also created the *John Carter of Mars* series, which depicted the red planet as teeming with life. But that's just the stuff of adventure novels, right? In 2004, a controversy arose about whether Mars was home to abundant supplies of methane gas. Methane is composed of four atoms of hydrogen bound to one atom of carbon. It's the main component of natural gas found on Earth. Geological processes release the same gases as do living organisms. Telescope and spacecraft data were debated until early 2009, when NASA and university scientists finally said they had the first definitive detection of methane in the Martian atmosphere. From this discovery they concluded that Mars is still alive, in either a biologic or geologic sense.

But does that mean you can live on the red planet? And how is the methane gas being produced there? NASA officials suggest that the large quantities of methane found in the northern hemisphere of the red planet suggest that some ongoing process is releasing the methane. One scientist compared the seepage of methane to the release rate of methane from Coal Oil Point in Santa Barbara, California. Such amounts of methane could indicate hot temperatures within the red planet. Gases might be being released from the ancient ice caves beneath volcanoes or even from bacteria deep within Mars. The 2009 discovery of methane followed several years of study of the Martian seasons by NASA's Infrared Telescope Facility located at Mauna Kea, Hawaii. Spectrometers attached to telescopes, which spread light like a prism into its component colors, were used in the study. Whether the discovery indicates that humans will be able to colonize Mars is yet to be seen.

> **OBSESSIVE BITE:** NASA's Kepler spacecraft was created to survey 100,000 stars within the Milky Way galaxy to search for Earth-sized planets.

COULD THERE HAVE BEEN NESSIE LAKE MONSTERS?

Whether Nessie—Scotland's Loch Ness monster—actually exists is a tough question, given the smattering of shadowy evidence and the number of hoaxes related to the legend. What should be asked is whether lake monsters like Nessie could have ever roamed the planet. The answer to that question is an overwhelming yes. A 2006 BBC article begins, "Australia was once home to ancient reptiles that swam in huge icy lakes, fossil evidence suggests." There you have it. Australia was said to have been covered with water during different periods of its history. Scientists say that 115 million years ago there were long-necked creatures with four flippers, a small head, and a short tail living on the continent. Those creatures resemble what many people say they have witnessed in Loch Ness.

UMOONASAURUS AND THE LOCH LAKE FOSSIL

While the remains of creatures such as plesiosaurs and umoonasaurus have been found in opal mines in Australia since the 1960s, it was a 2006 discovery that opened the possibility of such creatures being not just ocean dwellers, but lake monsters. After all, dinosaurs are monsters, aren't they? And they deserve some tasty saltless H_2O. Two specimens were found from two different species, one seven feet long and the other around 16 feet long. Both were thought to be juveniles in a breeding ground, which means that the creatures were likely not just traveling through and got caught in some seasonal patch of icy water cut off from the ocean, but lived and possibly bred in the area. Those icy lakes were home. Of course, findings from Australian opal mines, frozen lake monster theories, and small, four-flippered beasts are by no means proof of Scotland's Loch Ness monster, but the evidence suggests the idea of a monster in a lake is possible.

In 2003, a 67-year-old Scotsman, Gerald McSorley, stepped on a fossil at the shore of Loch Ness that was later found to be that of a plesiosaur. Loch Ness monster enthusiasts claimed that the 150-million-year-old vertebra was part of Nessie herself. Scientists said otherwise, that the fossil couldn't possibly be related to the legend, as they say Loch Ness didn't even exist until the last ice age, about 12,000 years ago. Another hoax? Possibly. Scientists at the National Museum of Scotland claimed the fossil was the first discovery of its kind ever at Loch Ness, and also the first in Scotland in more than a century. McSorley said his discovery confirmed his belief in the creature.

OBSESSIVE BITE: The Umoona opal mines of South Australia aren't just home to umoonasaurus fossils. Faye Nayler's underground Umoona opal mine home is a tourist attraction. She and two other women dug out rooms using pickaxes and shovels. The home is still lived in. There were also churches in the opal mines.

RANDOM CREATURES LINKING LAND AND SEA

GO-GO-BOOT-A-SAURUS: Its real name is Gogonasus and it is a primitive fish found in fossil limestone beds in Western Australia. The middle ear and limbs of this little fish uncannily resemble those of land vertebrates. Scientists could open and close the mouth of this fossil, it was in such remarkable shape. It's unknown whether it walked on land or wore go-go boots, though experts did find the beginnings of a wrist joint in its front fin.

IT'S IN THE JAW: Two fragments of a 370-million-year-old fish jawbone were all scientists found at a dig in Latvia in 2001. What's not known is whether this prehistoric tetrapod had legs or fins, though it is said to have stepped onto land.

FISH WITH FINGERS: In 2008, scientists at Uppsala University in Sweden stated that fingers didn't develop in fishy ancestors after they became land dwellers. The scientists found that fingers were already developing in fish before they began sloshing out of primordial swamps. The researchers studied a panderichthy fossil using a hospital CT scanner to come up with their analysis.

AN ALLURING SEX SCENT FOR VAMPIRE FISH

A woman might follow her man because of his scent, and vice versa, but it's doubtful a woman will wriggle her way upstream after sniffing her man's pheromones. Lampreys, on the other hand, known as "vampire fish," infest the North American Great Lakes and are slimy bloodsuckers driven not just by hunger, but the need to breed in creeks and rivers. Their lure? The scent of a male.

Lampreys are considered among the earliest relics of vertebrate evolution. Researchers say they have developed a synthetic chemical sex scent that could help control lamprey populations or perhaps even rid the Great Lakes of them completely. The sea lamprey has been an invasive species in the Great Lakes since its accidental introduction in the late 1800s when the completion of the Erie Canal linked New York to the lakes. Typically, they're birthed in streams and make their way to adulthood in the Atlantic Ocean. By the 1900s, canals provided access for the parasitic fish to the upper lakes, where they could devastate fish populations. The lamprey's devastating effects were felt as long ago as 1940.

A NEW WAY OF POPULATION CONTROL FOR THE LAMPREY

In the ocean, there are natural predators that help control the lamprey's numbers. But not in the Great Lakes. In the absence of natural predators, the vampire fish thrive. They have devastated the lake trout, of which a single lamprey can feed on about 40 pounds per year. Great Lakes lamprey populations have typically been controlled by the costly use of lampricides tanker-trucked in by the Great Lakes Fishery Commission. The program costs $20 million per year to implement and also kills off invertebrates within the spraying areas.

Universities such as Michigan State University and the University of Minnesota have done extensive studies of pheromones in lampreys. Complex animal behaviors are believed to be regulated in part by pheromones. Well-fed lampreys, engorged from feeding off their hosts, search for suitable breeding areas. When a team from Michigan State released synthetic lamprey hormones from a trap placed in a stream, females picked up the scent and swam into the traps. After breeding, adult lampreys typically die. But by tricking spawning lampreys, their behavior can be manipulated to work against the parasitic fish. While this doesn't mean that all lampreys will be eradicated, new methods of population control rather than the use of poisons are much less harmful to the environment. University officials didn't say what happens to sexually confused lampreys that don't find their way into the deadly traps.

> **OBSESSIVE BITE:** Lampreys are called "vampire fish" because of their circular, pointy-tooth-filled mouths and the ability to suck blood from a host, sometimes killing the host in the process.

BLUE LIGHTS, CITY LIGHTS, AND CONFUSED CREATURES

Eyes may have hidden perceptive abilities that help control the biological time clocks of animals. It's no mystery that light has an effect on just about every living creature, animals and plants alike—including the creatures that live in urban areas. Light can affect whether a person feels tired or awake and can confuse the animals in the urban environments in which we live. The discovery of output cells in the human eye that communicate directly with the brain to influence our biological clocks was an important step in learning how our bodies tick.

THE EYE-POPPING EFFECT OF BLUE LIGHT

Blue light, or short-wavelength light, was found to help people fight off tiredness in a study by the National Space Biomedical Research Institute. NSBRI has conducted dozens of experiments with blue light on test subjects. They even have a live-in laboratory. While the study is meant to help fight drowsiness during space flight, the program also aims to help the public battle late-night fatigue, as millions of people suffer from chronic sleep loss or circadian disorders. In the U.S., 22 million people do shift work that interferes with nocturnal sleep cycles. Those workers often suffer from ailments like gastrointestinal distress, cardiovascular disease, and emotional problems. Female shift workers are more likely to suffer from breast or colon cancer than day workers. Mental fatigue and diminished alertness can affect those who work at night. Some people practically become zombies while working the graveyard shift. Blue light, however, has been found to directly reduce sleepiness. Test subjects exposed to blue light were able to stay alert during the time of night when people feel sleepiest. The effects of the blue light lasted only as long as the blue light was on, usually a number of hours. The benefits for astronauts, pilots, truck drivers, and factory and hospital workers could be tremendous. But there are dangers.

POLARIZED LIGHT AS AN ECO-TRAP

Too much blue light can cause damage, just as too much polarized light in urban areas may be causing damage to animal environments. While bright light can help those who suffer from winter depression or jet lag, polarized light has been found to have a negative effect on urban areas, even creating eco-traps of light pollution. Polarized light that bounces off road surfaces and glass buildings could be confusing the very animals with which people live. Unknown to many is the idea that birds, insects, and reptiles react to light because of their own polarized vision. Such light helps animals find breeding grounds and feeding sites. For instance, baby turtles rely on starlight and moonlight bouncing off the ocean's surface to help them find their way from shore. But some turtles in urban areas get lost, and like moths and other nighttime bugs, head toward street lamps and bright buildings. Many bugs get confused by the polarized light of buildings. So, while bugs may think they're headed for water, the critters may actually be headed for a wall or a building. Stoneflies have been found to nest on asphalt rather than water.

> **OBSESSIVE BITE:** Light therapy? In one study, the leaves of cotton plants were used in a light experiment which determined that certain colors of light could affect the growth of leaves that typically attract hungry pests.

WHEN U.K. TEDDY BEARS INVADED SPACE

One British newspaper titled its article "Ground Control to Major Ted," a play on words referring to the fictional astronaut created by David Bowie. On December 1, 2008, four British teddynauts were launched to the edge of space in a flight that lasted an astounding two hours and nine minutes. The intricate payload that carried the four teddy bears was created by Cambridge University Spaceflight. Humans could not be used because Britain has no space program, and, well, aluminum foil was used for space suits—not very protective. But that didn't stop the team from developing a high-altitude latex helium balloon system that could carry a flight computer, cameras, GPS, radio, and four rather cuddly and stuffing-filled bears in flight suits to an altitude of 30 kilometers.

TWO-LITER-BOTTLE PRESSURE SUITS

One of the bears was outfitted in a remarkable plastic two-liter soda bottle converted into a pressure suit. It was also wrapped in aluminum foil and what looked like tape. A photo shows the bear's beady eyes staring into the cosmos, arms in a half-wave toward the camera. Earth looks like a fluffy playroom in the background. One of the bears, labeled M.A.T., looked rather cold, as it wasn't even wearing a helmet in the minus-53-degrees-Celsius atmosphere. "The sticker saying M.A.T. on one of the bears was the initials of the team members from the school who made that bear's space suit," said Fergus Noble of CU Spaceflight. "The other bears had similar name tags but sadly didn't reach the same celebrity status!" The aim of the experiment was for the group of 11- to 13-year-old schoolchildren to determine what would best insulate the bears from the cold reaches of space. Unfortunately, a note on the CU Spaceflight website reads, "We fear that the bears may all have frozen."

TEDDY BEARS INSTEAD OF ACTION FIGURES

Asked why teddy bears were used instead of something like action figures, Noble said, "The idea to use teddy bears was thought of through working with the children at the Parkside Secondary School in Cambridge. We were in contact with a teacher there and decided to do an outreach project with their science club to try and encourage more young people to take up science and engineering." Noble added that while there aren't any plans for the teddies to return to the edge of space, Spaceflight is planning to do more outreach projects with schools around the country and is currently running a competition for schools in the U.K. to fly scientific experiments they have designed. There wasn't much ceremony to the launch, but Noble said the children handled most of it, including filling the balloon with helium, rigging parachutes, and finally letting go of the spacecraft.

TEDDY BEAR TRIVIA

While Spaceflight sends teddy bears into the sky for science, others send them flying to help needy kids. Gravity works especially well when you're throwing teddy bears by the thousands. Just ask the ECHL Bakersfield Condors ice hockey team. Each year their fans bring thousands of stuffed animals to throw onto the ice during one special game called "The Teddy Bear Toss." Vice-President of Communications Kevin Bartl said there have been over 52,000 stuffed creatures sent onto the ice throughout the 10-year history of the event. On a personal note, in 2008 the author of this book was pegged in the head by a flying teddy bear at the event, sending his glasses flying under a sea of fluffy animals. Search YouTube to find the video.

A VERY "PLUSH" LANDING

None of the data collected in the Cambridge University study was new to science. Noble said the team did get a very nice measurement of how the air temperature changed with altitude, clearly showing the tropopause, at about 10 kilometers, where the air temperature stops decreasing and actually starts to increase as you get higher. Luckily, after the weather balloon burst and the chute opened, the payload didn't land in the sea; past experiments have splashed down and washed up on beaches. The craft eventually touched down four miles northeast of Ipswich (about 50 miles from launch). The team saw the payload come down too. Noble said: "We had made predictions about where it would land based on the wind speeds for the day, so we could be in the right kind of area ready to pick it up. However, we got lucky and actually saw the balloon fly overhead about 500 meters up and land less than a mile away from where we were waiting!"

> **OBSESSIVE BITE:** "It was a bit fraught at times and at one point it was looking like we didn't quite have enough helium left in the tank to get the payload to ascend fast enough that we wouldn't land in the sea! However it was great fun for kids and bigger kids alike."
> —**Fergus Noble, CU Spaceflight**

EXTREME CUISINE

In Malaysia, try some frog legs in a porridge with sliced ginger. Or have them cooked spicy *kung pao* style with dried chili. You can always do the kebab thing, stir fry, or travel to the Philippines and have *les cuisses de grenouilles* Filipino style with *adobong palaka*, simmering in a marinade of vinegar, soy sauce, garlic, and bay leaf. But don't get too hungry for them. Frogs are in a state of decline globally and their populations could run out.

GLOBAL FROG MEAT TRADE KILLS BILLIONS OF FROGS ANNUALLY

Just a peek at a research article by David Bickford and colleagues of the National University of Singapore and you'll see that amphibian populations have been ravaged by disease, declining habitats, and deformities. But that's not all. Frogs could be near extinction because of the added danger of being harvested and eaten to the point of no return. In case you didn't know, as many as one billion frogs are harvested for consumption in Indonesia and China each year. That doesn't account for all the other countries around the world that harvest the creatures for their tasty thighs. Conservationists have called for more monitoring and safeguards to be enforced at frog meat markets to prevent amphibians from reaching critical population declines.

FRENCH CHEFS GETTING HOPPING MAD

One news report cited the UN as saying that the global frog meat trade has been increasing since the late 1980s. France and the U.S. have been blamed as two of the largest importers of the creatures. Statistics are hard to come by, and French chefs are saying they're not even aware of what species they're cooking up, as most frogs are skinned, butchered, and frozen before being shipped. Some French chefs have called for local frogs in their kitchens. But that's a fat chance—France, Belgium, and Luxembourg import more frogs each year than are probably hopping around the French countryside. One report suggests that if frogs are being imported, local supplies have already been overharvested. While at least one expert said the Singapore report is inconclusive, the increasing demand for frogs and the growth of human populations world-wide can't be helping frogs, which truly are in decline.

> **OBSESSIVE BITE:** The frogs being exported from Asia are crab-eating frogs, giant Jana frogs, and American bull-frogs, all of which have large, delicious thighs and could be threatened with extinction.

RANDOM PECULIAR DELICACIES

FRIED SPIDERS: In the Cambodian town of Skuon, Thai Zebra tarantulas are bred in holes in the ground for frying in the local markets. **Flavor:** bland, pasty, scrawny-chicken-wings texture.

PALOLO WORMS: Samoan green-and-blue coral worm delicacy that fishermen catch in swarms. Fried or baked into a loaf with coconut milk and onions. **Flavor:** scratchy seaweed and caviar; fishy; salty; tart.

BAMBOO WORMS: These grubby worms that burrow in bamboo shoots are best eaten when three centimeters in length. Don't eat when hairy. They are a South Silk Road delicacy, deep fried and puffed like popcorn. **Flavor:** tasteless.

BEE PUPAE: Nurse bees feed bee pupae royal jelly. These critters are cooked in oil in China and eaten with a dipping sauce. **Flavor:** unknown.

CENTIPEDE ON A STICK: Fried on a stick is the way to eat these leggy arthropods. Sometimes made in a Chinese soup with licorice and slivered loofah. **Flavor:** unlike anything ever tasted.

STINKBUG SURPRISE: In Mexico these pests called *jumil* are a delicacy and eaten when only a centimeter long. They are eaten alive in tacos or cooked in sauces. **Flavor:** Certain breeds taste like cinnamon because of the leaves they feed on. Others taste bitter, like medicine.

GRILLED SNAIL: Make sure to cleanse by fasting them for three days on water only. Then feed flour and offer water for another week. Popular throughout Europe, especially in France, Portugal, Greece, and Spain. Often, snails are grilled in a butter sauce, though there are many ways to prepare them. **Flavor:** rubbery, like shellfish.

PUFFER FISH: This popular Japanese sushi dish, called *fugu*, must be prepared by a professional, otherwise you can die from it. Toxins are far more powerful than cyanide. Banned in Thailand. **Flavor:** subtle, fine.

PUFFIN ON ICE: These birds are a delicious Icelandic delicacy. You can get puffins in the supermarket if you're in the neighborhood of Iceland. When preparing them, make sure to carefully pluck and then singe. **Flavor:** fishy version of gamy chicken.

CROCODILE SURPRISE: Head to Queensland, Australia, for some Crocodile Surprise. Tail filets are good, though higher in cholesterol than other forms of meat. There are some interesting barbecue recipes on Google. **Flavor:** gristly chicken.

MONKFISH: Every part of this ugly fish (even the innards and skin) is eaten except for the lips, which are lined with sharp teeth. This Japanese delicacy is craved in winter months, when its flavor is condensed. **Flavor:** depends on which part of the fish you're eating, and whether hot or cold.

BLACK STURGEON CAVIAR: These tiny tasty eggs you plop in your mouth. They're also good on bagels and sandwiches. Unfortunately, sturgeon populations in places like the Caspian Sea have dwindled because of a global love for caviar. Beluga sturgeon can live 100 years and grow 30 feet in length. **Flavor:** subtle; crunchy texture.

SCIENTISTS EXCITED OVER WHALE SHARK POO?

It's odd to think that the first time a whale shark was ever filmed going to the bathroom in the ocean was in 2008. It's even odder to think that marine biologists would be terribly excited over collecting whale shark stool specimens. But the BBC reported, amid all the fanfare, "It is as thick as your arm, gungy, and smells disgusting—and it has just been caught on camera for what is thought to be the first time."

Scientists have only studied whale sharks, the largest known fishes in the sea, since the 1980s. Whale sharks are related to great white sharks but are peaceful creatures. Scientists say that studying both what goes in and what comes out of whale sharks will only lead to more telling discoveries about these animals. One of the scientists on the expedition filmed by the BBC observed that whale sharks usually do their poopy business at greater depths. DNA from stool samples was examined to determine what the sharks eat. It was found that the sharks were eating red crab larvae—which could be explained by the sharks' proximity to Christmas Island, off the coast of Australia.

FISH POO HELPS OCEANS THRIVE

Before you get sick to your stomach about fish poo in the open seas, it's important to understand that it helps control harmful acid levels. According to a Canadian study, fish waste helps neutralize carbon dioxide within marine ecosystems. Canadian scientists discovered that when fish drink seawater they excrete calcium as calcium carbonate, a chalky substance that makes seawater more alkaline as well as diminishing carbon dioxide. The discovery has helped researchers understand the marine carbon cycle and how even fish waste can reduce CO_2 levels. Elevated CO_2 levels can raise sea temperatures and harm global sea life.

OBSESSIVE BITE: Like the world's second-largest fish, the basking shark, the whale shark is a filter feeder. It swims with its giant mouth hanging open, gobbling plankton constantly, to the shark's delight.

CHAPTER 3

PUZZLING AILMENTS: MOST MYSTERIOUS MALADIES

If I mentioned simple words like the cold or flu, you might instantly draw from your own experiences with those ailments. You might think "runny nose" or running to the bathroom with the dry heaves. You might remember your last bout with such a sickness and all the boxes of tissue you went through. But what if I mentioned "Cotard's delusion" or "Alice in Wonderland syndrome"? Would you have any idea what I was talking about? Would you simply think "crazy person" and look politely away? Believe it or not, there are people out there with some really bizarre afflictions.

In "Puzzling Ailments" you will come across some of the most interesting maladies you could imagine. For instance, "Tree Man disease" is a real affliction that affects an Indonesian man. But does he really have tree roots growing out of his skin? "Guinea worm disease" is one of the weirdest and most horrific conditions imaginable. Worms can literally crawl from your stomach into your arms, hands, and feet. What are the world's disease-control centers doing about such a bizarre sickness? "Morgellons disease" could just be a form of Internet paranoia sweeping the planet. Then again, it might really be a condition that sprouts fibers from lesions. Do you know anyone whose hands seem to think independently of each other? Could someone actually have a monster hand? "Alien hand syndrome" explores the realities of people who suffer from a monstrous hand that simply seems to do whatever the heck it wants.

While there seems to be no end to the types of creepy ailments afflicting humanity, after reading this chapter you'll get the sense for sure that the common cold you have occasionally battled was never as severe as you imagined it to be. You might even be thankful that that's all you ever had to deal with.

TREE MAN DISEASE

The Discovery Channel said tree man was half tree, half man. That's not really true, though parts of the former Indonesian fisherman named Dede don't look much different from a tree. His hands look like they've been ripped from tangles of tree roots. Branchlike brown growths shoot from the wide stumps where his hands are supposed to be. Unseen, his fingers lie hidden. Curls of brown growths shoot from his feet. In a video, the tree man says his feet and hands are heavy. He moves his limbs slowly, as you would expect a tree to move.

When Dede was a teenager, the roots began to grow out of his hands and feet after he got a cut on his knee in an accident. The Discovery Channel said the rootlike protrusions sometimes grow five centimeters per year. The U.K. *Telegraph* reported on December 22, 2008, that Dede, who is in his mid-thirties and lives near Jakarta, might actually have an immunodeficiency that prevents his body from battling the wartlike growths covering his body. The newspaper said that as the disease ravaged Dede's body, he lost his wife and his job. Living through years of ridicule, he joined a freak show, where he was paraded in front of audiences alongside others with grotesque and fantastic diseases.

The *Telegraph* reported that an American dermatologist, Dr. Anthony Gaspari of Maryland University, flew to Indonesia and examined Dede. The doctor determined that Dede's condition is caused by human papillomavirus. HPV is a common infection that causes warts, but because of Dede's genetic immunodeficiency, the warts are growing out of control. Gaspari claimed that Dede's treelike growths may be treated with a synthetic form of vitamin A. Gaspari, who thinks tree man will one day regain control of his hands, told the newspaper, "I have never seen anything like this in my entire career."

Symptoms: Hellish treelike growths and fast-growing warts.

VARIOLATION, ANYONE?
Prior to the advent of a smallpox vaccine, throughout the 18th century an inoculation method called *variolation* was used. The smallpox virus was taken out of the pus of an infected victim's sore and placed in a small incision in a healthy person. Only the wealthy could afford it. About one out of 50 people died after the procedure.

BAD DOCTORS
In Florence, Italy, in the 14th century the plague raised doubts about the credibility of the medical profession. Doctors couldn't manage the disease, which was the leading cause of death at that time.

PATIENTS
Or maybe patience? The idea of being a patient is universal.

We all eventually become one. So, have patience. Your turn cometh.

GUINEA WORM DISEASE

It's the kind of disease that you might think only afflicts the unsuspecting in horror movies: two-foot long worms seen burrowing beneath the skin after having traveled from the stomach.

According to *Scientific American*, Guinea worm disease is a debilitating parasitic infection that has been around since antiquity, affecting extremely poverty-stricken people who live in unsanitary conditions in Africa and Asia. The disease is caused by a roundworm parasite called *Dracunculus medinensis*, whose larvae live in microscopic water fleas. People contract Guinea worm disease by drinking unfiltered water that harbors the larvae-infected fleas. Once imbibed and passed through the stomach, the larvae burrow into intestinal tissues and reproduce. The wormy offspring then migrate through the body on a slow journey toward the outer skin. It takes about a year for the noodlelike worm to complete its journey. Often resembling spaghetti, the worms can be as long as 2–3 feet. Those afflicted see the worm moving beneath their skin as it prepares to break the surface, which in itself causes excruciating burning.

In a tormenting cycle of infection, those afflicted by Guinea worm disease often get relief by dipping their infected areas back into the tainted local water supply. When they do so, the worm releases millions of larvae. Those are then eaten by water fleas, the very bugs that transmit the worm to the afflicted. In 1986, there were 3.5 million infected with Guinea worm disease. Efforts have now reduced the disease to the point where it may be eradicated altogether.

Symptoms: After about a year with no symptoms, those afflicted develop a malaria-like fever. A lethargic week or so later, an intensely burning skin ulcer develops. A blister forms within the ulcer, from which the worm soon emerges. The worm's exit is a week and a half of agonizing torture. Those afflicted have multiple worms on different areas of the body, rendering them practically paralyzed with pain. If the worm pulls back inside the body, actual paralysis can result from the cutting off of blood supply and calcification.

MORGELLONS DISEASE

Bizarre red, blue, and black microscopic fibers under the skin? Bouts of itching and intense pain? Not good. People's lives have become transformed as they seek answers to their suffering after finding tangles of stringlike filaments beneath their skin. Yet, strangely, it could be that those who think they are infected with Morgellons disease—an ailment unrecognized by many doctors—are suffering from delusions brought on by an Internet paranoia sweeping the planet. But then again, it could be a real disease with strange fibers found in lesions. Confused?

Either way, Morgellons disease, named by a mother who swore she was finding fibers embedded in her child's skin lesions, has gained notoriety with major news sources across the globe discussing the validity of the ailment. In January 2008 the *Washington Post* reported, "Thousands of people around the world say they have a disease that causes mysterious fibers to sprout painfully through the skin, and they've given it a name. The spread of 'Morgellons disease' could be Internet hysteria, or it could be an emerging illness demanding our attention."

The newspaper reported that in 2004 Sue Laws said she felt she was being attacked by a swarm of bees. She claimed red fibers were found across her back but she was never wearing anything red. Over the next month her itching and pain intensified and she said it felt like thousands of tiny bugs were beneath her skin. She told the newspaper that eventually she coughed up a springtail fly, and a pink worm came out of one of her eyeballs.

According to the Morgellons disease website, the U.S. Centers for Disease Control and Prevention has now undertaken the task of helping to further characterize the illness. It seems that those afflicted, as the website says, just want the truth, whatever it may be, and an end to their suffering.

Many doctors call the ailment delusions of parasitosis, with people self-diagnosing common ailments during paranoid fits because of websites claiming that the disease is real. Some doctors have said the fibers are textile in origin, possibly from clothes or carpets.

But other experts claim there are too many commonalities among the sufferers. Why would people from around the world all report the same colors and kinds of fibers mysteriously appearing in lesions? Fibers whose composition many experts can't determine? Inorganic, silicon based, metal based, or organic? Experts can't seem to agree. Now the Centers for Disease Control is looking into Morgellons to determine whether it is real. That's a step in finding out if thousands of possible sufferers are deluded or afflicted with a disease not previously known to science.

In a twist of fate, a 22-year-old relative of Laws who died from cancer was found to be covered in lesions filled with fibers. Yet doctors have consistently told Laws she is deluded.

Symptoms: While Morgellons disease is not recognized by the medical profession, those who suffer symptoms often report disturbing crawling, stinging, and biting sensations. They also suffer from skin lesions that don't heal, and they claim to pull out fibers and filaments from their wounds. Some sufferers are afflicted with seedlike granules and black specklike material.

In addition to their skin ailments, those afflicted suffer from chronic fatigue syndrome (CFS), fibromyalgia, joint pain, weakness in concentration, and memory loss.

> **OBSESSIVE BITE:** While it wasn't Morgellons disease, the author of this book once had a third-of-an-inch-long filament that looked like a transparent pencil lead come out of his finger. It happened on New Year's Day, 2009— nearly 20 years after the author had worked in a Fiberglas factory.

ALICE IN WONDERLAND SYNDROME

If you wake up and it looks like your fingers are stretching for a mile, or you peer out a window and the seagulls flying 100 meters away look like they're about to land on you, then you might be one of the rare sufferers of Alice in Wonderland syndrome, a peculiar depth-perception ailment named after the popular book by Lewis Carroll.

Strangely, there's nothing wrong with the sufferer's actual eyes. People suffering from AIWS often experience distorted depth perceptions such as micropsia, where objects appear to shrink and seem farther away, or macropsia, where items appear larger than normal. "Everything shrinks. It's like I'm looking through a telescope backwards. I don't feel huge, though. I actually feel very small as well, which is strange since everything around me also feels small. It's like I've been miniaturized along with everything else around me." So wrote one man in January 2009 in a forum on an AIWS website run by Rik Hemsley, an actual sufferer of the ailment.

Some people experience the opposite reaction: not miniaturization but enlargement. They might be looking at someone whose extremities suddenly appear to balloon. Others claim they can induce the experience at any time and then shake their head, or shake their own weirdly transformed body part, to make the sensation stop. Some have said they feel as if their brain is being stretched like a rubber band.

Hemsley said to the U.K. *Guardian* in 2008: "When it first happened, I was a 21-year-old undergraduate. I had been up late the night before writing my dissertation and drinking a lot of coffee, but on that particular morning I was stone cold sober and hangover-free. I stood up, reached down to pick up the TV remote control from the floor, and felt my foot sink into the ground. Glancing down, I saw that my leg was plunging into the carpet. It was a disturbing sensation, but it lasted only a few seconds, so I put it down to overtiredness and forgot all about it."

Since writing for the *Guardian* in early 2008, Hemsley said no medical researchers have offered to study his affliction. "None, though I have answered questions for an article in a Polish magazine named *Medical Tribune*," he said.

Hemsley said he's still dealing with the affliction. "I am still improving, yes. I had a couple of days over the [2008] Christmas holiday where I noticed it, as a result of typical migraine-inducing behavior. I hadn't had anything for about three months before that."

It's hard to imagine that even if the affliction went away, as it usually does with AIWS, Hemsley could ever forget about a syndrome as puzzling as his. While he is married, has a job, and continues on with his life, many others in the world who suffer from this ailment rarely go outside, fearful of experiencing these surreally distorted perceptions. "The most bizarre thing I can think of, off the top of my head, is that often when I sit with my legs crossed, with my shin on the other leg's thigh, I would perceive that the upper leg was partially sunk into the lower.

This seemed to be caused by a combination of odd sensation and imagination. Whatever it was, it was quite unpleasant and occurred often. I would expect it is related to the more commonly quoted perception of a 'spongy' floor," said Hemsley.

Some of the possible causes cited are migraines, temporal lobe epilepsy, and Epstein-Barr virus.

Symptoms: The AIWS website describes the main symptom as that of altered body image. Those afflicted are usually confused as to the size and shape of parts of their own body. Heads and hands commonly undergo a metamorphosis, shrinking or growing. Visual perception of the surrounding world gets skewed. People, scenery, buildings, animals appear smaller or larger, while distances appear too close or too far away. Some of those afflicted experience distorted time, touch, and sound perception.

ELIXIR OF LIFE

Have you heard of the Philosopher's Stone, the *quinta essentia, elixir vitae*? It was sought after in China centuries before Christ. This miraculous plant or potion is supposed to cleanse the body of all illness and turn metal into gold. It could be hidden in a stone, bound by an occult sort of enchantment, and it is considered the dream of all Indo-European peoples.

COXSACKIEVIRUSES

These strange enteroviruses can be passed from mother to infant in utero but are not thought to cause spontaneous abortions.

FOREIGN ACCENT SYNDROME

A man I met once at a pizza parlor, who promoted music shows, was accused of having a fake accent because he suddenly started speaking as if he had spent many years in Europe. Others around the world have been accused of this, too. One woman in Michigan sounded like she was British though she was born in a small American town. Whether these people are faking it or not, most actual sufferers of foreign accent syndrome are accused of falsifying their speech.

The reality is, the 40 or so documented cases of FAS usually stem from a brain injury or stroke that may have caused damage to the speech centers of the brain. While the person's speech sounds otherwise normal, there is a foreign-sounding accent that overlays syllables and sometimes sentences. Some people are more fluent with their accents than others. Some of those afflicted are reported to have mysteriously recovered within just a few months time.

The BBC reported that one British woman, after a stroke, started speaking with an idiosyncratic accent that sounded alternately French Canadian, Slovakian, Italian, or Jamaican. "I didn't realize what I sounded like, but then my speech therapist played a tape of me talking. I was just devastated," Linda Walker said. She added, "I've lost my identity, because I never talked like this before. I'm a very different person and it's strange and I don't like it."

The best-known case of foreign accent syndrome occurred in Oslo, Norway, after a British bombing raid on September 6, 1941. A 28-year-old Norwegian woman was seriously injured in the head by a bomb fragment. She lay unconscious for several days and was not expected to live. Two months later, she was discharged from the hospital—suddenly with a German-sounding accent. During the remainder of the war she was often mistaken for a German and suffered discrimination because of it.

Symptoms: Sudden strange foreign accent.

TWENTY-FIVE RANDOM REMEDIES

APHRODISIAC: If you're looking to increase your libido and you don't want all the nasty potential side effects of Viagra, find some horny goat weed. It has been helping the Chinese since the days of the ancients. In lab experiments it works just as well as the little blue pill.

CONSTIPATION: Laughter has a massaging effect on the intestines.

NOSEBLEED: Run something cold down the back of your neck. Sudden chills can cause blood vessels to contract.

MOUTH ULCERS: Try a pinch of baking soda or dissolve some in a glass of warm water and use as a mouthwash for neutralizing acids in mouth ulcers.

GREEN HAIR: For blondes in chlorine pools whose hair has turned green, just add ketchup and cover with cling wrap for 30 minutes.

HEADACHE: Draw blood to your feet by soaking them in hot water. Add some mustard powder for exceptional thumpers.

DECONGESTANT: The University of Nebraska found that traditional homemade chicken soup (not from a packet) contains the amino acid cysteine, which is a decongestant.

PMS BLOATING: The yeast extract Marmite can help fight PMS bloating. Fish eggs and brazil nuts can help too.

BRUISES: Vinegar heals bruises. Soak cotton and apply.

COUGHING: Try a nice bar of chocolate. Theobromine in cocoa suppresses sensory nerves.

PMS: Boil a cup of water and pour over a teaspoon of dried rosemary. Cover and let brew for 15 minutes, then drink a warm cup twice daily.

INSECT BITES: Dab on toothpaste to fight itching and swelling.

OBESITY: Turmeric, which is found in curry, has many medicinal uses and helps prevent obesity in lab rats. So eat hearty.

CANCER: In 2008, it was announced that medical experts in the U.S. are now studying the ancient Chinese remedy of potentially deadly toad venom for cancer patients. Often cancer patients try a blend of Western and Chinese remedies to fight tumors.

TOXIC BLOOD: Actress Demi Moore once had 45 leeches gorge on her blood— a creepy Austrian treatment for toxic blood. Apparently the little critters release a helpful enzyme as they chomp down.

STROKE: Consider acupuncture to help you in your recovery. Millions of patients each year do so in China. Could they all be wrong? Get in harmony with yourself.

SKIN DISORDERS: A urine-mixture ointment can help clear up blotchy skin. Singer Amy Winehouse tried it. In another curious case of urine therapy, actress Sarah Miles drank her own urine for 30 years, claiming that it immunized her against allergies.

CELLULITE: Mix a little olive oil with warm coffee grounds. Spread on thighs twice a week. Cover with cling wrap for several minutes. The caffeine helps circulation.

ICKY BREATH: Chomp on a raw coffee bean.

SORE THROAT: Manuka honey from New Zealand can kill over 250 bacteria strains. It can help heal burns too. Add some lemon.

BEAUTY TREATMENT: Actress Gwyneth Paltrow once used a type of acutherapy for beauty called "cupping." Heated glass cups applied to different areas of the body can supposedly relieve stress.

STINKY TOES: Soak your feet in two cups of hot tea diluted with extra water.

DANDRUFF: Three aspirin dissolved in shampoo can help with flaking scalp.

SNIFFLES: Warm feet in hot water. Soak pair of thin socks in cold water. Wring out and wear. Add thick, dry socks and put feet up (go to bed). Boosts circulation, which can help with the sniffles.

STAINED TEETH: Rubbing strawberries on your teeth can rid you of superficial stains.

ALIEN HAND SYNDROME

A Discovery Channel video uploaded to YouTube shows a woman's hands being examined. "This is Vern and this is Skip," she smiles, holding up her hands. The woman claims she named her right hand after her intellectual brother, Skip, and the left after her more volatile brother, Vern. "Because I can control the right one far better than the left," she adds. The video shows the woman feeling a marble in her left hand, which fidgets uncontrollably. She can't tell what she is holding until the object is placed in her right palm.

Like a few dozen people around the world, the woman suffers from alien hand syndrome, an affliction that causes people's arms to work independently of each other. Some sufferers have a monstrous loss of control, with reports of their rogue hand trying to take control of the car while driving. Others' hands are a nuisance because they can unbutton shirts or pull out hairpins independently of whatever task the person may be performing with the other hand.

One YouTube video posted on the Internet in 2006 shows a California woman lying on her back on a gurney as she recovers from a brain aneurysm. Her left hand fidgets and moves uncontrollably. The woman admitted she often thought someone else was in the room because of the way her alien hand syndrome caused her hand to act. In a video update in September 2008, the woman said she had regained much of the control of her hand.

Some experts say the key to alien hand syndrome is a loss of use or damage to the corpus callosum, the superhighway that connects the left and right sides of the brain. Possible causes of damage to the corpus callosum include brain injury, stroke, aneurysm, and infection. There is no cure for this monstrous condition. People with the affliction try to keep the rogue hand occupied. One man was even reported to have placed an oven mitt over his rogue hand to help keep it under control because it was creeping around on him at night.

Symptoms: Loss of control over a limb that still has feeling and movement and seems to operate independently.

MEDICINE IS MAGIC

Medicine and art both descended from the same roots: both originated in magic.

HYPOPLASTIC LEFT HEART SYNDROME

Both heart ventricles are the same size at birth. In the rare case that a baby is born with a tiny left ventricle, 91 percent die in the first month. But some can survive.

MULTIFETAL PREGNANCIES

The incidence of twins has dramatically increased in the United States since the 1970s, to epidemic proportions.

SPASMODIC DYSPHONIA

The cartoon character *Dilbert* doesn't have a mouth. Coincidence? Maybe.

Certain parts of the brain control speech. But these parts can break down or go haywire, leaving some people with a rare disorder that renders them only able to speak in riddles, laughter, or whispers. Victims of spasmodic dysphonia are unable to speak to others in their normal tone—a man might speak in a falsetto voice or a woman in a baritone voice. Oddly, they are able to speak normally after sneezing, laughing, or while reciting poetry and riddles. Experts say the voice disorder is caused by involuntary movements of at least one muscle of the larynx. The disorder causes the voice to break or to have a strained and sometimes strangled quality. The voice is often normal when those afflicted laugh, sing, or speak in rhymes. Many with the disorder speak in a breathy whisper.

Sometimes the disorder runs in families, as it is thought to be inherited. Spasmodic dysphonia also sometimes accompanies other involuntary muscle disorders that affect eye twitching or other parts of the body. There is no known cure, though Botox injections are often used as a temporary fix to help sufferers speak normally again.

Cartoonist Scott Adams, the creator of *Dilbert*, is the most famous of those affected with spasmodic dysphonia. As many as 30,000 Americans between 40 and 50 years of age are afflicted with the condition. In 2006, Adams was able to beat the disease, though it's unknown whether he beat it for good. It was reported that Adams didn't like getting Botox injections. His only comfort was singing and reciting poetry, which caused only slight gasping and stammering. He recited nursery rhymes in hopes of remapping his brain and was chanting "Jack Be Nimble" when he suddenly realized his voice sounded mostly normal again. Adams's character Dilbert is one of very few cartoon characters ever created without a mouth.

Symptoms: Muscle tremors in voice box, breathy voice. Can only speak normally while singing.

COTARD'S DELUSION

Imagine feeling hopeless and unable to recognize people or places anymore. Would you feel as if you were dead? You might. Those afflicted with Cotard's delusion are so impaired by self-deprecating feelings of despair that they are in denial of self and the external world and believe they are dead. Those who have such feelings also experience buildings, places, and people as unfamiliar.

In one case of Cotard's, a 61-year-old man who was depressed after a bowel resection was transferred to a hospital psychiatric ward. Soon his depression worsened, and he began to say he had been dead since the previous week. He constantly looked at the ward clock, and when asked why, said he couldn't understand why it was still working. He thought the clock should have stopped when he died. The man claimed to be somewhere between Heaven and Hell.

Jules Cotard, a Parisian neurologist and psychiatrist and former military surgeon, made discoveries about the disorder in the 1800s. Cotard's delusion is said to comprise any of a series of delusions varying from the belief that blood, body parts, or organs are missing to believing that one is dead or that one's soul is lost. The condition is encountered mostly in psychoses such as schizophrenia and bipolar disorder. There has even been a report of a pregnant woman who was convinced that her pregnancy was nonexistent, even though she was in an advanced stage of gestation.

It wasn't until after 1980 that experts determined that those with the disorder also suffer from recognition loss. Capgras syndrome, a related disorder discovered in the 1920s, is the delusion that one is an imposter, or that others are imposters. Imagine looking into a mirror and not recognizing your own face!

There are even odder twists on the disorder. Some with Capgras syndrome tend toward violent behavior and attempt to attack those they believe to be imposters. Some even think their pets are imposters. One patient believed his jogging shoes were replaced by identical fakes each night. One woman, looking into a mirror and seeing an imposter, screamed and called herself a hussy.

Symptoms: Depression, disassociation with self, reality. Facial recognition loss.

TWENTY-FIVE CURIOUS PHOBIAS

ARRHENOPHOBIA: Fear of male offspring.

BAROPHOBIA: Fear of gravity.

CALIGYNEPHOBIA: Fear of beautiful women.

CELTOPHOBIA: Fear of Celts.

CHEROPHOBIA: Irrational fear of merriment or gaiety.

CHROMETOPHOBIA: Fear of making money.

COPROPHOBIA: Abnormal fear of feces.

DEXTROPHOBIA: Fear of objects on the right side of your body.

EMETOPHOBIA: Irrational fear of vomiting.

ERGASIOPHOBIA: Fear of work or functioning.

EUPHOBIA: Fear of good news.

GELIOPHOBIA: Fear of laughter.

GENUPHOBIA: Fear of knees.

GRAPHOPHOBIA: Fear of writing.

GYMNOPHOBIA: Fear of being seen naked.

HELIOPHOBIA: Fear of the sun.

HIPPOPOTOMONSTROSESQUIPPEDALIO-PHOBIA: Fear of long words. (No, really.)

IDEOPHOBIA: Fear of ideas.

ITHYPHALLOPHOBIA: Fear of erections.

MYCOPHOBIA: Fear of mushrooms.

NOMOPHOBIA: Fear of being out of cell phone range.

OPTOPHOBIA: Fear of opening your eyes.

SELENOPHOBIA: Fear of the moon.

TELEPHONOPHOBIA: Fear of cell phones and other communication devices.

URANOPHOBIA: Fear of Heaven.

STENDHAL SYNDROME

You're a tourist traveling by yourself without a guide. You go to see a great work of art in Florence, Italy, perhaps Michelangelo's *David* or Botticelli's *The Birth of Venus*. Emotionally, you're devastated by the experience. You hallucinate, you feel panicked, anxious. Was this the experience you hoped for? How long will these feelings last?

Stendhal syndrome affects those who expose themselves to the grandeur of great artworks. In 1989, Italian psychologist Graziella Magherini examined 106 patients over a 10-year period at Santa Maria Nuova Hospital in Florence. She determined that those afflicted were young, single persons who were sensitive, impressionable, and mostly traveling on their own while coming in contact with great works of art without a professional guide. Magherini determined that many patients fell into a 2-to-8-day disturbed mental or psychosomatic state. Those in a disturbed mental state experienced a disturbing sense of reality characterized by feelings of strangeness or alienation and altered perception of sounds and colors. In their delirium patients described being persecuted in relation to their immediate environment.

Magherini came to her conclusions after comparing notes with the French writer Marie-Henri Beyle, better known as

Stendhal, who lived in Italy in the early 1800s. Stendhal's diaries, contained in the book "Rome, Naples et Florence," depict an important day in his life, January 22, 1817, when he went to see various works of art in Florence. After visiting the Franciscan church of Santa Croce, where several Italian artists, writers, and scholars are buried, including Michelangelo, Galileo, and the poet Vittório Alfieri, Stendhal wrote: "There, to the right of the door, is Michelangelo's tomb; beyond this is Alfieri's tomb ... Then I notice Machiavelli's tomb and, in front of Michelangelo, there rests Galileo. Such men! What a magnificent collection! My emotion is so deep that it almost reaches piety. The melancholic religiousness of this church and its simple wooden vaulted arches, still unfinished: all this speaks vividly within my soul."

In a portion of the church where Stendhal could see the cupola decorated with the frescoes of the 17th-century Florentine painter Volterrano, his emotions bordered on hallucination: "Sitting on the step of a genuflection stool, with my eyes diverted from the pulpit to be able to contemplate the ceiling, Volterrano's Sibyls gave me perhaps the greatest pleasure that any painting had ever given me ... I reached the emotional state in which we experience the celestial feelings that only the beauties of art and sentiments of passion can offer. Upon leaving Santa Croce, my heart was beating irregularly ... life was ebbing out of me and I went onwards in fear of swooning."

There's also evidence that the Russian writer Fyodor Dostoyevsky, who suffered from epilepsy, experienced Stendhal syndrome. On his way to Geneva with his wife, Anna Grigorievna, Dostoyevsky had an ecstatic experience while viewing the painting *The Body of the Dead Christ in the Tomb*, by the German artist Hans Holbein.

Dostoyevsky, author of *The Idiot*, *Crime and Punishment*, *The Possessed*, and *The Brothers Karamazov*, stood at the painting dazed, in a state of ecstasy. His novel *The Idiot* depicts his transcendent experience with the artwork, as does his wife's diary: "During the journey to Geneva, we stopped in Basle to visit the museum, where there was a painting that my husband had heard about ... representing Christ after his inhuman martyrdom, now taken down from the cross and in the process of decomposition. The vision of the tumescent face, full of bloody wounds, was terrible. The painting had an oppressive impact on Fyodor Mikhailovich. He remained standing in front of it as if stunned."

Dostoyevsky describes the painting in great detail in *The Idiot*, which seems to characterize its stunning effect on him. Grigorievna recorded Dostoyevsky's reaction after viewing the painting: "Faced with a picture like this, a man could lose his faith."

Stendhal syndrome may not be limited to Europe. Comedy websites can be found in relation to the ailment, and there's even a 1996 film of the same name about a policewoman who suffers from a psychosomatic disease that gives her dizziness and hallucinations when she is exposed to artistic masterpieces.

While many people are inspired by great works of art, it's unknown whether Stendhal syndrome has resulted in artistic epiphanies in the works of other creative persons. David Hackett Fischer writes, at the beginning of his 1989 historical work, *Albion's Seed*, that he had an emotionally moving epiphany after standing in Boston's Museum of Fine Arts and viewing a painting of Polynesian women by Paul Gauguin. In the painting's corner Gauguin wrote three questions in French: "Where do we come from? What are we? Where are we going?"

"Everything I've written is an answer to that," Fischer said in a 2008 interview promoting his latest book, *Champlain's Dream*. The painting caused Fischer to question who he was and where he was going, and the same about America. He spent several years working on *Albion's Seed*, a historical work about waves of immigrants and the influence of their folkways on American culture.

Paris syndrome is a variation of Stendhal syndrome, affecting Japanese tourists who have emotional breakdowns when visiting the city. About a dozen women are reported to be affected each year, of the million or so who visit the city annually from Japan. Many Japanese visitors are reported to travel to Paris with a deeply romantic vision. Apparently, the reality can come as a mental shock.

Symptoms: Viewing artworks causes psychosomatic symptom to appear, including tachycardia, chest pains, weakness, sweating, and stomach pains. Those afflicted also experience anxiety and confusion.

THE IDEA OF MEDICINE

In medicine the recollection does not have to reach so far back, only to the beginning of the illness, though it tries to investigate the very first symptoms, hovers about in the border zone, and crosses into another, earlier world, the world of good health, the world without illness.

—Andrzej Szczeklik,
Catharsis: On the Art of Medicine

RANDOM FAMOUS SICK PEOPLE

CHARLES DARWIN: Between the ages of 30 and 33 Charles Darwin became an invalid recluse and wrote *On the Origin of Species.*

FLORENCE NIGHTINGALE: She nursed thousands

during the Crimean War. After the war she became tyrannical and bedridden with a psychoneurosis. She lived to 90, yet constantly believed she only had months to live.

LOU GEHRIG: New York Yankees first baseman who contracted amyotrophic lateral sclerosis, or ALS, in the 1930s. He was a reluctant spokesperson for what became known to many as Lou Gehrig's disease.

FERDINAND MARCOS: In 1967, the once popular leader of the Philippines had snail fever, or schistosomiasis, which is transmitted by freshwater snails that harbor the parasite. He told a doctor that he would name an archipelago in the Philippines after him for helping rid the leader of the disease.

SHAH OF IRAN: When a doctor removed the shah's cancerous spleen in 1980, it was 20 times its normal size. Stretched out on a table, the organ was measured as a foot long and weighed 1,990 grams.

HALLE BERRY: This Hollywood star suffers from Type 2 diabetes. Slightly overweight in school but otherwise healthy, the actress was once unconscious for a week because of her illness. Other celebrities with diabetes include Tommy Lee, Mae West, Spencer Tracy, and Elvis Presley.

CARRIE FISHER: Princess Leia's toughest battle wasn't against Jabba the Hut but in battling bipolar disorder. A doctor first diagnosed her with manic depression when she was 24 years old. She went for years before seeking treatment. Other famous people with bipolar disorder include Phil Spector, DMX, Sylvia Plath, Axl Rose, and Virginia Woolf.

MUHAMMAD ALI: This famous world-champion boxer once known as Cassius Clay fought the "Rumble in the Jungle" and the infamous 1975 bout "Thrilla in Manila" against Joe Frazier. Seven years after his thrilling victory, he contracted Parkinson's disease. The ailment attacks the central nervous system, which controls balance, coordination, and body movement.

ROBIN WILLIAMS. One of the world's funniest men in television, film, and stand-up comedy suffers from ADHD (Attention Deficit Hyperactivity Disorder). As much as 5 percent of the population worldwide suffers from this energetic, lively, inattention-causing ailment. Will Smith, Michael Jordan, and Jim Carrey are also known sufferers.

HOWARD HUGHES: The American film producer, industrialist, and aviator (1905–1976) contracted syphilis when he was young. He had neurosyphilis in his later years, which caused degenerative brain disease, paranoia, and other bizarre behavior. In addition, he was obsessive compulsive, a condition some believe his mother also suffered from. Other sufferers of syphilis include Ivan the Terrible, Winston Churchill, Guy de Maupassant, and Al Capone.

JERUSALEM SYNDROME

When some people travel, they have an agenda of touristy places to visit where they can get a sense of history and culture. Others actually slip into their own religious psychosis as soon as they step off an airplane. At least that's how those with Jerusalem syndrome are described.

Between 1980 and 1993, 1,200 tourists visiting the Holy Land had severe Jerusalem-generated mental problems and were referred to the Kfar Shaul Mental Health Centre. Of those who visited the hospital, 470 were admitted. On average, 40 tourists are admitted to Kfar Shaul each year.

According to the *British Journal of Psychiatry*, there are varying types of people who experience Jerusalem syndrome. Some already have a psychosis and are impelled to visit Israel by their mental condition and preexisting delusional religious ideas. Some have fantastic or magical ideas, such as thinking they can heal others, or violent agendas like wanting to destroy mosques. Some are loners; others are part of a group. (One group, following biblical prophesy, is searching for an unblemished red heifer born in the Holy Land—a sign of the Messiah.) Some people visit the Holy Land without any mental problems whatsoever but fall victim to Jerusalem syndrome while visiting.

Others identify with characters from the New or Old Testament. In one report, a 40-year-old American tourist with a mental condition, who liked to work out and identified with Samson, traveled to Israel so he could move one of the stone blocks of the Western (Wailing) Wall. He caused a commotion as he tried to move one of the blocks. Police were called, and he was hospitalized. After being told he wasn't Samson, he broke a window and escaped. He was later found at a bus stop. Hospital officials determined him to be in an acute psychotic state.

While reports of pilgrims to Jerusalem being seized by religious psychosis date back as far as the Middle Ages, it wasn't until the 1930s that Israeli psychiatrists formally described the condition.

Symptoms: While symptoms vary, if you're not normally mentally disturbed, while visiting Jerusalem you might experience agitation, the desire to break off from your touring group, a strong desire to be clean and pure, the need to scream or shout out Bible verses, the need to wear a toga made of white bed linen, the need to march to a holy place, or the desire to deliver a moralistic sermon at the holy place.

JUMPING FRENCHMEN OF MAINE DISORDER

Like Japanese tourists with Paris syndrome, other culture-bound syndromes can affect the unsuspecting. One of the strangest is an exaggerated response to being startled called the jumping Frenchmen of Maine disorder.

Most people have a response to being startled that lasts only a few seconds: muscles tense up, the heart pounds, and senses go on high alert. Sometimes there's a scream. First observed in 1878 among French Canadian lumberjacks in Maine's Moosehead Lake area, people with jumping Frenchmen disorder have an exaggerated reaction. Those afflicted jump and twitch. They flail their arms and legs and impulsively obey sudden commands, even if that means injuring someone.

The disorder is called *latah* in Malaysia and Indonesia and *myriachit* in Siberia, where it has been observed in factory workers. Among the Ainu people of Japan, it is known as *imu*. Some experts have said the disorder is a genetic mutation that blocks glycine, a neurotransmitter that calms the central nervous system during sudden stimulus. Others suggest it's a psychological condition developed as a heightened defense mechanism to living and working in close proximity to other people.

In Malaysia and Indonesia, the hyperstartling response to stimuli leads to a highly flustered state where people may say things that are obscene or irreverent. Symptoms tend to improve with age, experts say.

Symptoms: An unnatural response to being startled that makes a person susceptible to the power of suggestion.

PENIS PANIC

Who would have thought that mass hysteria could come about over the fear of penises shrinking, disappearing into one's body, or being snatched?

Genital retraction syndrome, also known as koro syndrome (from the Malay word for "turtle's head"), was first recorded in 300 B.C. China in a text titled "The Yellow Emperor's Classic of Internal Medicine." Epidemics have occurred in both Asia and Africa and can cause a penis panic. Sometimes the condition is affiliated with a belief in witchcraft or sorcery. Either way, men with this syndrome believe that their penises are retracting into their bodies, or have been stolen; this is often accompanied by the belief that they will die as a result.

Those who believe in penis snatching believe that the penis is given back, reappearing at the time people begin to make accusations about the unsettling ordeal. An epidemic of penis theft swept Nigeria between 1975 and 1977, according to a 2008 *Harper's* magazine article. One doctor wrote that after a resurgence of the belief in penis theft in 1990, "men could be seen in the streets of Lagos holding on to their genitalia either openly or discreetly with their hand in their pockets."

During the panic, people yell that their genitals are missing. The accused are often tormented or killed. In April 2001, at least a dozen accused penis thieves were lynched in Nigeria. Dozens were killed in Benin, West Africa, between 1997 and 2003. In

China, penis retraction is diagnosed as *suo-yang*, a type of fever that arises from too much cold. In 1967, hundreds, possibly thousands, were afflicted with koro, all believing their penises were shrinking. In 1976, at least 2,000 people, both men and women, believed their genitals were retracting into their bodies, and in 1982, epidemics of koro swept India and China, affecting thousands of villagers.

In the 1950s, Hong Kong–based psychiatrist Pow Meng Yap noticed men coming into his office in fear of imminent death from their penises retracting into their bodies. He determined that the ailment was a culture-bound syndrome. In modern terms, this means a culture-related disorder rather than one bound to any single area. After all, there are reports of American koro as well.

Some women are affected by the affliction, believing their breasts or nipples are retracting into their body or shrinking.

Symptoms: Strong belief that genitalia are shrinking, disappearing into the body, or stolen.

CHAPTER 4

IDIOSYNCRATIC INVENTIONS: TECHNOLOGIES WE DEPEND ON EVERY DAY AND SOME USELESS CONTRAPTIONS

Inventions can push water over mountains or help people to get from point A to point B more efficiently. They help people live longer and look better. They help flowers grow and they entertain us. Inventors have been with us through history. Some inventors were nameless individuals who created technologies tens of thousands of years ago. Others aren't well known, like Samuel O'Reilly, who invented a tattoo machine in 1891. And yet others are household names like Thomas Edison, known for inventing the long-lasting lightbulb and the phonograph. He recorded 1,093 patents.

Benjamin Franklin was one of America's great early inventors. He invented bifocals, an extending arm to reach books off tall library shelves, the lightning rod, and swim fins. In a letter to the editor of the *Journal of Paris* in 1784 about his idea to observe daylight savings time, Franklin wrote, "For the great benefit of this discovery, thus freely communicated and bestowed by me on the public, I demand neither place, pension, exclusive privilege, nor any other reward whatever. I expect only to have the honour of it." Franklin never may have wanted payment for his invention, but most people do. They spend great amounts of money on patents and sell them to manufacturers for the possibility of mass production.

In "Idiosyncratic Inventions" you're going to find some of the more bizarre inventions ever created. Take the Neolithic ax. No one knows who the inventor was, but it surely revolutionized the world. "Greek fire" brought about new ways of killing and terrorizing one's enemies, as did man-bearing kites, in a gruesome way. You will learn that some inventions were thought of as wild or unlikely to succeed, while others came about totally by accident. An unlikely invention, the MRI scanner, is one of the oddest medical machines ever devised, with an ability to see into people. The microwave oven was a big accident that developed as the result of a melted candy bar. Other inventions have provided unexpected uses, as robot faces suggested the use of synthetic skin for medical purposes. Read on. You may discover a few offbeat inventions in your house as you read this chapter.

NEOLITHIC AX

Take a polished stone blade, fix it with a deer antler wedged into a wooden handle, and you've got one of the craziest inventions ever made: the Neolithic ax. Great for all kinds of uses, including chopping trees and killing enemies. Easy to carve your initials on, too. It's hard to say when the ax was invented. Evidence includes hollowed-out canoes and wooden utensils from as long as 7,500 years ago.

CHARIOT RIMS

Drive down any California street and you'll find two cars competing for the coolest rims on their lowered rice burners. But don't think the use of rims on decorated vehicles started when you were a teenager. A Celtic chariot dating to the early Iron Age used high-quality steel *tyres* that were standard on heavy vehicles in the 4th century and possibly earlier. Braking wasn't so good, though, according to one account of a slave getting run over on a steep street in Rome. The slave owner was compensated.

DILDOS OF THE ANCIENTS

Put away that sex catalog and go to the nearest museum of antiquities. You can do some serious studying there. The Greeks may not have invented dildos, but a discussion of them in the 3rd-century comedy *A Private Chat*, by Herondas of Alexandria, proves that women have used sex toys for centuries. While the Greeks used dildos (*olisbos*) made of the softest leather available, and though dildos can be made of anything, the Greeks came up with a unique material for them: breadsticks, which they called *kollix*. In 1986, a professor studying inscriptions found the word *olisbokollix* in a lexicon of classical 5th-century Greek, with pictorial evidence to match. That was proof enough that the phallus-shaped loaves were once both sexual as well as edible delights.

ANCIENT CHINESE SEISMOGRAPH

The earliest known earthquake-detecting device was created by Cheng Heng in China between A.D. 78 and 139. The device was kept in an earthquake room in the center of a building in the Forbidden City. It consisted of a huge copper caldron that held the inner workings of a pendulum that was attached to eight dragons outside the caldron. The foot of the vessel was set on foundations hidden from sight beneath the floor. The eight dragons held metal marbles in their mouths and were positioned above carved toads with their mouths open, one for each dragon. If a dragon dropped its marble into the mouth of the toad, an earthquake occurred in the direction it faced. Up to the 17th century, 908 earthquakes were recorded on the device. Cheng is also reported to have created a flying machine that lifted him into the air.

GREEK FIRE

Imagine you're taking a joyride along the coast in a tiny boat. Suddenly a ship with gilded bronze lion heads fixed to the side shoots liquid fire from the beasts' mouths. Terrifying? It's supposed to be. Greek fire actually originated around A.D. 674 in Byzantium—modern-day Istanbul, Turkey. The inventor, Callinicus, created a formula that was so closely guarded that the makeup of the mixture is unknown to this day. The Chinese utilized Greek fire by the year 900. Around 150,000 supposedly died in a battle that took place on the Yangtze River in 975. In the heat of battle the warriors failed to check wind patterns before they cut loose streams of fire from a 10-deck-high ship. Apparently, the admiral of the vessel, Chu Ling-Pin, was so distraught over the ordeal that he cast himself into the flames.

TWENTY-FIVE RANDOM ODD INVENTIONS

FLYING SAUCER CAMERA: Created by the U.S. Air Force in 1953. It would take regular photos and also separate light colors, because, as you know, that's how spaceships hide.

TINY GLASSES: These glasses strapped to a band worn around the head were so tiny they were smaller than dimes. In 1936, they were meant to shield the eyes from glare while driving.

BALL-SHAPED TRAIN: In 1935, a magnetic train was invented. Or rather, a ball pulled by magnets on a track was invented, called the "bullet flash." The ball was expected to roll at upwards of 300 miles per hour and could be used on or off tracks. The entire idea for this invention seems to have rolled away somewhere.

CLAIRVOYANCE DRUGS: It must be true, since *Modern Mechanix* magazine ran an article in 1932 about a South American plant called *Yage* that caused people to see great distances and through objects. It's unfortunate that the compound wasn't mass-marketed in a little invisible pill.

PHONOGRAPH DISK ARMY TANK: In 1934, someone had the brilliant idea that sounds recorded onto phonograph disks could be used for automatic control. It would be a shame if, during a war, someone might spin some jazz music rather than play directions for a tank to explode an enemy bunker.

GRENADE THAT PUTS OUT FIRES: It's unknown what this 1890 gizmo looked like, but since it exploded, you'd likely not want to double the damage if there was already a fire.

MECHANICAL PAGE-TURNER: The first such invention was built in 1890 and is now on display at the British Library. More than 100 years later, an MIT student built another version. They're still not available at Wal-Mart.

ELABORATE MECHANISM WORKS AND WORKS TO DO NOTHING WELL: Featured in *Popular Mechanics* in 1954, this bizarre mechanism had over 700 working parts that rotated, twisted, and oscillated. It was all for the sake of movement. The inventor called it a flying-saucer detector.

THE TWO-HANDLED SELF-POURING TEAPOT: Built in 1886, this invention was quite the catch. One press of the lid and an entire teacup was filled.

TOOTHPICK GRAND PIANO: *Popular Science* in 1940 reported that a two-inch-square grand piano had been constructed. It was so small it could be played with a toothpick.

BREATHING BALLOON FOR BIG BREASTS: *Mechanix Illustrated* magazine showed off a breathing balloon for women to use to develop their lung capacity. This 1949 invention was wrapped with a tape measure that somehow corresponded to breast size.

INFLATABLE SHORTS: In 1971, you could find magazine ads for ordering inflatable air shorts that offered pneumatic support. The shorts kind of looked like a waffle. And they promised to massage you in unspoken places.

MOTORIZED ROCKING CHAIR: This 1955 invention even came with a gearshift. The motor mechanism was as big as the chair.

SPEED MASK: Strap it on. It had a built-in snorkel and once helped a man swim from Catalina Island to San Pedro, California. That was in 1968. The inventor claimed that drag was cut by 35 percent. It resembled a full-faced superhero mask. Only it was transparent.

KEROSENE RADIO: In 1955, *Popular Science* showed off this gas-powered all-wave radio made in Moscow. The advertisement in the magazine said the invention worked best in a room with open windows.

NONSKID HOT DOG BUN: In 1939, some wacky inventor created a hot dog bun that weenies couldn't escape from. These rolls with ridges had quite a grip.

MECHANICAL "WILLIE": He was a laboratory robot built in 1934 that could be quite the servant. Westinghouse claimed Willie could salute, raise flags, smoke, sit, stand, and bow via voice command.

WRISTWATCH RADIO: It would have been easier to strap bricks to your arm and pretend they were radios. This 1947 invention claimed to have the world's smallest microtube.

MOBILE PLASTIC EYE: In 1947, you could finally get a fake eye designed to help your eye move in conjunction with eye muscles. Of course, doctors also had to sew the eye muscles to a metal mesh that was attached to the back of the plastic eye.

SOLAR BATH APPARATUS: All you did was sit down and put your head in this machine, built in 1933, that shot out ultraviolet light to your entire noggin. It was supposed to cure every head ailment known to man.

WARM PILLS: In 1957, *Science Digest* claimed that pills had been invented that could keep you warm. The pills caused the body to create more heat than the body could naturally produce. The makers claimed to have tested the pills on blacks, whites, and Eskimos.

MIDAIR FLYSWATTER: This invention looked like giant tongs created by an insane fly hater. It was shown at the International Patent Exhibition in Philadelphia in 1932.

SPURISCOPE: Just dial in the serial numbers on your money in your pocket, and this 1949 invention would tell you if the money was counterfeit. It's unknown if this handheld device could also double as a magic 8 ball.

CROSS-EYED CONTRAPTION: In 1939, the American Optical Company created what it called a stereoscopic optical machine, meant to strengthen eye muscles. Of course, the article discussing this peculiar contraption shows a man with his eyes crossed.

ROBOT SUITS FOR ANIMATED YOUNGSTERS: *Science and Mechanics* magazine claimed in 1957 that these contraptions were great for costume parties, parades, or trips to outer space. It was fairly certain you had to supply your own cardboard box to use for the head.

BONE SKATES

The earliest known skates were made out of bone and looked like tiny skis. Forget those turn-back-the-clock jerseys they sometimes wear in the NHL—lets see them fight while skating on some ancient bone skates!

TATTOOS

It's clear that tattooing started with the ancients, who used various techniques including placing powdered charcoal in cuts with small needles. In 1991, "the Iceman" was found melting in an Italian glacier. The 5,300-year-old corpse had several tattoos, including one of a cross on his left knee.

AFTERLIFE LEGS

A mummy of a 14-year-old girl discovered in 1975 had fake legs made out of reeds and mud. Why? Apparently, ancient Egyptians believed bodies must be whole in preparation for the afterlife, so false limbs were constructed for the girl, post-death. The earliest known recorded evidence of false limbs was found in the writings of Herodotus. He recounted the story of Hegesistratus, who sawed off his own foot so that he could escape a leg iron and fight against the Spartans in 479 B.C. He made a foot out of wood to use as an attachment to his leg.

MAN-BEARING KITES

By the year 559, the first Ch'i emperor of China, Kao Yang, was regularly using prisoners as test pilots for kites to see if the contraptions could bear human weight. The kites were actually controlled from the ground. One of his man-bearing kites held

Prince Yuan Huang-T'ou, who flew for nearly two miles. The prince was rewarded by being starved to death. Yang's invention was based on an earlier idea of his to tie bamboo mats to prisoners who had been condemned to death and watch them fly (fall) to a dismal end from a 100-foot-high tower.

GLOVES

Who invented gloves nobody knows. But they're important enough to mention. Written about in *Beowulf* in the 8th century, gloves are believed to have been used by early Germanic tribes. In Shakespeare's day, the ancient half-moon knife was used by glovemakers who invented a way to cut deerskin while paying attention to every direction the glove would be stretched when it was sewn together. It's also not known when the first glove was used to slap a poorly behaving man in the face. An unhappy woman invented that, for sure.

THE CAMERA OBSCURA

There was something called a camera before there was a camera? Try sometime between A.D. 965 and 1039, when Alhazen invented the camera obscura. The camera obscura was a dark room with a small hole in the wall through which the view outside was projected upside down onto the opposite wall or onto a white screen. It was originally designed so that people's eyes wouldn't be harmed when looking directly at the sun during a solar eclipse. Of course, people also found it fun to watch projected images of what went on outside the room.

MASS-PRODUCED PAPER

Don't go taking for granted that just because the world is turning paperless, paper isn't needed—nor was it always easy to come by. Around 1850, the demand for paper was at an all-time high as printers and stationers were taking major innovative leaps in their fields of expertise. At first, straw was added to rags. That didn't help much. Then, in 1855, esparto grass was added. That wasn't much better. But then wood pulp began to be used on a major scale. By 1873, major improvements had been made thanks to the discovery of chemical methods of extracting impurities through boiling in certain chemicals.

ZINC YELLOW

It's said that paints didn't become sophisticated until the 20th century. The development of paint increased rapidly where industrialization developed the fastest. Ready-mixed paints didn't have a heyday until then. Zinc chromate, better known as zinc yellow, wasn't used much before 1914. But during World War II millions of pounds of it was used to protect metal objects such as military equipment, because it was rust-inhibiting.

ICE FACTORY

At the supermarket you might take for granted that shelf of fish kept on ice. Fish is affected by microbial spoilage more than any other type of protein, but a revolutionary invention called the ice factory extended the shelf life of fish. While sea ice was used at first to protect fish from spoiling on ships, it wasn't until 1891 that the first ice factory was capable of producing 50 tons a day for outgoing trawlers. Think of the preservative effect of ice: cod will spoil within 4–5 days at 5 degrees Celsius. Put the same fish on ice and it will last for over 16 days at zero degrees Celsius. Ice for transport was used in England as early as 1786, but in China much earlier. Of course, ice could only last for a limited amount of time, so distances were limited.

TWENTY-FIVE RATHER USELESS PATENTS

FLEXIBLE MUSTACHE CUP: U.S. Patent No. 3733021 is a drinking cup with a movable upper lip protector.

DIAPER ALARM: U.S. Patent No. 4205672 is a sensor that clamps onto a baby's diaper. It is a rather shocking invention.

CHICKEN SPECTACLES: What else can be said here? You should mass-produce them so your chickens don't peck one another's eyes out.

SHOCK GAME: U.S. Patent No. 6561905 is a skin-irritating game machine. Do you really want to play? What garage was this invented in?

TOILET LANDING LIGHTS: U.S. Patent No. 5263209 is for those with poor toilet etiquette. Makes for great middle-of-the-night trips to the potty.

INSIDE-OUT CLOTHING: U.S. Patent No. 7350242 was issued on April 1, 2008. Someone who wore hand-me-downs must have invented this in a fit of vengeance.

TWO-HANDED GLOVE: Perfectly weird patent for hand-holding lovers.

BUNNY SYRINGE: U.S. Patent No. 3299891 changes the shape of unfriendly needles into harmless bunnies. What would happen to the idea of the Easter Bunny after a few years of mass use?

HEAD-MOUNTED LETTER M: U.S. Patent No. 6834453 is exactly what the name suggests: a hatlike contraption that supports a giant letter M.

PARACHUTE HAT: U.S. patent No. 3345646 is a balloon cap. The BBC shows a related image of a man suspended from a balloon by strings connected to his cap with a chin strap.

HOSPITAL HAPPINESS: U.S. Patent No. 6012168 provides a modest flap for hospital gowns so everyone won't see your rear.

BEERBRELLA: U.S. Patent No. 6637447 is exactly what America needs, don't you think? The small umbrellas clip on to beer bottles.

SPORTS JERSEY CHAIR: U.S. Patent No. 6637447 should go well with those who manufacture, sell, and buy Beerbrellas. It's simply a chair made out of sports jerseys.

PEST DEATH RAY: U.S. Patent No. 6647661 locates pests with a microwave scanner. The pests are then killed by a "lethal impact" of radiation that can blast for three minutes.

RIFLE HELMET: You might not want a rifle sticking out of a helmet, especially if you get whiplash easily. One man's neck was broken testing the device, the BBC pointed out in a report on the patently absurd.

HUMAN-SHAPED DECORATIVE VEGGIES: U.S. Patent No. 4827666 lets veggies grow into the shapes of human heads. Edible Elvis, anyone?

DOGGY COLOSTOMY BAG: U.S. Patent No. 7461616 could actually be used for nice walks through the park without having to use a pooper scooper for the dog. However, the invention looks more painful and time consuming than just cleaning up after Fido.

MAGNETIC THERAPY DEVICE: U.S. Patent No. 6648812 is a round magnet centered in a gyroscope. It's a toy. A fancy magnet toy that makes you feel better? Doubtful.

THE LOVE BOX: U.S. Patent No. 4194629 is a simple box with the word "love" carved into the outside and inside. Unfortunately, it's not very attractive.

FINGER-MOUNTED STEALTH FLYSWATTER: A fly lands on a little bar attached to your finger. Another bar, a sort of flicker, is attached to your index finger. The rest is just practice. U.S. Patent No. 7484328 was issued in February 2009.

THREE-LEGGED PANTYHOSE: U.S. Patent No. 5713081 is really called "Panty Hose x 3." When one leg gets damaged, apparently you would have a spare.

THE DOG UMBRELLA & LEASH: U.S. Patent No. 6871616 attaches directly to your pet. In your other hand you can hold an umbrella for yourself. Be careful getting out the front door.

DISPOSABLE BOXER SHORTS: U.S. Patent No. 6539554 was issued on April Fools Day 2003. As the patent says: "The need for clean underwear is universal."

CLOTHES PROTECTION SYSTEM: U.S. Patent No. 7350239 is just a Velcro bib. Or is it? It is.

BOXER ADVERTISING SYSTEM: U.S. Patent No. 6742293 is for a sign to be carried by a person, yet how can one do that while boxing? This patent caused great confusion on the website IPWatchdog. com, which wrote a good summary of this entire section: "The patent classification system is extremely strange ..."

THE GREAT WONDER-WORKER OF THE AGE

You might be thinking "the computer," "modern film," or "the automobile." Maybe you're even considering "automatic banking." Nope. First you have to know the era we're talking about. When discussing the technological innovation that pushed forward the great material advances associated with the first Industrial Revolution, there's one word for it: the railway. The railway linked the Western world to non-Western peoples and was the core of industrial transformation. Railways crossed Africa, Asia, Europe, and the Americas. It was truly the great wonder-worker of its age, bringing people and products to new places in a revolutionary system of transportation.

VOLTA BATTERY

It was considered a momentous discovery when Alessandro Volta discovered in 1800 that electricity could be generated utilizing a battery of plates made of dissimilar metals in the presence of saline, alkaline, or acid electrolytes. Apparently, the laboratories of electricians in the European scientific institutions of the time had all but given up. Of course, Volta's discovery led to many inventions in battery power generation throughout the 1800s, which eventually led, via many related innovations, to your iPod. Thank goodness Volta didn't give up!

MILE-HIGH BUILDING

Although it never came to be built, in 1956 Frank Lloyd Wright sketched out ideas for a mile-high building. He wanted it to be an urban focal point, a place that would meet social and cultural needs. The design consisted of a load-bearing structure with a central tripod-shaped column that tapered toward the top. He compared his idea to a tree with roots that stretched far into the ground.

MRI SCANNER

In 1977, Dr. Raymond Damadian and his assistants needed an indomitable name for the huge, complicated machine they had been working on for several years. They finally decided on "magnetic resonance imager." Not only did their invention, the MRI scanner, allow for early cancer detection, it provided a window into the functioning of the body as a whole. Unfortunately, when Damadian first announced in 1971 that he was building such a machine, he opened himself to years of torment and ridicule, as scientists said his ideas were wild.

MICROWAVE OVEN

Believe it or not, microwave ovens have been around for as long as there has been radar. Magnetrons, if you didn't know, help send out radio waves. In 1946, Percy Spencer was testing a magnetron when he discovered that the chocolate bar in his pocket had melted. Of course, magnetrons were huge and expensive. It wasn't until 1967 that they became compact and affordable. It took another 10 years for people not to be terribly frightened to use them.

GYROSCOPE COMPASS

Elmer Sperry was really into gyroscopes. He loved them so much that in 1907 he took the novelty and created a gyroscopic compass that would always point north. But it didn't stop there. He utilized heavy gyroscopes in what he called a gyrostabilizer to help ships counteract the rolling caused by high seas.

COB BUILDINGS

Forget all those cookie-cutter homes lining the hills of suburbia. Build a natural house with clean, green, natural 24-inch earthen walls. Make them thicker if you want. What's holding you back? There's a modern architectural home-building revival that's going green around the world, and it has natural aesthetic flair, not to mention fire resistance. Cob structures first appeared in the 11th and 12th centuries in Europe; in England, cob structures have stood for 500 years. Old cob structures can also be found in Africa, the Middle East, and the eastern United States. No, it's not corn cobs—cob is a mixture of clay or other soil, sand, straw, and water. These homes are sturdy, environmentally safe, and don't destroy resources. They use building materials that can be replenished and sustain themselves.

The natural building and sustainability movements in

England and Ireland beginning in the 1990s caused a modern green resurgence in cob structures. In 1994, Kevin McCabe built a cob house two stories tall, with four bedrooms. His home was reported to be the first cob home built in England in 70 years. His innovation was simply to add sand to the mixture to reduce shrinkage. Cob builders in the northwest U.S. use a process called the "Oregon cob," a wall lay-up technique using loaves of sand-and-straw-mixed mud. The technique has been used by House Alive, which provides cob workshops around the globe. As do the people at www.cobworks.com. And cob homes are economical. In 2007, a 2,150-square-foot home was built in British Columbia for the equivalent of $171,484 U.S. It has solar power and subfloor heating.

ARCADE VIDEO GAMES

Before arcade video games, the first video game wasn't *Pong*, but *Spacewar*, which required a $7 million computer to run in the early 1960s. Not very efficient when you want an arcade game to only cost a quarter. In 1971, Nolan Bushnell designed an arcade version of *Spacewar* that wasn't too much of a hit. Of course, when one of his recruits built *Pong* a few years later, that turned out differently. But not at first: Bally Games initially turned down the idea, but when a test model was placed in a bar in Sunnyvale, California, it shorted out because it got overloaded with quarters so fast. Bushnell hired Steve Jobs in 1978, who, along with Steve Wozniak, built the game *Breakout* while working the night shift. Wozniak and Jobs also built the first Apple computer that year, too.

COMPUTER MOUSE

It's the name of a rodent and a device most people use to move their cursor around on their computer screen. But where did it come from? Douglas Engelbart used a chunky square box as the first mouse in 1968. He and his coworkers called it a mouse because of its long tail of a cord. He got the idea for the function of the mouse from the way he thought people were meant to utilize their hands to control writing instruments. It took 18 years for Engelbart to develop that simple vision into a reality. By the way, computers have advanced at such a fast rate that no mouse was used in the writing of this book.

KOOBFACE COMPUTER VIRUS

Computer viruses are manufactured like viruses in sci-fi movies and are often meant to cause mass hysteria. Koobface was built to spread through social networking on the Internet, causing hard drive meltdowns. Journalist Matthew Shaer, who reports on innovation trends, said that by December 2008 Koobface had infected thousands of users in dozens of countries, prompting Facebook to release a set of safety instructions. Among them: Download an antivirus scanner and immediately reset your password. Then, on a Monday morning, the Web was rocked by a second attack, a "phishing" scam targeting the popular microblogging network Twitter.

Viruses like Koobface are spread from computer to friend's computer, sometimes between unsuspecting, trusted friends; they are a grave security threat. "Koobface showed us that social networks, which we expect to be relatively bombproof, are in fact as susceptible to all sorts of nasty infestations." Shaer said. "The implications are manifold: a PR problem for Facebook; an adjustment in the way many users approach social networks; a warning that all that personal information which we store on our profiles isn't quite as safe as we once expected. Plus, we got that great name—'Koobface.' I read somewhere that the name of the virus came from a stray piece of coding that a particularly savvy geek somewhere managed to extract. It's certainly an evocative word, no?"

A VIRUS INVENTION THAT AFFECTS TRUST ISSUES

So is trust the real issue? Shaer said, "A security expert at McAfee told me that the best way to avoid getting viruses is to read the subject line of incoming messages. Solid advice, and when people have asked me how to avoid malware, I always pass along that particular bit of received wisdom. Read the message title! If it says, 'Paris Hilton throws up on my shoe,' it's fake. If there is any question at all as to the veracity of the message, check with your friend before opening it. And use a little common sense. Obviously social networks work at least in part on mutual trust—we trust our friends not to send pictures of us drinking beers to our bosses or grandmothers, and our friends trust us not to scrawl curse words all over our walls. I hope Koobface doesn't damage that mutual trust, but I also hope that people are a little more aware of the kind of malware that circulates through many social networks."

And that's tough, because social networking, as Shaer points out, is like candy to hackers. "The week before I started the article, a friend sent me a message on Facebook. There was an embedded video link, and some lame come-on—"check out this cool/crazy video of you," or something similar. I realized it was malware of some sort but didn't yet know about the Koobface attack. If I'd clicked on the link and launched the .exe file, the story certainly would have taken on a more personal dimension! At any rate, yes, of course—I was surprised by how effective Koobface was, and how little most users knew about it. Facebook posted a short item on the site somewhere, but the majority of friends and coworkers hadn't the slightest idea what was going on and could easily have had their computers infected. I was also impressed at how quickly the hackers had sent Koobface spiraling out into the digital world. We'll likely never know the identity of the team or individual that created the virus, but in a horrible sort of way, the malware was quite an achievement."

> **OBSESSIVE BITE:** Matthew Shaer can be found on his Tumblrlog at http://mattshaer.tumblr.com. He writes for the *Christian Science Monitor,* which after 100 years switched from a daily newspaper to magazine format.

ROBOT FACES

When many people think of lifelike robots, singing Disneyland pirates usually come to mind. Yet those animatronic faces are devoid of life compared to Bristol Robotics Laboratories' service robot head, which can talk and show emotion. In 2008, BRL, at the University of West England, revealed its newest lifelike robot head, marking the latest achievement in service robot technology trends. Service robots are still a way from being mass-produced and available to common households. BRL and other robotics companies seek to find new ways to design humanlike robots. By designing complex computerized facial features such as frowns, smiles, and even contemplation, their robots seem empathetic. But why? BRL's belief is that service-class robots will be the future's caregivers, tour guides, domestic servants, hotel porters, and so on. And who wants a boring tour guide?

Some robot facial features are cartoonish and childlike, as in Zeno, by Hanson Robotics. Zeno's boyish robot's face uses imitation skin patented as Frubber™. The skin is an elastic polymer that makes realistic facial movements and talking possible. It also has the potential to help in real-life facial reconstruction and many other uses. Hanson Robotics' Character Engine software provides facial enhancements with 62 preprogrammed facial features. That means even more lifelike behavior from such service-class robot innovations. Everyone wants a child robot, right? Now go watch Steven Spielberg's *Pinocchio*-like movie, *A.I.*, about a robot boy, and dream. Because the future of marionettes without their strings is here.

802.11B

No, this isn't the name of a TV show. The Institute of Electrical and Electronics Engineers (IEEE) established what is known as the 802.11 working group around 1990 as a standard in wireless technology. When 802.11b was adopted as a standard in 1999, in just two years there was a shift from fixed computer networks in every industry imaginable. Where the world had once used cables, there began a transformation into a wireless world.

PENDULUM CLOCKS

People all live by the clock. Blame it on 14th-century inventors whose development of giant pendulum clock towers in European city centers eventually led to the idea of regulating sleeping patterns and corporate workdays.

PAPER CLIPS

Since the first bent-wire paper clip was invented in 1867, there have been many styles and brands, including the Fay, Gem, Eureka, and more. If you spend a moment pondering all the nasty things kids do with paper clips, you'll understand why this invention is so rebellious.

FISH TANKS

People take the idea of aquariums for granted—as if ocean life was meant to be recreated in false habitats literally poured out of the sea. Blame Chinese and Roman inventors for creating the revolutionary idea of fish out of water. But it was British and German fascination with the idea that really took root.

CHAPTER 5

ODD OCCUPATIONS: SOME OF THE DIRTIEST, WEIRDEST JOBS THAT YOU NEVER WANTED BUT HAVE TO KNOW ABOUT

ome jobs don't seem normal, because movies like *Office Space* or TV shows about cubicle dwellers make normalcy seem like it should be behind a desk. And sure, there are plenty of those desk jobs in corporate offices and government buildings. But while work is what people do to pay the rent and have money for material items like hobbies or fast cars, the idea gets in people's heads that crazy jobs are for people who are a little different. Astronauts risk their lives to enter outer space for the sake of science. Fire-eaters and sword swallowers risk their health and well-being to entertain people like you and me. The reality is, people aren't all working behind a desk. People work all kinds of jobs, from retail at the local mall to airline pilots, entertainers, and soldiers battling on war fronts. The world needs them all—even those fire-eating entertainers. Whether a job seems eccentric or not really depends on your perspective. If you're loaded with tattoos you're not going to think a tattoo artist is out of the ordinary, and if you work in the sex industry you're probably not going to think being a professional dancer on Broadway is all that glamorous.

In the meantime, check out " 'Obama Wonderama' Burlesque Performer," about a woman who works the Washington, D.C., burlesque circuit entertaining lawmakers and other interesting clientele. The guy profiled in "Wastewater Operator" claims that every city needs people like him willing to wade into the cesspools of humanity. "Bean Pimp" may not be the kind of summer job you thought you wanted, but you sure can learn a lot about life. A pawnbroker can perform good deeds while catering to some of the most desperate people in society who need to cash in. And if you need to learn how to tell what's a fresh catch at the seafood market, read "The Art of Gutting Fish."

Most people will find as they read "Odd Occupations" that they can easily add to this list of job descriptions. I've added a few of my own, including "Bottle Washer" and "Creative Writer," just so you won't feel alone. Now, have a friend read along so you can ask each other about the normal life, whatever that may be.

'OBAMA WONDERAMA' BURLESQUE PERFORMER

If you live in Washington, D.C., and you need side work, there just might be a career for you. Burlesque performer Candy del Rio has had an affinity for showgirls and burlesque her entire life. She watched the 1962 movie *Gypsy* when she was about eight years old on a small black-and-white TV and was intrigued by Gypsy Rose Lee. After moving to the D.C. area, she watched her belly dance teacher perform at the Palace of Wonders show bar, which focuses on live burlesque and sideshow acts. She said she immediately fell in love with burlesque and sideshow culture that night.

SEXY JOB EMPOWERS WOMAN AFTER 40

Del Rio performs a few times a month and was even photographed by the renowned photographer Elliott Erwitt for his photography feature "Visions of the Inauguration" in *Newsweek* during the inauguration of Barack Obama. Her show at the Warehouse Theater on January 18, 2009, was titled "Obama Wonderama." She said her burlesque job involves creating acts or numbers around a piece of music or a concept, sometimes humorous, sometimes a political statement, or sometimes just a glorification of the glamorous burlesque stars of the past. Something she loves about burlesque is that it embraces the beauty of all kinds of women. While classic beauty always gets the most attention, so will funny, outlandish, and just plain courageous burlesque, del Rio says. She added that not many professions would afford a 40-year-old woman a chance to perform a routine where she transforms from Marilyn Monroe to Jackie Onassis to the tune of Kill Hannah's "I Wanna Be a Kennedy."

NOT AS BAD AS WHAT HAPPENED TO THE SWORD SWALLOWER

As for craziness onstage, del Rio said she has shared the stage with dogs that jump through hoops of fire, hula-hoopers, fire-eaters, fire dancers, sword swallowers, magicians, bagpipers, trapeze artists, and more. She said she also performed a duet with an old guy who looked like Cap'n Crunch and showed off his private parts. She said she became an expert on what is the best adhesive for pasties (in her opinion, carpet tape is the best) and how to hook fishnet pantyhose into a thong without showing a waistband. Yet, del Rio said the weirdest thing that happened was during "The Weirdo Show" variety act. She said one of the performers, a new sword swallower, punctured his esophagus. She said the guy was in the hospital for a month and still had a huge scar on his throat. "I think I'll just stick to dancing around like a drag queen and flashing my pastie-covered boobs to quirky music," she said. "At the very least, I know that glitter, sequins, and eyelash glue are not life-threatening."

WASTEWATER OPERATOR

There's a job that needs to be done at your local wastewater treatment plant, and maybe you're the right person to do it. Chris Bell is a California wastewater treatment plant operator. A normal day for Chris might involve doing mechanical work on a pump or on one of two methane-operated cogeneration units. When he first started, he never thought it was odd, and even to this day still doesn't see it as offbeat. He said people probably can't imagine being in charge of their own food and waste.

WAIST DEEP IN WASTEWATER, AND THE WALL OF SHAME

Bell said he has been waist deep in raw wastewater and on the business end of a 10-inch industrial vacuum line, with more condoms, feminine hygiene items, and hypodermic needles than you would care to know. One of the unique aspects of Bell's job is a humorous and rather interesting bit of evidence recreation—a sort of wastewater CSI. Bell said staffers created a "wall of shame" out of a small collection of adult photos that people had torn up and flushed down the toilet. People go through the trouble of tearing up a photo and flushing it down the john without destroying the face. Bell said it's funny when he sometimes recognizes people on the street from pieced-together photos of them on the wall of shame. "One day I found all but two parts of a photo that was torn into about twelve parts. What are the odds of that?" He added that it's almost unbelievable he could find so many pieces of a dirty photo when 16.5 million gallons of raw sewage pour through in a 24-hour period.

TWENTY-FIVE RANDOM WEIRD JOBS

FORTUNE COOKIE FORTUNE WRITER: In 2005, Lisa Yang was writing about 20 fortunes a week for a fortune cookie company. Her strengths were copy-editing and a love for movies, books, and famous quotes.

PROFESSIONAL WRESTLER: It's amazing the kinds of jobs you can find when surfing the Internet. MySpace has listings for pro wrestlers at $92/hour.

ODOR TESTER: There are all kinds of jobs where you can be an odor tester. Factories, mines, and waste-water facilities are just a few. Don't forget perfume and deodorant companies.

MASCOT: Sure, being a high school mascot might be cool. And you might aspire to become the next San Diego Chicken. But some mascots are more offbeat than that. One hockey team has mascots dressed up as produce that race around their ice rink. Other mascots stand on street corners as pizza slices or the Statue of Liberty. At a bowling alley the author frequents there is often a fluffy human bowling pin.

ISLAND CARETAKER: You can find the listing for this job, billed as the "Best Job in the World," at Islandreefjob.com. The caretaker of the Islands of the Great Barrier Reef has a fantasy job description: write a blog while living in paradise. The job was easily filled.

PROFESSIONAL MUSE: Can you make $10,000 per week if you know how to inspire as a personal life coach? While a related ad was run on NYSocialdiary. com in 2008, it's unknown if anyone actually spends that kind of cash on pro muses these days. But then, everyone needs their own personal cheerleader.

LIGHT CHASER: The Selfridges store on Oxford Street in London has 26,000 light bulbs. The light chaser's sole job is to replace them. The store occupies six floors.

DOG TREAT TASTER: Does being a dog treat taster mean you have to eat dog treats? Maybe in some secret societies of dog treat tasters, but not for most pet food and pet snack makers. You do have to learn how to interpret pet behavior, though.

MERMAIDS: There's a Las Vegas casino by this name where employees dress up in extravagant aquatic costumes. But there are also women who float in fish tanks, as they do at the Coral Room nightclub in New York. Could you be in a fish tank all day?

ABATTOIR WORKER: There are careers all over the world for people who carry out the various tasks concerning the slaughter of animals and the preparation of carcasses. Some workers have the daunting task of sorting innards.

TOILET CLEANER: Can't imagine this is an especially good job if you work at a constipation clinic.

Every school needs a janitor. Think of the stories you'll hear.

GUM BUSTER: We would all be surprised if we really knew how much gum was out there in the world. Thank goodness some of us don't have to ponder such sticky thoughts, since people like Duane Cummins, with his GumBusters company, make it their job to clean gum off sidewalks and buildings. Try it as a start-up. Gum can be your friend.

FLAVOR CHEMIST: Create natural and artificial flavors in a laboratory. Work for more than 10 years at it and you're in the $150,000 range.

FECAL ARCHAEOLOGIST: Being a pathoecologist means establishing relationships between human behavior, environment, and disease. The travel to ancient sewage sites could have some glamorous aspects. Just ask Karl Reinhard, who pays the bills studying ancient fecal matter.

PRODUCT BREAKER: Being an evaluation engineer means you might have a difficult and challenging time breaking dishwashers, microwaves, or toasters. There's a spin-off called a video game tester. Imagine the endless hours of fun as you try to see if you can break the most innovative video games that aren't even out to market yet.

CELEBRITY PERSONAL ASSISTANT: If you have to hold up your boss's drink with a straw so she doesn't smudge her lipstick, you're probably in the world of celebrities. There are many types of assistants, from bag carriers to tea makers and those who run homes and private offices. In 2008, Jennifer Lopez was said to have two assistants, while Mariah Carey had an entourage of nine. Some celebrity PAs have moved on to run entire companies.

BOLLYWOOD EXTRA: It's said that foreign tourists visiting Mumbai, India, are often asked to be extras in street scenes being filmed for Bollywood pictures.

SHEEPSKIN FACTORY WORKER: In some factories sheepskins come right off a truck. Workers have to scrape the excess meat from the hide, stretch them out, and salt them down. Not for the timid.

CARPOOLER: Some companies pay up to $11 dollars an hour for people to sit in the passenger seats so delivery trucks can enter carpool lanes.

WEIRD THEME PARK WORKER: Forget Disney-land—anyone can be a Mickey Mouse, right? What about working at Holyland in Buenos Aires, Argentina, as a regular for the nativity? How about Wannado City in Florida, where "kidizens" try out for grown-up jobs (all make-believe). Or Dubailand—could you really hang with fun-loving sheiks? Top it off with an application to Japan's Skycycle, in Okayama, where there's a Brazilian-themed amusement park.

GOLF BALL DIVER: Brett Parker is a salvage diver

in Dallas, Texas. He finds an average of 3,300 golf balls each day and has made as much as $100,000 in one year.

SALMON STUNNER: At salmon fish farms some lucky job seeker is assigned the task of stunning fish so they can get tagged.

LAWYER LISTENER: Some lawyers hire people to listen to dry runs of their court grandstanding. Advice: wear dark glasses and take a nap on the job.

ICE STATION BUS DRIVER: Any outdoor job at McMurdo science station in Antarctica has to be tough. Imagine being Marty Gilligan, who was once the station's equivalent of a bus driver.

CHICKEN SEXER: If you have the right qualifications and can tell male chicks from female chicks, then you might find yourself at a factory farm where there are chickens in the tens of thousands. Be careful what you wish for.

BEAN PIMP

One of the more unusual jobs anyone could have is the job of marrying male and female soybean plants. Not in the religious sense, of course. At the age of 12, Julia Heatherwick considered herself a working girl. But instead of working the streets, she worked soybean fields with a pair of tweezers, a Dixie cup, and two carpet squares. She said the purpose of hand pollination was to control the soybean plant crosses and to create a soybean hybrid with strength and resistance to disease. For seven summers Heatherwick toiled in the soybean fields at Funk's Seed Hybrid Company, where she was paid about three dollars an hour. During the mornings she weeded acres of soybeans and in the afternoon she carefully pollinated them.

According to Heatherwick, the romancing of the soybeans started with a quick session that she jokingly called speed dating. Her overall goal was to create the highest number of successful unions each summer. Heatherwick said she's not embarrassed about her seedy past. "I blossomed from a child to a young woman. I learned about life. I created life. Some folks called us bean pimps. Maybe we were, but I felt more like a match-maker and a cultivator of connections. I was a soybean artist," she said.

PAWNBROKER'S GOOD DEEDS

Chance and circumstance. That's what brings a pawnbroker together with a client. Aaron Mauldin earns a living as a pawn-broker by purchasing and loaning money against valuables such as gold jewelry, electronics, instruments, and tools. Mauldin said his day-to-day work consists of processing and redeeming loans as well as buying and selling merchandise. With a direct line to the community's dark underbelly, Mauldin said his job is often fulfilling. He once helped catch a teenage thief who was stealing Belkin wireless routers and DVDs from trucks destined for Target. He said the case made its way to cargo theft detec-tives in Los Angeles who determined that the teen worked for a trucking company. He also once helped a pastor get his stolen computer back after hacking into a computer a teenager brought in to his pawn shop. Mauldin was only 22 years old when he started his business.

THE ART OF GUTTING FISH

Who would have thought that working at a stinky fish market could teach you good seafood purchasing habits? As a teenager in the early 1990s earning money for her first car, Sherry Zaun said she cleaned and packed fish on ice. She said the job was a little tricky and gross and the smell got everywhere, earning her a few nicknames. Having worked in a California fish market, she said there's an art to actually cleaning fish and that the weirdest fish she ever had to gut was a catfish twice the length of her arm.

As for shopping tips, Zaun said to look out for bloody eyes. "If you buy a fish alive, that's the freshest you're going to get. But if you have to choose from a selection of dead fish, beware of the eyes and gills." Eyes aren't just the windows to the soul for people, according to Zaun. She said eyes should look almost alive and clear, practically fresh out of the sea. Bloodshot eyes are never a good sign. And neither is a brownish tone to either the eyes or the gills. Zaun added that discoloration means the fish has been dead longer than it should be for consumption. Fresh fish will still have a reddish or dark tone to the gills, and the scales won't just loosely fall off or look pale.

GRANDFATHER CLOCK WINDER

For Melinda Carroll, worrying about Big Brother was the least of her worries in 1984. Imagine being a young girl whose job it was to turn a skeleton key around and around to ensure that dozens of clocks all kept the same time. Carroll said the clock company where she worked had two showrooms, one of which was a grandfather clock showroom that she had to keep meticulously dusted. What kind of maddening tasks were included in winding grandfather clocks? Carroll said there were two ways to wind them: pulling the weighted chains located behind the pendulum until the weights hung at the bottom of the clock, or, with some clocks, endlessly turning a skeleton key. Once the clock was wound, she pushed the pendulum into motion until it moved back and forth like a metronome. Carroll was so bored at times that she would time her heart rate to the ticking of the 30 or so grandfather clocks in the showroom. She added that she would often amuse herself by setting all the clocks to different times so they chimed all day long. "I had my own grandfather clock musical opus every day," she said.

PERSONAL REPORT: BOTTLE WASHER

The bottle washing machine looked like some kind of gizmo from a Dr. Seuss book, minus bright orange trumpets and *Whoville*-looking creatures. The machine had at its core a large rotating carriage that dipped down into a soapy mixture and looked like a futuristic water wheel. The wheel itself chugged and crunched along and held rows with four slots in each where bottles got fed into the machine. Route trucks would come into the facility and the drivers would unload cases of half-gallon glass bottles. I would have to grab two at a time and, like a speedy madman, drop the bottles just right into their slots. It was all about numbers. If I missed a bottle, maybe only three in that row would get washed, or two. That meant bottling production could slow down. And for a small, privately owned bottling plant, that could spell disaster. I was only 18 years old.

A JOB WHERE LOTS OF GLASS GETS SMASHED

Back then, disaster was my middle name. One of the workers always gave me sideways glances when I placed too few bottles into the machine. And no matter how hard I tried, I broke bottles. I still remember the first time. I had been grabbing bottles from crates and dropping them into the bottle washer as fast as I could. When I misjudged, that meant glass shattered against the steel carriage. Big pieces of glass fell into the machine, which I didn't know how to turn off. Other glass bottles shattered from being shifted and forced against the odd angles of glass in the machine.

HOW DIRTY CAN A MILK BOTTLE GET?

The bottling plant made nonfat, lowfat, and chocolate milk. It also bottled orange juice and fruit punch. The bottles would go sliding out of the machine looking shiny and new, ready to be filled with whatever the guys in the bottling side of the plant had on their schedule. The bottles themselves were sometimes extremely dirty. We never knew how long people would leave bottles on their porch, in the rain, or out in a shed where they collected spiders and dirt. Maybe kids kept marbles or adults spit tobacco in them. In the world of recyclable bottles even the route truck drivers kept an empty bottle or two from their long morning routes. And if they had to go to the bathroom? Well, why not a nice, big milk bottle? Sure, they rinsed them out. But I never knew if I was sticking my fingers into one of their piss bottles when I was busily shoving glass into the bottle washing machine.

TAROT CARD READER

In the early 1990s, Maria Gordon worked as a single parent when she decided she needed to supplement her income. In the back of a *Dell Horoscope Magazine* she found an ad for tarot card readers for a psychic readers network. The ad said she could work from home. All she needed was an additional phone line exclusively for incoming 900 calls. She said part of her routine was all about small talk—she had to keep each client on the phone for at least 30 minutes.

Sometimes, Gordon said, she performed cold call readings without using her tarot cards at all, just telling clients obvious information. Gordon said she once spoke with a woman from

Louisiana who was in tears because her daughter had been missing for eight months. "From what she described, it sounded as if she would never hear from her again," Gordon said. She would also get calls from people who were disabled or on fixed incomes, wondering if they were ever going to get back on their feet. She added that she didn't really believe in tarot cards, and she thought that people would call for more superficial reasons, like whether coworkers liked each other. Gordon said she eventually found a better job and didn't need to work the tarot card phone line anymore.

SHOVELING COW POOP

Yes, you can learn to love cow poop. It's a rough road, but if Matt Webster, today the president of a Washington, D.C., firm that designs field-programmable gate arrays and semiconductors can do it, so can you.

Webster said that when people are young and need money they are willing to put in day after day of honest hard work and will do just about anything. Years ago, when Webster was 17, he and a friend hit up the usual 17-year-old venues for jobs: fast-food joints, video stores, even T-ball umpiring. Then they had an epiphany. Webster realized that his buddy's dad, a cow veterinarian, had lots of odd jobs. Webster and his friend were both interested in science. They planned on going into engineering in college and were excited about the possibility of working in medicine. The possibility of getting their hands dirty to help animals appealed to their budding science minds.

But dirty would barely be the word for what Webster was getting himself into. Upon arriving at the farm, they took a guided tour of the cow intake area, pens, vaccine lab, and a waiting room. He said they were counting their blessings when his buddy's dad came out of his office, formally greeted them, and said, "Let's get to work." To his son he said, "You and I will be drawing blood and working on the next generation of my vaccine. And you," he smiled to Webster, "will be cleaning up outside." Webster said he was soon handed a wide-lipped shovel and was directed to his new job emptying a never-ending stream of cow excrement. His job was to shovel until the concrete was visible.

LEARNING TO LOVE COW PIES

It was a never-ending cycle that when finished simply meant he had to start all over again. Webster spent the next three months getting very familiar with the endgame of cows. The first week was almost unbearable and the second even worse. It wasn't until the third week that he said he realized shoveling cow poop would be his job, at least for the summer. He said, "Instead of scrunching my nose, I inhaled. Instead of stepping gingerly, I stomped. By the end of the summer, I became one with my situation and could shovel all day without a second thought." He added that to this day cow piles hold a special place in his heart. "When I find myself in central California, at a petting zoo, or anywhere where large animals live and s***, I see and inhale."

PERSONAL REPORT: CREATIVE WRITER

The Fremont Street Experience in downtown Las Vegas is four and a half blocks long and arches over the street pavilion connecting a dozen casinos. It's in the old Block 16—that was Las Vegas in the Old West. Working as a creative writer and story-board artist was hands down the most fun I ever had at a job. You have to think about the crazy locale where you're working when you have a job that entails creating 3-D animated sound-and-light shows for the largest video screen on the planet.

ARTISTS ARE INSANE

I worked with a zany cast of characters at the Golden Nugget Hotel-Casino that included a boss who had worked on the *Lion King* video game and video slot machine animations. One guy I worked with looked like a bulldog. He was particularly good at animating cats. Another guy created a character named Agent Zero, while another made freaky animations of characters that looked like Greek gods. An intern named Brad Alexander went on to achieve the most fame of anyone, working on *Star Wars* films, Steven Spielberg's *War of the Worlds*, James Cameron's *Avatar*, and a host of other films. My job was to sit around thinking up silly concepts for the Fremont Street Experience shows. I'm not sure everybody liked my ideas, but when I look back, it wasn't just about having good ideas or not. It was about working downtown in the heart of Las Vegas in a festive atmosphere, where I could see my artwork on a giant lighted canopy. We were a team of insane artists working in one of the craziest cities on earth.

GETTING PAID FOR CREATIVITY

Being a creative writer and storyboard artist meant coming up with funny, fresh ideas. Some stuck, others didn't. I drew them out on a computer using Photoshop and added dialogue here and there. We spent a lot of time playing video games because our boss nurtured our creativity by allowing our minds freedom to roam. You can't beat that. Of course, we worked in a room next to propane tanks in the Big Red Garage for a while. That was stinky. It got much nicer when we moved across the street from the giant statue of Mr. O'Lucky at Fitzgeralds Casino.

We made the *Motown Show*, *The Rescue*, *Swing Cat Blues*, and a host of other shows, including one about bugs called *Sting* that the president of the Golden Nugget and others didn't like for some reason. I remember seeing the mayor a lot—Oscar Goodman, who had a bit part in the movie *Casino*. He would always eat lunch at a little Subway sandwich shop on the Strip near where I worked. I was always sitting at the bar whenever he arrived with his entourage.

CHAPTER 6

SATURDAY NIGHT FEVER: POPULAR FILMS FOR OBSESSIVE FANS

Have you ever been to a midnight showing of a film? It could be you saw *Toxic Avenger* (1984) at the witching hour and now you're a closet geek when it shows on cable television in full mutant glory. Maybe you were dressed as a dreadlock-wearing pirate with dozens of children who looked exactly the same as you while waiting in line for *Pirates of the Caribbean: The Curse of the Black Pearl* (2003). It's okay, that's just modern movie culture at its best—staying up late and fighting sleep while overloaded with popcorn and red licorice. And sure, there are others of you too. You could be the kind of person who frequents film festivals. What hard-core Harrison Ford fan can resist the actor as Rick Deckard in *Blade Runner* (1982) or as the whip-toting action hero Henry Jones Jr. in *Indiana Jones* (1981) when there are so few big screen moments that fans can relive? Showings of *Touch of Evil* (1958), *Citizen Kane* (1941), or *Casablanca* (1942) have a special place in the hearts of cultured moviegoers. Don't forget foreign films, for their captivating story lines and filmmaking. You shouldn't miss *Central Station* (1998), *Amelie* (2001), or *City of God* (2002) when they're projected at your neighborhood dollar theater.

What makes a movie last through the years? While actors and actresses age, occasional films have a timeless quality that makes people watch them over and over. Occult obsessions driven by marketing schemes, crazy fan rituals, and even ideologies can spin off films. While the media may help fuel some of the culture, like the *Star Wars* franchise with its toy lines, video games, and TV spin-offs, it's hard to say whether media influences every aspect of a film's sometimes obsessive fan culture. Take *Scarface* (1983), which had an unintended pull on hip-hop culture. Can you predict such an influence? Probably not. But films have an influence on just about everyone, in one way or another. Just how obsessed you are really depends on you and your pocketbook.

This section takes a look at some of that film culture and the movies such fans obsess over. There's a *Star Trek* remake (2009) that is energizing new fans and reinvigorating the old diehards. Did a YouTube video help influence the film trailer because fans had already gobbled up images? A discussion of obsessive *Star Wars* culture inevitably leads to a discussion of *Avatar* (2009) and what that film could mean for sci-fi fans—it's already one of the films that's spent the longest time ever in postproduction. The bizarre *Hedwig and the Angry Inch* (2001) represents an entire subculture of gay cult followers. The *Lord of the Rings* trilogy (2001–2003) spawned not just legions of fans unfamiliar with J.R.R. Tolkien, but an entire film industry in New Zealand known as Wellywood. There are a few trivia surprises in this section too, though what may prove most unsettling about reading it is coming to realize that you probably fit into more than one obsessive film fan group.

PERSONAL REPORT: STAR TREK REVISITED

Sure, I grew up having in my possession blueprints to the Starship *Enterprise*. I can remember eating on TV trays in the 1970s in front of reruns of *Star Trek* and seeing Captain Kirk trading punches with giant space lizards. As for giant tribbles—I thought those were really cool powder puffs. I watched every episode of *Star Trek: The Next Generation* too. I was a big fan of Jean-Luc Piccard, though I never thought he could throw a punch—not like Kirk. Yet Piccard was the kind of bad-ass captain you wanted driving your school bus when all the kids were exceptionally rowdy. So years later while working for an ABC affiliate, I found out that a portion of J.J. Abrams's new *Star Trek* movie (2009) was being filmed near Bakersfield, California, along some corn fields. Bakersfield has this knack for resembling the American Midwest with its giant patches of quilt-work farmland. I couldn't help but get even more excited when a cameraman at the news station was able to snag some footage of Captain Kirk's supposed boyhood car during a film shoot. I slammed that onto YouTube and got several thousand tasty Web hits. To this day I wonder whether the trailer they released for the film showed the car and the cornfields because I had already exposed that footage on the Web. Or is that just wishful thinking by a Trekkie?

STAR WARS AND THE CULTURE OF FAN INSANITY

When the original *Star Wars* trilogy hit the big screen, its culture seemed to involve mainly children addicted to the film's cowboy-style battles, as if it were a modernized movie Western with blasters on hips and shootouts among tumbleweed stars. In a way, Darth Vader was the ultimate cowboy villain, not only garbed but encased in black from head to toe. Princess Leia was the film trilogy's prized damsel in distress (with a mean side, of course). Kids would go home and act out movie scenes in their backyards with sticks. Others had action figures by the bucketload. That was early *Star Wars* culture.

GENERATION X, STAR WARS TOYS, AND VIDEO GAMES

Most people who stood in line to watch early installments of film series such as *Star Wars* or *The Empire Strikes Back* probably never thought George Lucas's franchise would morph into a television cartoon series, or interactive LEGO video games, or that the world would see hordes of followers dressed to the hilt as Chewbacca, storm troopers, and Jedi knights at movie premieres. The *Star Wars* trilogy and prequel trilogy product-related culture has brought those who were once Gen X kids into happy and often frustrated Gen X adulthood. Many are now with children and grandchildren who likely have similar, yet more complex and obsessive, *Star Wars* needs. Perhaps that's the true multidimensional capability of film culture: legions of fans and the moneymaking industries that bank on fandom's perpetual desire for more.

At the 2008 San Diego Comicon there were massive draws of fans that flocked to workshops and panels on *Star Wars* art, filmmaking, toys, specialty books, and comic books. People were also on hand to play demos of the game *Star Wars Unleashed*, a multiplayer game of intense proportions for those with a Sony PlayStation. Of course, those addicted to their Wiis and those who anticipated waving joysticks madly like lightsabers were unfortunately let down by the game's rigidity, though GameSpot said in its review that *Force Unleashed* for Wii is "possibly the most waggle-heavy action game available on the system."

More than a million copies sold in the first month of *Star Wars Unleashed*'s release, which offers a bridge between the story lines of the films *Revenge of the Sith* and *Star Wars: A New Hope*.

Whether people like the game or not, it's a perfect example of just how much businesses do invest in a franchise that always seems to exist on a cliffhanger where people want more.

HARRISON FORD ISN'T AN OBSESSED HAN SOLO FAN

Sure, there are comic books like those from *Star Wars: Legacy*, *The Clone Wars*, and *Knights of the Republic* that take the *Star Wars* sagas into new territories. Yet the future of the franchise might be not in expanding the story lines between films but in expanding the story beyond the first three films. But don't expect Harrison Ford to play an aging Han Solo telling his adventures to Jedi younglings. Ford was reported to have said in the *Daily Stab* in May 2008 that Han Solo isn't interesting and has a very narrow story-line utility. He added that while it was fun and great for his career, he wouldn't return to the role. "Some characters are decidedly one-off kinds of characters. Some characters don't outlive the movie," Ford said. On the website RottenTomatoes. com Scott Weinberg went so far as to report that Harrison Ford may have turned down a $47 million paycheck for a Han Solo spin-off movie. Imagine all the saddened middle-aged Gen Xers. The site reported that Ford chose instead to do a fourth installment of *Indiana Jones*. Nevertheless, *Star Wars* culture, whether or not aged actors have left their roles in a galaxy far, far away, still rages on.

FAN FANATICS WORSHIP THE JEDI FAITH

Right here on planet Earth there are roving bands of Ben Kenobis as well as protesting hordes of Luke and Anakin Skywalkers screaming their belief that their sacred Force is not a farce. Movie culture gone to the heads of the fanatical faithful? Try what some people call the Jedi religion. It has spun off *Star Wars* and scooped into an off-branch of film culture that takes film philosophy to a new level. And it's happening around the world in English-speaking countries. Some worshippers are even protesting because they want the world to be tolerant of Jedi worshippers. In New Zealand there's been a huge push to fulfill the destiny of the Jedi Church, founded on the belief that there is an all-powerful Force that "binds all things in the universe together."

The website of the Jedi Church claims to get as many as 21,000 visitors per month (though not all Jedi religious orders claim such strong numbers). In a Google search for "Jedi religion" the Jediism Way was the third item returned, but it had only four total users online at the time of that site study. Temple of the Jedi Order had only 122 active members of 1,276 registered members logged in within the last 30 days as of early 2009. A dying religion? Hard to believe after a grassroots campaign caused a ruckus in Britain, Australia, and New Zealand by calling for people to list the Jedi religion as their faith. Just a prank? Hundreds of thousands across the planet listed "Jedi" as their faith. Could be just a silly aftereffect of *Star Wars* culture. But then, that might depend on whether George Lucas ever proclaims his faith as something akin to the Force.

ANIMATOR BRAD ALEXANDER TALKS *STAR WARS* CULTURE AND MEDIA

"*Star Wars* culture is a movement of society driven by media. In my eyes it is nothing more or nothing less," said previsualization animator Brad Alexander, who worked on *Star Wars: Episode II* and *Star Wars: Episode III*. Alexander says the media serves the human mind a fantasy world that allows the person exploring to be set free from his or her own life. He says it's like a drug and helps people escape from mundane lives. He adds that being under the influence of a media form of this type allows the viewer to be taken to another world to explore the vast imagination of someone else. It's basically like taking a trip to a faraway planet, especially when visualized as a well-told story in an epic cinematic event.

Asked if he is still a part of *Star Wars* in some way, Alexander said *Star Wars* would always be in his heart. He said it was a dream to work on the prequels. When his dad asked what he wanted to do when he grew up, he said, "I want to do *Star Wars* stuff." He added, "The weird thing is, it actually manifested." Alexander said there were no secret Jedi initiation parties when he worked on the films, only really genuine people who truly wanted to make the best movies they could with the resources available.

Asked what he thinks will happen to the *Star Wars* franchise, Alexander said he thinks *Star Wars* will live forever. "It's a masterpiece of cinema and storytelling that is epic, and it revolutionized filmmaking," he said.

AVATAR: GREAT SCI-FI MOVIE-MAKING

The question remains whether such far-reaching movie culture can ever be predicted. Really, what else could there be for science fiction fans post *Star Wars*? *Harry Potter* films, like *Lord of the Rings*, are fantasy and highly popular, but seem to have their limits. Just who could be the next George Lucas? Brad Alexander, who is also a previsualization supervisor on the James Cameron film *Avatar*, was asked if that film is the kind of movie that will create a new fan base of psycho viewers and new action figure toy lines. The film, which is about a group of humans pitted in battle against a distant planet's indigenous population, has already reached records with some of the longest postproduction on a film ever. Reports indicate that the film's precedent-setting 3-D animation is the reason. "I can't say much at this time," Alexander said during an early 2009 interview.

"I can say this: It may very well be the best sci-fi movie ever made." He added, "It better be. I've spent the last four years on it with the most talented artists, director, producers, story-tellers, editors, visual effects companies, and model makers." *Avatar* was written by Cameron in the 1990s in the fashion of *John Carter of Mars*, a series of adventure novels by Edgar Rice Burroughs, the author of *Tarzan*. Cameron also wrote and directed *Aliens* (1986), the sequel to Ridley Scott's *Alien* (1979). *Avatar* stars Sam Worthington, Sigourney Weaver, and Michelle Rodriguez.

TWENTY-FIVE RANDOM CULT MOVIES

BRAZIL (1985): This Orwellian masterpiece was directed by Terry Gilliam. It's the ultimate office-dystopian film. Gilliam has cult followings for several of his films. And since Robert DeNiro also has a crazed fan following, you will be happy to know he has a cameo in *Brazil*.

NAKED LUNCH (1991): Based on the William Burroughs novel of the same name and directed by David Cronenberg, *Naked Lunch* is filled with hallu-cinatory strangeness. Fans of the Beat generation hearken to this drug-culture flick.

MULHOLLAND DRIVE (2001): If ever there was a David Lynch film more bizarre than other David Lynch films, this is it. There's a car wreck and twisting dreams. Fans of David Lynch are usually just as confused as the rest of us.

THIS IS SPINAL TAP (1984): The ultimate fake rockumentary for metal fans. As awkward as it is hilarious. No other film really captures the metal of the 1980s the way *Spinal Tap* does. Don't tell that to Wayne and Garth fans.

EVIL DEAD (1981): It's a mystery why the *Evil Dead* movies are such a cult hit. It's famous for the line "This is my boomstick."

FIGHT CLUB (1999): How many yard fights, street fights, office fights have resulted from this film based on the Chuck Palahniuk novel? Countless. Enough said. No boxing gloves required.

ROCKY HORROR PICTURE SHOW (1975): One of the greatest midnight theater cult films, which has fans throwing objects at each other and dressing up. Stage versions are still a hit across the U.S.

PLAN 9 FROM OUTER SPACE (1959): It's possibly the most awful yet popular cult film of all time. Flying saucers on strings, terrible dialogue. Fans can't help but love the film and its star, Bela Lugosi, who died during filming.

THE PRINCESS BRIDE (1987): People can't stop quoting this Rob Reiner fairy tale featuring Andre the Giant. No other movie has lampooned the Middle Ages quite as well. Monty Python followers are probably angry that *The Princess Bride* was included in this list instead of *Monty Python and the Holy Grail* (1975).

BLADE RUNNER (1982): Possibly Harrison Ford's greatest role was Rick Deckard, in this haunting masterpiece by Ridley Scott about a futuristic U.S. city and renegade androids. Based on Philip K. Dick's novel *Do Androids Dream of Electric Sheep?*, the film was digitized and rereleased for its 25th anniversary.

THE TEXAS CHAINSAW MASSACRE (1974): Cult horror film fans love their slasher pics, and this is no exception. You can't disregard the influence this low-budget film, with its family of cannibals, has had on the horror film genre. One critic was terrified just watching the film because so many people cheered for its villain, Leatherface.

REEFER MADNESS (1936): It's campy and supposed to scare you away from smoking marijuana, but it doesn't because it's ridiculous. People love to watch it at midnight for a good laugh.

A CLOCKWORK ORANGE (1971): Stanley Kubrick's highly controversial and haunting film about future shock is based on the 1962 novel of the same name by Anthony Burgess. This film originally had an X rating.

DONNIE DARKO (2001): A demonic rabbit and a teenager in a time-traveling story are at the center of director Richard Kelly's bizarre film. A big hit on DVD.

HAIRSPRAY (1988): This John Waters musical starring Ricki Lake is so popular that in 2007 there was already a remake.

FEAR AND LOATHING IN LAS VEGAS (1998): Based on the life of Hunter S. Thompson, this Terry Gilliam film starring Johnny Depp as the gonzo journalist and Benicio Del Toro gets psychopathic and psychedelic.

WILLY WONKA AND THE CHOCOLATE FACTORY (1971): It's a dark yet colorful tale of a haunted candy factory, complete with creepy songs and some creatures called Oompa-Loopas. Based on the Roald Dahl classic. It causes both candy fetishes and nightmares.

AKIRA (1988): Katsuhiro Otomo's grandiose anime film, an apocalyptic, futuristic tale set after World War III, grabbed the attention of the West and spawned a genre of films, trading cards, and TV cartoons.

THE GOONIES (1985): Kids on a treasure quest in an '80s film with a cult resurgence. The author of this book can't get enough of it either. Will the Goonies live forever?

2001: A SPACE ODYSSEY (1968): Some people who understand this Stanley Kubrick sci-fi epic have seen it more than 100 times, and not just for its grand musical score. The movie is based on an Arthur C. Clarke novel and deals with evolution, artificial intelligence, technology, and extraterrestrials. A richly detailed film that rivals today's special effects.

ERASERHEAD (1977): This surreal art-horror film by David Lynch in his directing debut is set in a sexless future. Captures midnight audiences all over. It took five years to film—that's a long time for the actor who portrayed the protagonist to have kept his giant hairdo.

FREAKS (1932): Some say this is the most disturbing movie ever made. And it used real sideshow freaks: Siamese twins, living skeletons, midgets, and giants. It was cut from distribution by MGM but was later discovered and played to midnight audiences in the 1970s and 1980s.

TOXIC AVENGER (1986): One of the kings of the B-movies simply because of its fan base, which won't melt away. Seriously, try a Google search and you'll even find a band by the same name with more than 30,000 friends.

NIGHT OF THE LIVING DEAD (1968): Zombie movies always seem to be popular. But without George A. Romero's classic, we might not have had such great films as *28 Days Later* (2002), *Resident Evil* (2002), and *Quarantine* (2008). That includes video games like *Left for Dead* (2008) as well as websites like Yourzombieplan.com

CLERKS (1994): This indie classic was a pop culture phenomenon on video that launched the careers of Ben Affleck and Kevin Smith. It spawned such sequels as a comic book and an animated series. Here's to Jay and Silent Bob.

FORGET HISTORY CLASS—I HAVE HOLLYWOOD

If you thought you were an expert on the history of cowboys or Native Americans, think again. You've probably just watched too many movies. One of the unexpected cultural influences of the film industry is the fact that movies are constantly giving history lessons. Try thinking about what the American cowboy really means. Who was he? What did he wear? What were his values? Did he have a rugged sense of individualism? Did he save the damsel in distress? Did he even call himself a cowboy? For many years people didn't think African Americans ever were cowboys, lived in the West, or ran cattle. Unfortunately, Hollywood culture is to blame for such misconceptions. Might also want to blame your grade-school history teacher too, but don't blame the trained historians. It's not as if they have the marketing power of Clint Eastwood. In *Cowboy Imperialism and Hollywood Film*, Mark Cronlund Anderson writes that since movies portray past events with historical significance, people can't help but be influenced by what they see in theaters.

GAY FILM CULTURE: *HEDWIG AND THE ANGRY INCH*

John Cameron Mitchell's *Hedwig and the Angry Inch* (2001) is one of the oddest films about gay culture you could ever see. If people learn about their sexuality from films, they're definitely in for a roller-coaster ride from *Hedwig*. Part biopic, part musical, part concert, the film follows a glam-punk rocker named Hedwig who undergoes a botched sex change and is left with what she describes as "a Barbie doll crotch." The film's songs are hilarious and disturbing, leaving the viewer thinking about concepts such as identity and acceptance. Before the film version the story was originally a drag show and an off-Broadway hit. Go to any film festival showing of the movie and you'll see an entire culture of fans singing, acting out, and generally having a great time.

The music is far better than that of another film popular with gays and lesbians, the most successful midnight cult film ever: *The Rocky Horror Picture Show*. While theater groups across America aren't as fanatical about *Hedwig* as they are about *Rocky Horror*, there's definitely a following that will amaze film-goers. Be prepared to sing along with "The Origin of Love."

WHERE DID YOU GET THAT *SCARFACE* JACKET?

Walk into many smoke shops or video stores and you can find a leather jacket advertising the 1983 Brian De Palma film, *Scarface*. The image on the jacket might show Al Pacino's famous F-word-screaming character Tony Montana grimacing as he blasts a machine gun. And the impact of the film appears not just on jackets. You're sure to find all the curse words from the film on edited YouTube versions of the movie, in video games, and in hip-hop songs.

That's quite an impact for a film that didn't do so well at the box office. Most people can't even name a movie from 1983, let alone the top 10 grossing movies from that year. The list doesn't include *Scarface*. Try *Star Wars: Return of the Jedi*, *Flashdance*, and *Terms of Endearment*. In fact, it was reported that many people in Hollywood hated *Scarface*. The following year, De Palma was even nominated for a Razzie, an award for worst director. The culture factor comes into play because of the long-lasting effect of the film on pop culture. It's not just that people like to shout out, "Say 'ello to my little friend!" The hip-hop artist of the same name, Houston rapper Scarface, described his curious connection with the fictitious main character of the film to *USA Today*: "Me and (Montana) went through the same stuff, going from nothing to something. I'm just not dead. For years to come, that movie will be relevant because it's the truth." The impact of the film is felt in hip-hop culture across America.

There's even an album of hip-hop tribute music that accompanied the 25-year rerelease of the film on DVD.

A strange cultural fact about *Scarface* is that it's a Latino gangster film made by white filmmakers who have admitted to having trouble accepting the sweeping urban-cultural influence of the film in America. After all, *Scarface* is a movie about those affected by street crime, drugs, and the search for success and power. Why wouldn't Americans love it?

PIRATES OF THE CARIBBEAN: THE WATER RIDE FACTOR

Three films, three midnight releases, three times Johnny Depp as a drunken swashbuckling pirate stumbled onto the silver screen between 2003 and 2007. And each time, fans just wanted more of his irreverent antics, his seafaring one-liners, and the goofy walk that mocked famed Rolling Stones guitarist Keith Richards.

The lasting cultural impact of the films can be easily witnessed just by walking into Disneyland, where the legendary Tom Sawyer's Island was recast with a pirate theme and renamed "Pirate Island." Step onto the boat ride. After bobbing through a bayou, zooming down a couple of waterfalls, and being surrounded by skeletons and treasure, before you know it, there's an animatronic version of Johnny Depp as Captain Jack Sparrow poking out of a barrel. Not too many films have made the leap from a Disneyland ride to a movie and back again, with images from the movie transplanted to the ride. And with thousands of visitors to the theme park each day, thousands of Johnny Depp dolls, plastic hooks, eye patches, pirate hats, treasure maps, and more are being sold, reinforcing that crazy pirate culture that infects Americans and international tourists of all shapes and sizes.

But it doesn't stop there. The film also inspired pirate guilds across America. One group, called the Kern Pirates Guild, claims to have actual sword props from the films and shows up at an annual Pirate Day dressed in authentic handmade costumes. As you probably know already, 2012 marks the tentative release date for the fourth installment of *Pirates of the Caribbean*. Pirates, it seems, will never get old—as long as kids want to be Captain Jack on Halloween.

FIVE RANDOM PIRATE FILMS NOT TO WATCH

VENGEANCE OF THE SPACE PIRATE (1987): In this animated film, Captain Harlock becomes a lawless space pirate. At the time this book was written, no one had even taken the time to review it on Yahoo! Movies.

YELLOWBEARD THE PIRATE (1995): This horrible 30-minute long puppet film about a pirate cruise ship should be used as a torture technique. Don't confuse it with the hilarious 1983 film *Yellowbeard*, starring Graham Chapman, Cheech and Chong, Peter Boyle, Marty Feldman, and John Cleese.

TREASURE PLANET (2002): This cartoon is one giant Disney-themed bomb. Roger Ebert said it best: "Do we really need this zapped-up version of the Robert Louis Stevenson classic?" You can find a plethora of films with Stevenson's title, *Treasure Island*. Try the 1950 version.

SWASHBUCKLER (1976): Robert Shaw, of *Jaws* fame, was much better at hunting sharks than being a sword-swinging pirate. It's safe to say he was no Errol Flynn.

SKY PIRATES (1986): One reviewer called this sci-fi film "limp," while another classified it as "action, adventure, cheese." John Hargreaves stars as Harris, who flies a time-warping airplane. It really is as bad as pirate films get.

WELLYWOOD, FIGWIT, AND *LORD OF THE RINGS*

If you haven't had enough from Peter Jackson regarding plump hobbits, grumpy dwarves, and dexterous elves, you might want to take a sightseeing trip to New Zealand. Between 1998 and 2004, roughly 95 percent of the $330 million film budget of *The Lord of the Rings* (2001–2003) was spent in New Zealand and about 22,000 people were employed. Take a ride to the park atop Mount Victoria to find a film location where scared hobbits once encountered gruesome black riders. There's even a tour. Sure, many kiwis in this nation of only four million think movie tours in their country are silly. But not the profiteers. More planes, more safari vehicles, and just plain more manpower was needed to feed the demand of all the people wanting to see film locations. One farmer whose land was used for the film was even able to keep some stripped-out buildings of Hobbiton while the rest were razed.

Sorry, Hollywood, but Peter Jackson was able to create the entire *Lord of the Rings* series outside California—in a place people now call Wellywood. An entire sound stage was built there for *King Kong* (2005). *The Hobbit* (2012) and *Water Horse: Legend of the Deep* (2007) also make full use of Wellywood, as do some Bollywood films and a slew of Christian-themed movies, including both of Disney's *Narnia* films (2005–2010) and *Kingdom Come* (2010). Postproduction for segments of James Cameron's sci-fi epic, *Avatar* (2009), was completed in Wellywood.

Of course, some of the biggest achievements in the culture of *The Lord of the Rings* weren't accomplished in New Zealand but in cyberspace. The films' influence on the Internet reached monumental proportions in a plethora of fan sites. After watching the first film, *The Lord or the Rings: The Fellowship of the Ring* (2001), two students, Iris Hadad from Israel and Sherry de Andres from England, created a fan site for an unnamed elf who had no speaking lines in a Council of Elrond scene. The two fans' acronym "Figwit" (for "Frodo is great—who is that?") ended up landing the actor who first played Figwit an actual speaking role in the last film in the trilogy, *The Lord of the Rings: Return of the King* (2003). Unfortunately, the name Figwit didn't make the credits; actor Bret McKenzie was simply listed as "elf escort."

SAVING PRIVATE RYAN AND TRIUMPHANT WAR FILMS

World War II has made a positive comeback in triumphant film memorializations of the Second World War. Steven Spielberg's *Saving Private Ryan* (1998) was followed by the popular television series *Band of Brothers* (2001) and Clint Eastwood's *Flags of Our Fathers* (2006). There's also Quentin Tarantino's *Inglourious Basterds* (2009), which takes gore and war films to their stomach-churning limits. Add Spike Lee's *Miracle At St. Anna* (2008) to the bunch too. And if you think war films don't tie into the larger culture, think again. The U.S. government decided to build a controversial $100 million National World War II Memorial on the Mall in Washington, D.C. The site opened on April 29, 2004, and honors the 16 million Americans who served in uniform between 1941 and 1945.

But does the realistic violence in the latest batch of triumphant World War II films reflect an antiwar sentiment? And do such films resonate with the children and grandchildren of America's World War II veterans? That's tough to measure, since the only visible fan base for World War II films may be the throngs of users riveted to ultraviolent first-person-shooter video games like *Call of Duty*. Nonetheless, the popularity of such war-era films means that they continue to resonate soundly through the American consciousness.

PERSONAL REPORT: HARRY POTTER AND THE WIZROCKERS

The *Harry Potter* phenomenon may live on, like *Star Wars*, in one form or another. At least, that's what die-hard fans are hoping. At the writing of this book, there were still two films in the series yet to hit the silver screen. The last book, *Harry Potter and the Deathly Hallows*, has already come out—surely one of the greatest nights for fiction books ever. But there is another phenomenon associated with the films: the music. A unique musical culture accompanies *Harry Potter*, and it's called "wrock."

"HOTS FOR HERMIONE" AND OTHER WROCK HITS

At Vromans in Pasadena—the oldest and largest bookstore in Southern California—the same night the book *Harry Potter and the Deathly Hallows* came out, in 2007, wizard-dressed girls danced to the song "Hots for Hermione." Wizrock, or wrock, is the peculiar music culture of *Harry Potter*–themed bands and songs that have swept the likes of MySpace and spawned websites like Wizrocklopedia.com.

"Harry Potter came out when I was in the third grade," said vocalist/guitarist Landen Belardes, the son of this book's author. His teen band, Dirty Spanglish, which includes Shaun Alaniz and Nick Alvarado, performed their *Harry Potter*–themed song twice that night in 2007 and performed a rousing encore that led right up to the midnight book release frenzy. Believe it or not, there are nearly 200 bands around the world that exclusively perform *Harry Potter*–themed songs. Although Dirty

Spanglish isn't a full-fledged wrock band, they don't feel so bad. An online article about that night titled "Under Their Spell" continues to get thousands of visitors and is the most popular article ever on Bakotopia.com, the home page for *Bakotopia* magazine. In 2007, MTV listed its top 10 wizard-rock bands, including: Switchblade Kittens, Harry and the Potters, the Parselmouths, the Remus Lupins, Draco and the Malfoys, and the Whomping Willows.

TWENTY-FIVE OF THE LONGEST FILMS EVER MADE

THE CURE FOR INSOMNIA (87 HOURS): This 1987 film meant to cure insomnia runs 5,220 minutes. By John Henry Timmis IV, the film has no plot and features poet Lee Groban reading a poem over clips of action that include car crashes and pornography.

THE BURNING OF THE RED LOTUS TEMPLE (27 HOURS): Based on the novel *The Tale of the Extraordinary Swordsman*, the film (1928–1931) focuses on the rescue of a commander held captive in a temple full of traps. This Chinese film has been labeled the longest major release.

LEAVING HOME (25 HOURS): Made in 1992, *Die Zweite Heimat* (*The Second Homeland*) is the second of three lengthy chronicles of life in Germany between 1919 and 2000, seen through the eyes of a family from the Hunsrück area of the Rhineland.

GRANDMOTHER MARTHA (24 HOURS): This 1996 documentary out of Holland follows the last days and thoughts in the life of Martha Stello.

A GERMAN CHRONICLE (15 HOURS): This first in the series of three chronicles of life in Germany in the 20th century premiered in 1984. The story spans the years between 1919 and 1982.

THE JOURNEY (14 HOURS): Presented at the Toronto Film Festival, this 1987 Swedish documentary by Peter Watkins (original title: *Resan*) is structured around the theme of nuclear weapons.

OUT 1 (13 HOURS): This 1971 French film (subtitle: *Noli Me Tangere*) is about loosely connected characters with independent stories. Its subplots weave among each other and continually uncover new characters.

CHRONICLE OF A CHANGING TIME (11 HOURS): *Chronik Einer Zeitenwende,* made in 2004, is the third of three chronicles in the series about life in Germany during the 20th century. The story takes place between 1989 and 2000.

EVOLUTION OF A FILIPINO FAMILY (11 HOURS): With a film shoot lasting from March 1994 to April 2003, it took 11 years to complete this film. More scenes were added as late as 2005. The film is also known by its Tagalog title, *Ebolusyon ng isang pamilyang pilipino*.

SHOAH (9 HOURS): Claude Lanzmann's 1985 documentary is about the Holocaust. The film consists of interviews with people involved with the Holocaust and visits to locales associated with the atrocities.

DEATH IN THE LAND OF THE ENCANTOS (9 HOURS): *Kagadanan sa banwaan ning mga engkanto* was made in 2007 and is set in the Bicol region of the eastern Philippines, devastated by Typhoon Durian in December 2006. The film follows Filipino poet Benjamin Agusan as he returns from Russia and wanders through a ravaged landscape of devastation, old friends, and lovers.

HEREMIAS BOOK ONE: THE LEGEND OF THE LIZARD PRINCESS (9 HOURS): This 2006 drama set in the Philippines follows a traveling craftsman who gets caught in a hurricane. Helpless, he meets various people on his journey and ends up fasting in a deal with God to help save a possible rape victim.

TAIGA (8 HOURS): This 1992 German film follows a nomadic tribe through the desolate Darkhad Valley in northern Mongolia.

LIBERATION (8 HOURS): This 1969 Russian World War II docudrama was released in the 1970s as two separate movies.

WAR AND PEACE (8 HOURS): This 1968 Soviet film took seven years to make and might be the costliest film of its time, at over $100 million. One battle scene alone included 120,000 soldiers. Thank goodness for CGI today.

MELANCHOLIA (8 HOURS): Another film set in the Philippines, this 2008 movie follows a cast of characters trying to survive the sadness and insanity of the world.

THE PHOTO-DRAMA OF CREATION (8 HOURS): This 1914 religious film is based on a book of the same name that was also published in 1914.

IMITATION OF CHRIST (8 HOURS): Renowned artist and experimental filmmaker Andy Warhol made this enigmatic 1967 film about a young boy who reflects on his place in the world.

EL PROTEGIDO DE SATÁN (8 HOURS): This 1917 film was directed by José María Codina, who directed 23 films in the early 20th century.

SATANTANGO (8 HOURS): This 1994 film, a coproduction of Hungary, Germany, and Switzerland, follows the collapse of a collective farm in Hungary near the end of Soviet rule in 1989.

HITLER: A FILM FROM GERMANY (7 HOURS): This 1978 film, a coproduction of West Germany, France, and the U.K., is a series of monologues based on the histories of Hitler and other high-ranking Nazis, and people who knew Hitler.

THE CLOTH PEDDLER (7 HOURS): This 1916 Russian silent film, also known as *Archin Mal Alan*, explores Azerbaijani marriage customs.

THE SATIN SLIPPER (7 HOURS): Film crews from multiple European countries contributed to this 1985 epic about Spanish conquistadors in America and Africa.

THE BEST OF YOUTH (7 HOURS): Released in 2003, this Italian film follows Italy out of the chaos and ruins of World War II.

BÁBOLNA (7 HOURS): This 1985 Hungarian film was directed by Sándor Sára. She has written and directed for film and television since the 1960s.

GIRLS WHO WEAR HELLO KITTY

Sometimes film reflects pop culture, and sometimes it's the other way around. In the case of Hello Kitty, there's a franchise of products that influence a television series or a set of films. The television series *Hello Kitty* isn't all that wonderful—unless, of course, you're a die-hard fan of the products.

Go to the Sanrio website (they own Hello Kitty) and you will read: "It's more than just a catchy phrase; it's the foundation of everything we do, and we're proud to say we've been creating smiles for over 40 years. At Sanrio, we believe that a gift … is a means of expressing our heartfelt feelings for others. This philosophy guides all Sanrio activities, whether we're designing a stationery set … or an animated television series." Spoken like true entrepreneurs—Hello Kitty products can be found in just about every mall in America. There's really no escaping them. And though the Hello Kitty culture has legions of pink-clad, fluffy-kitty backpack wearers, it's the haters who seem to take the cake.

DO HELLO KITTY HATERS REALLY HATE?

Do a Google search for "Hello Kitty," and one of the first sites you come across is a hate site called KittyHell.com. The site, possibly a thinly veiled marketing ploy, purports to be run by the boyfriend of a Hello Kitty-obsessed girl. An early 2009 entry on the site about a Lisa Loeb video with a dancing, guitar-strapped Hello Kitty in the background reads, "I guess it could have gone without saying, since anything that involves Hello Kitty is 'creepy' to some extent, but it seems to take on horror film dimensions when a Hello Kitty plush comes to life in the back of a music video." Given its position in the Google search rankings, the site might have a lot of corporate search engine optimization (SEO) behind it. Yet it can't be denied—there are Hello Kitty haters. A popular phrase found on more than one website reads: "Guns don't kill people. Hello Kitty kills people."

ONE HUNDRED YEARS OF *THE WAR OF THE WORLDS*

Filmgoers always love a good film about invading extraterrestrials that, without explanation, lay waste to planet Earth. Such films may have their origins in a novel, a radio show, or an earlier film. The original version of *The War of the Worlds* was an 1898 H.G. Wells science fiction novel describing the invasion of Victorian England by angry Martians using tripodlike fighting machines. While that book provided a foundation for many science fiction writers, including Ray Bradbury, L. Ron Hubbard, and Arthur C. Clarke, it was a radio show of the same name by Orson Wells, broadcast on *Mercury Theatre On the Air*, that caused a fright among listeners.

The War of the Worlds was broadcast on Halloween 1938 as a series of simulated news bulletins, which many listeners took as an actual attack by Martians. The show ran without commercial breaks, which added to the fright of the listeners. The radio reading was modeled after radio reports of the 1937 Hindenburg disaster.

In 1953, the film version of *The War of the Worlds*, starring

Gene Barry and Ann Robinson, began its own run of influencing decades of pop culture, including television and movie remakes. In the 1988 *War of the Worlds* TV series, Ann Robinson reprised her role as Sylvia Van Buren. She went on to make two more films in that role. *Mystery Science Theater 3000* named one of its characters after Dr. Clayton Forrester in homage to the film. Other films have paid homage too, including *Independence Day* (1996) and *Mars Attacks!* (1996). The 2005 film *War of the Worlds*, directed by Steven Spielberg, was yet another modern adaptation of the H.G. Wells classic. That film drew elements from the 1898 novel, the 1938 radio play, and the 1953 film.

THE SPELL OF *THE WIZARD OF OZ*

There are some films that people grow up with in every decade, thanks to perennial, popular holiday rebroadcasts. Think of *It's a Wonderful Life* (1946), *The Ten Commandments* (1956), *The Sound of Music* (1965), and even the television classic *Rudolph, the Red-Nosed Reindeer* (1964). Viewers simply can't get enough of them. Yet none seem to have the far-reaching cultural impact of *The Wizard of Oz* (1939), a film that keeps getting remade and reformed, sometimes in lackluster attempts at outdoing the original.

Some observers call 1939 the greatest year in Hollywood history, a year in which 365 films were released and moviegoers bought tickets at a rate of 80 million per week. Not many people know that there's a 1910 version of *The Wizard of Oz*, based on a 1902 musical stage play that was one of Broadway's greatest successes. Some are aware of the L. Frank Baum book titled *The Wonderful Wizard of Oz*, published in 1900, which contained strongly Populist political metaphors and which American historians still discuss in college courses. Post-1939, few will likely remember *The Wiz* (1978), starring Diana Ross, which featured

Michael Jackson as a boogieing Scarecrow and Nipsey Russell as a sort of drunken Tinman. Fewer will remember *The Return of Oz* (1985), about Dorothy getting rescued from a psychological experiment, or *Oz* (1976), about Dorothy in a rock band, or *Thanksgiving in the Land of Oz* (1980), about Dorothy in a turkey balloon. The Sci-Fi Channel's 2007 futuristic snoozer *Tin Man* was another hopeless attempt. There is an animated film titled *Oz* slated for a summer 2010 release. At least one website begged the filmmakers to cease production on the film, which is not slated to be a musical.

RANDOM *WIZARD OF OZ* SLIPPER TRIVIA

STOLEN SLIPPERS: In 2005, a pair of ruby slippers worn by Judy Garland in the film were stolen from a Minnesota museum.

SILVER SLIPPERS: In the original L. Frank Baum story, Dorothy's magic slippers were silver. They were changed to ruby red for the film to show up more vividly against the yellow brick road.

SEVEN PAIRS: The actual number may be lost to Hollywood film history, but at least seven pairs were made, four of which can be accounted for. You can view a pair at the Smithsonian in Washington, D.C. An elaborate curled-toe pair not used in the film is owned by actress Debbie Reynolds.

WHITE SILK PUMPS: Four pairs used in the film were white silk pumps from the Innes Shoe Company in Los Angeles. White silk pumps were inexpensive and easy to dye.

FORGET THE SEQUINS: In the 1985 Disney film *Return to Oz*, handmade British spool-heeled shoes were covered in red crystals.

$5,000 SHOE FLOP: In 1989, the Western Costume Company created limited-edition sequined and jeweled official reproductions that sold for $5,000 each. They halted the project after only selling only 16 pairs.

WORLD OF WARCRAFT: Get a pair of epic-level cloth shoes in this popular video game and you can do some serious teleporting. (Only in the game. Sorry.)

CHAPTER 7

ECCENTRIC AUTHORS AND FANTASTIC ART: GREAT AND LITTLE-KNOWN WORKS BY THE WILDLY (AND WEIRDLY) CREATIVE

Everyone wants to be a writer or an artist—until they figure out how much creative energy it takes to write a book or create a series of paintings; or until they realize that creativity is both a gift and a learned talent that is nurtured over years. Brad Listi, who supplied the foreword to this book, wrote on TheNervousBreakdown.com, "Personally I don't know a single writer who has an easy time writing. Especially fiction. Fiction seems to be a special kind of pain in the ass. Or maybe I'm just projecting."

Creative discipline has a way of producing weirdness, oddness, oddballs, and odd works of art. You'll find plenty of examples in this section. There is information about some of the great writers of the world and their idiosyncrasies. Each entry includes a portion of a letter or diary by the author, and you'll also find related trivia about the writers and painters discussed here.

I couldn't help but start off with the Nobel Prize–winning author V.S. Naipaul. If you visit the official website of the Nobel

Prize (http://nobelprize.org) you can hear him speaking about how difficult it was to retrain himself to be a writer. He had to throw out everything that he thought he knew. Here, you'll get to know him as a young expatriate struggling at Oxford. You'll get to know a few expatriates in the world of art as well. After a brief look at Jack Kerouac's scroll, you'll read about some scrolls in Asian art, including one that's 250 meters long. A tour of Jessica Anya Blau's highly recommended 2008 book, *The Summer of Naked Swim Parties*, will leave you with a rather interesting perspective on nudes in art. Further along, there is a glimpse into the sickness of James Joyce, as well as a poignant letter from him. Afterward, you'll read about some paintings that touch on the subject of sickness. And there's more, including a snippet from Byron and random Don Juan trivia. Read on and enjoy the odd world of the arts.

V.S. NAIPAUL: EXPATRIATE WINNER OF THE NOBEL PRIZE

Few writers seem to write sentences that are seemingly perfect, as if spun one after another from a wheel. V.S. Naipaul is one of them. An ethnic Indian born in Trinidad on August 17, 1932, he spent much of his life in exile in Britain. Many writers find themselves in London, Paris, or Morocco, often staying for years. Ernest Hemingway, e.e. cummings, and Jack Kerouac are just a few notable writers who lived outside their native countries for a time. Naipaul, the author of many works of fiction and nonfiction travel histories, received the Nobel Prize in literature in 2001. He has rarely given speeches or lectures, though he did so upon receiving the prestigious award. He has been criticized for his realistic approach to the post-colonial Third World and for the realism of his writing. Some of his notable fiction and nonfiction books are *The Mystic Masseur* (1957), *Miguel Street* (1959), *A House for Mr. Biswas* (1961),

A Bend in the River (1979), *Magic Seeds* (2004), *The Loss of El Dorado* (1969), and *India: A Million Mutinies Now* (1990). Travel writer Paul Theroux, who met Naipaul in Africa in the 1960s, wrote about their turbulent 30-year friendship in his 1998 nonfiction work *Sir Vidia's Shadow*.

EXCERPT FROM V.S. NAIPAUL LETTER
TO HIS FAMILY, OCTOBER 12, 1950

The atmosphere of this college is more of a club than anything else. There is a Junior Common Room where the students meet and drink and smoke and talk, as though they were in any club. I have got to learn how to dance. Even Capo has advised me to try and learn. The lectures are dull and uninformative. I am going mainly to make social contact. It would surprise you to see the vast flock of people reading English. Most want to become writers. You are not obliged to attend lectures or write essays. You can do no work at all, if that is your inclination. But I have so much to read.

I am going out after this letter to see about the books Pa wants. Chenwing has also asked for some books. I am going to send him some too. It is slowly becoming colder and colder. I shall soon start wearing my overcoat. Up to now I have been sticking to the unlined rubber raincoat. Please don't call a raincoat a cloak. England is teaching me to say thank you and please.

The beauty of Oxford grows on you.

I think I have exhausted myself now. I have rambled conversationally in the hope of making this letter more conversational.

Incidentally, I have a favour: could you send me a carton of cigarettes? Everyone here smokes and everyone offers you, and I have fallen back into the habit. But don't be horrified. But please send the cigarettes. They are so expensive here.

Your loving son (and brother to the rest)
Vidia

[Handwritten note]: Pardon the faults in typing. I have no time nor the desire to correct.

RANDOM TRIVIA ABOUT EXPATRIATION

THE HARLEM OF PARIS: Many African Americans lived in Paris in the 1920s, in the district called Montmartre. The name derives from the hill that is the district's most prominent feature. It was there that jazz was popularized in Parisian nightclubs. Famous painters who worked in the district include Salvador Dalí, Amedeo Modigliani, Pablo Picasso, Vincent van Gogh, and Claude Monet.

THE BEAT GENERATION: In the 1950s and 1960s a group of American writers known as the Beats, including Jack Kerouac, Allen Ginsberg, Gregory Corso, and William S. Burroughs, lived abroad in Mexico, Africa, and France. Those who lived in Paris stayed in a seedy hotel that's since been called the "Beat Hotel."

THE NEW BOHEMIAN BERLIN: In 2008, an article in the *International Herald Tribune* claimed that Berlin, having emerged as the new creative capital of Europe, was now what New York had been in the 1980s: a haven for artists of all types. Rent was one-third cheaper than in Paris or London. In 2006, 13,100 Americans were calling Berlin home, citing its bohemian culture as what drew them.

THE LOST GENERATION: Take a look at this notable list of writers—all disillusioned with the idea of fighting for America during WWI, and full of zest at the idea of living for art: Ernest Hemingway, John Dos Passos, Julian Green, William Seabrook, e.e. cummings, Harry Crosby, Sidney Howard, Louis Bromfield, Robert Hillyer, Sherwood Anderson, and Dashiell Hammett. Discontent with America upon their return sent many back to Europe in the 1920s.

THE MERLIN JUVENILES: Another wave of American writers who traveled to Paris were associated with the expatriate periodical *Merlin*. They include Samuel Beckett, Alexander Trocchi, Christopher Logue, Patrick Bowles, and Richard Seavers.

WALT WHITMAN

In photographs the gray-bearded and wizened Walt Whitman (1819–1892) almost seems like the Albus Dumbledore of American poets. He could magically produce poems, many of which he reworked until his death. Although he wasn't just a poet, but an essayist, journalist, and humanist, he was known as the father of free verse. His poem "Beat! Beat! Drums!" was considered a rallying cry for the North during the Civil War, and the famous writer volunteered as a nurse during the conflict. His major work, *Leaves of Grass*, was self-published in 1855;

Ralph Waldo Emerson praised it considerably. Nowadays self-publishing typically suggests a lack of credibility. Like that of the fictitious Dumbledore, Whitman's sexual orientation has been scrutinized. The homoeroticism of his poetry is generally taken as evidence that he was gay.

WALT WHITMAN LETTER TO RALPH WALDO EMERSON, DECEMBER 29, 1862

Dear Friend,

Breaking up a few weeks since, and for good, my New York stagnation—wandering since through camp and battle scenes—I fetch up here in harsh and superb plight—wretchedly poor, excellent well, (my only torment, family matters)—realizing at last that it is necessary for me to fall for a time in the wise old way, to push my fortune, to be brazen, and get employment, and have an income—determined to do it, (at any rate until I get out of horrible sloughs) I write you, asking you as follows:

I design to apply personally direct at headquarters, for some place. I would apply on literary grounds, not political.

I wish you would write for me something like the enclosed form of letter, that I can present, opening my interview with the great man. I wish you to write two copies—put the one in an envelope directed to Mr. Seward, Secretary of State—and the other in an envelope directed to Mr. Chase, Secretary of the Treasury—and enclose both envelopes in the one I send herewith so that I can use either one or the other. I wish you also to send me a note of introduction to Charles Sumner.

It is pretty certain that, armed in that way, I shall conquer my object. Answer me by next mail, for I am waiting here like a ship waiting for the welcome breath of the wind.

Indeed yours, &c
Walt Whitman

FAMOUS SELF-PUBLISHED WORKS

HUCKLEBERRY FINN (1885), by Mark Twain
THE TALE OF PETER RABBIT (1866),
by Beatrix Potter
WAR AND PEACE (1865), by Leo Tolstoy
FUGITIVE PIECES (1806), by George Gordon Byron
THE CELESTINE PROPHECY (1993),
by James Redfield
TAMERLANE AND OTHER POEMS (1827),
by Edgar Allan Poe
THE ELEMENTS OF STYLE (1918),
by William Strunk, Jr.
TARZAN OF THE APES (1914),
by Edgar Rice Burroughs

J.R.R. TOLKIEN: FROM THE TRENCHES OF WORLD WAR I

When people think of J.R.R. Tolkien (1892–1973), they likely don't consider that he contributed a landmark study of the epic poem *Beowulf* in 1936, or that he volunteered for military service in World War I. During the war he was commissioned as a second lieutenant and contracted trench fever after participating in the Battles of the Somme and Thiepval Ridge. He claimed to not have been a good officer, often working on the Elvish languages for his books even while in a dugout under fire. He became medically unfit after the war, but not too unfit to write *The Hobbit* (1937) and *The Lord of the Rings* (1954–1955).

EXCERPT FROM J.R.R. TOLKIEN LETTER TO HUGH BROGAN, DECEMBER 14, 1955

Dismiss the nightmare! I can stand criticism—not being unduly puffed up by the success (v. unexpected) of 'The Lord of the Rings'—even when stupid, or unfair, or even (as I occasionally suspect) a little malicious. Otherwise I should be in a fine taking, what with 'emasculate' and other kind adjectives. But you are welcome to let your pen run as it will (it is horrible writing letters to people with whom you have to be 'careful'), since you give me such close attention, and sensitive perception.

RANDOM FAMOUS ART DEPICTING WAR

NICHOLAS POCOCK (1740–1821): Famous painter of sea battles and maritime art who commanded ships and witnessed many naval battles. In 1794, Pocock was aboard the frigate *Pegasus* during the Battle of the Glorious First of June. He filled a journal with sketches and notes and later painted scenes of the battle.

ANCIENT GREEK ART: THE TROJAN WAR: At the Musée du Louvre in Paris you'll find a famous vase depicting the Trojan War. Created around 485 B.C., the artwork shows the duel of Paris and Menelaus and another battle described in Homer's *Iliad*. The pottery of ancient Greece fills a large portion of the archaeological record of such warring times.

GEORGE WASHINGTON CROSSING THE DELA-WARE: This famous 1851 painting by the German American artist Emanuel Gottlieb Leutze (1816–1868) is more than 12 feet tall and 21 feet wide. A replica hangs in the West Wing of the White House. Leutze used American tourists as models. One of the original versions was destroyed in a bombing raid in 1942 by the British Royal Air Force. Retaliation for losing the War of Independence?

THE BOER WAR: This famous 1901 painting by John Byam Shaw (1872–1919) depicts a woman stricken by grief because of a soldier killed in Britain's Imperial War in South Africa. The painting evokes the great distance often felt between peace and war.

LOUISA MAY ALCOTT

Louisa May Alcott (1832–1888) lived on an 18th-century estate known as "The Orchard House" that encompassed 12 acres of apples. It was there that she wrote her classic, *Little Women* (1868), based on her childhood experiences with her three sisters. The family once housed a fugitive slave for a week.

EXCERPT FROM THE JOURNAL OF LOUISA MAY ALCOTT, APRIL 5, 1887

April 5

Weighed—143. One pd. Less than a month ago. But am much better. Sleeping well, eat bread & butter, some meat, & take water. Hooray! Cut out my dress, took a walk. Headache discharged & felt better.

RANDOM FAMOUS ART DEPICTING WOMEN:

THE MONA LISA: This famous painting, titled *La Gioconda*, by Leonardo da Vinci (1503–1506) is a portrait of a woman with just a hint of a smile. Mysteries surround the painting, including the function of the two columns, thought to be a later addition, which make for a confusing background. The smile is a source of much discussion and may depict the confusing nature of relationships between men and women, among other interpretations.

WHISTLER'S MOTHER: This 1871 portrait by James McNeill Whistler is titled *Arrangement in Grey and Black: The Artist's Mother*. There are several legends relating to the painting. One story has it that the original subject was late, so Whistler's mother took her place. Another is that Mrs. Whistler grew tired of standing, so she sat down for the painting.

THE CREATION OF EVE: Michelangelo Buonarotti created this painting in the Sistine Chapel between 1508 and 1512. It was a commission by Pope Paul II. While the public called the painting scandalous for its nontraditional nude figures, the pope defended the work.

JACK KEROUAC'S *ON THE ROAD* SCROLL

In the late 1950s, the torrid lives of a group of artists and writers including Jack Kerouac were labeled collectively as the Beat Generation, and the notion of "Beat" became popular. While it is well known that Kerouac's novel *On the Road* enlivened generations of youth, celebrated the coolness of pop culture, and inspired a loose-knit group of anti-mainstream American writers, it's not so well known how Kerouac came by his literary methods.

Like many writers, Kerouac pondered new ideas in fiction for many years. During poverty-stricken cross-country travels in the late 1940s, Kerouac wrote extensive notes and journal entries as he sped across America with friend Neal Cassady and lived among friends in places like Denver, San Francisco, and the outlying areas of Bakersfield, California. But it wasn't until the early 1950s that Kerouac realized that he could capture his novel through a method of spontaneous prose. His words flowed like musical notes of free-flowing be-bop music as he wrote an experimental draft of *On the Road* that he taped together into one 120-foot-long single-spaced scroll.

Could Kerouac's scroll idea have been one of the best promotional and literary gimmicks of the modern era? It very well could have been if it were published that way. Several drafts and several years later, a paragraph-friendly version of Kerouac's novel made bookshelves and was a national sensation. But it wasn't until nearly 50 years later, in 2007, that Kerouac's *On the Road* scroll was published as a collector's item for fans of his work.

RANDOM FAMOUS SCROLL PAINTINGS

CATALOG NUMBER 116027: Though it sounds like the sequel to *THX 1138*, this is really an ancient Chinese watercolor paper scroll with a cloth backing that depicts Christianity in the Far East. Until 2008, the scroll sat in a dimly lit case, its details difficult to make out. After its restoration, the scroll gained importance with its Chinese-style madonna and infant, showing Christianity's ability to cross cultural borders. The scroll was dated to the 17th century. A mystery in the scroll involves a forged painter's name, which was placed on the painting to conceal evidence of the piety of the family that owned the painting.

CHINESE HAND SCROLL: One of the best-known Chinese painters of Buddhist and Taoist figures was Liang Kai, who from 1201–1204 served as a painter at the court of the Southern Song Dynasty. Not many of his works remain. One in particular used a technique called *baimaio*, showing six narrative scenes surrounding a seated figure who emanates radiance. Saintly figures also adorn the painting, and a mysterious title strip mounted on the work has inspired much scholarly debate. In 2009, the painting can be found at the Huntington Library in California.

JAPANESE "TIGER" SCROLL: According to the *Japan Times*, this is one of the British Museum's most famous Japanese hanging scrolls. Created by Gan Ku in the 1790s and since restored, the scroll painting, nearly six feet long, depicts a fearsome tiger. The painting is on loan so often to other museums that as of 2008 it was said to have been absent from its location for a total of seven years.

GIANT SILK THANGKA: In 2008, dozens of monks carried and hung a giant silk thangka painting on the side of the Zhaibung Monastery in Tibet. It was the first time the building was opened since a riot had occurred months earlier. Many tourists stood on hillsides for a distant view of the giant 1,000-square-meter scroll painting that depicted the Buddha.

THE 250-YARD SCROLL: Between 1994 and 1997, Li Yushan, an elderly painter in Beijing, China, visited the Three Gorges of the Yangtze River, an area that was scheduled to be dammed and flooded. Wanting to capture the area's beauty, he made many drawings of it, and afterward spent five years creating the scroll painting, which he finished in 2002. He often made his sketches while standing in a boat. Boatmen in the area, hearing of the painter standing in a boat, revealed the area's most beautiful locations to him.

ANAÏS NIN

Anaïs Nin (1903–1977) was a Cuban-French author, the daughter of a singer and a composer. She is hailed as one of the first writers of female erotica but is best known for writing about her own life, in *The Diary of Anaïs Nin, Volumes I–VII* (1966–1980). She is also known as the lover of the American author Henry Miller. In 1995, over coffee and muffins, three friends who met through their connections with Nin founded the website Anaisnin.com, devoted to her life and work. According to the site, they started it because books and reviews didn't accurately depict the writer.

EXCERPT FROM THE DIARY OF ANAÏS NIN, 1934

This great passivity in action which makes Henry take all the blows, never fight for what he loves, write despairingly but act in no way to change his surroundings; which makes him write violently, curse, and take whatever woman comes his way: this great passivity seems to be necessary to the flowering of life, because it means enjoyment, effortlessness. His yieldingness to life. He expresses nonchalance, relaxation, looseness, easygoingness. The will only expresses itself in a negative way, by contradicting others, attacking others, opposing what others have done. His physical relaxation is the expression of a defect, a defect in action. Perhaps the world needed that loosening, that untying, unknotting, unleashing of controls, oiling, de-mentalization. In any case, that is Henry's gift. Certain qualities were lost by organization, by the forms of the old novel, the old way to tell things.

THE SUMMER OF NAKED SWIM PARTIES

With so much nudity on television and in film, you'd think there were American novels galore about families who are less modest than most. But not so. One book may stand alone in postmillennial nude-family storytelling. Voted "Best of 2008" by the *San Francisco Chronicle* and one of the top summer picks by the *Today Show*, *The Summer of Naked Swim Parties*, by Jessica Anya Blau, redefines families and the idea of nudity. The novel is set in the buzzing year of 1976, during that rather formative summer when people were reminded of America's bicentennial every time they turned on their televisions. Blau gathered experiences from that year, when she was coming of age. The mostly fictitious story revolves around 14-year-old Jamie, who loves surfers and has best friends into tanning, boys, and sex. The catch is, her parents are into throwing naked swim parties.

MODERN-DAY NUDITY JUST ISN'T THE SAME

Don't blame Jessica Anya Blau if the notion of "naked summer swim clubs" hasn't caught on. Her book may actually reinforce the idea that people are just as uncomfortable with their own nudity as they are with other naked bodies in a semipublic setting. Or perhaps nudity itself is just plain sacred. Blau has said that because the book takes place in a particular era, the naked swimming and the nudity don't really translate to modern-day life. She said she deliberately set the novel in 1976 because it was a time before AIDS and widespread chlamydia and herpes. "Sexuality was freedom and it was liberation and it wasn't bogged down by all the terrors there are surrounding sex today," Blau said.

Maybe an American coming-of-age novel about growing up in a family that throws naked swim parties found success because comedy and nudity just sort of go together. As Blau put it, "When you take away all the current ideas about bodies and sex, you're left with these floppy, ridiculous mounds of flesh."

THE INCREDIBLE WORLD OF NUDES

TIME UNVEILING TRUTH: In 2008, the Italian government was criticized for covering the breast of a female nude in a reproduction of this famous 1743 painting by Giambattista Tiepolo. "One cannot hide truth," an angry curator said about the cover-up.

PAINTING CARNAVAL MODELS: It was said in early 2009 that Betto Almeida had possibly the best job in Brazil. That's because the 36-year-old artist toils away each day painting the bodies of gorgeous women. Almeida said to a reporter, "You wouldn't believe how many applications I get for an assistant." He gets paid roughly $1,000 per model, each of which takes about two hours to paint.

NO NUDES FOR INDIA: In 2006, Maqbool Fida Husain withdrew a controversial nude painting from a charity auction. The 90-year-old artist had painted

India's mother goddess without any clothes. His home in the city of Mumbai was once ransacked after he painted a series of naked Hindu goddesses. Even his paintings have been attacked.

SARAH PALIN IN THE BUFF: In 2008, a Chicago bar hung a nude portrait of Republican vice-presidential candidate Sarah Palin that was created by the bar owner's husband, Bill Elliott. The bar has displayed more than 200 racy celebrity portraits. Elliott's daughter, who resembles Palin, served as the model.

JACK LONDON: AUTHOR WITH A STRANGE BEGINNING

The circumstances of Jack London's (1876–1916) birth are among the oddest of any author. London's mother, Flora Wellman, was a music teacher and spiritualist who believed the dead could be contacted. When she became pregnant by William Chaney, he asked her to have an abortion. In desperation, she shot and injured herself. During the time his mother was deranged, baby Jack was raised by an ex-slave named Virginia Prentiss. London is known as the author of *Call of the Wild* (1903), *White Fang* (1906), and *The Sea Wolf* (1904).

JACK LONDON LETTER TO ANNA STRUNSKY, FEBRUARY 20, 1900

Dear Anna:

You have done me a great wrong. I hardly know whether I can ever forgive you; for you have put into my life a great unrest which will continue for at least a year to come. Yes; out of the largeness of my heart I will forgive you, for I do believe that you did it without malice aforethought. You remember,—O surely you do,—that evening at Glenholm when you told me of Barrie's new story? It's your fault. It was because of you that I looked up the January Scribner's and could not lay it down again until I reached "to be continued." Your fault that I am unhinged, my life thrown out of joint, and that I can hardly contain myself until the March Number arrives. No; on second thought I shall never forgive you. NEVER!!! But say, isn't Tommy and Grizel splendid? Barrie is a master. And in the whimsical delineation of character do you not notice a trace of Dickens at his best?

Now I feel comfortable. Nobody ever "Mr. London's" me, so every time I open a letter of yours I felt a starched collar draw around my neck. Pray permit me softer neck-gear for the remainder of our correspondence.

Now about Thursday. I have to be down in Oakland at two o'clock in the afternoon. An old chum of mine, (Class of 1900, U.C.), who died on the way to Manila, has come home. I have to attend the funeral. But the morning is free. Can I see you at any time between 9:30 A.M. and 1 P.M.? Tramp if the weather prophet be gracious, or anything you wish. Reply immediately on receipt of this so I may know.

Most Sincerely Yours,
Jack London

JAMES JOYCE: PORTRAIT OF A PHOBIA

As you've read elsewhere in this book, phobias can have a drastic effect on a person's life. The Irish writer James Joyce (1882–1941) was no stranger to phobias. The author of *A Portrait of the Artist as a Young Man* (1916), *Ulysses* (1922), and *Finnegan's Wake* (1939) was the unfortunate victim of a dog bite suffered when he was young. That bite led to a lifelong canine phobia—Joyce always carried an ashplant walking stick. He also suffered social phobias and had a fear of thunder, lightning, violence, and water. At least one doctor thought Joyce's mysterious stomach ailments were psychosomatic.

JAMES JOYCE LETTER TO ROBERT MCALMON, MARCH 1, 1922

Dear McAlmon: God only knows when I am likely to get that holiday. Darantiere is driving me out of any wits I have left. In a month he has not sent me any copies and it is impossible to get press copies out of him. I have to stay on and sign the rest of the deluxe lot. Besides I was on the track of two flats. One has collapsed but the other is still possible. How long are you staying there? I hope you are not annoyed at my not writing one way or the other. If you were at this end you would appreciate the situation. Have you finished Ulysses? If so I should like to hear your complete opinion. There are heaps of misprints in the last two episodes.

I suppose you have done a bundle by now instead of a bunch. A journalist called on me yesterday to ask what I was writing now!!!

I am sure it is very pleasant down there. The only thing that would give me any consolation is a nice necktie so if you feel inclined to throw any into the winedark sea remember me. A child is easily satisfied. But don't send me more than one or I shall feel very mean ...

Please let me hear from you in any case and excuse this bewildered bewildering author.

RANDOM PAINTINGS OF SICKNESS

THE TRIUMPH OF DEATH: FLEMISH PAINTER PIETER BRUEGEL THE ELDER (1525–1569) created a depiction of Hell on Earth in this mid-16th-century painting, which reflected the social upheaval and terror of the scourge of the plague, known as the Black Death. Paintings of the Black Death between 1500 and 1800 were often presented as Christian messages that God wanted people to clean up their ways. Other plague-like calamities, caused by cholera and typhus, swept Europe as well.

NATURE'S SICKNESS IN *THE SCREAM:* The subject of this 1893 painting by Edvard Munch (1863–1944), which shows horror in the face of a screaming man, might actually be the sickness of nature. In his 1892 diary, Munch writes that he was walking with friends as the sun was setting and the sky suddenly turned red. He paused, feeling exhausted, and leaned on a fence. He said the sky looked like blood and tongues of fire. As his friends walked on, he trembled and "sensed an infinite scream passing through nature."

CONQUERORS OF YELLOW FEVER: DEAN CORN-WELL (1892–1960) created this allegory of one of the great moments in medical history. The image depicts experimental treatments for yellow fever being conducted on Dr. James Carroll. Dr. Jesse Lazear, shown in the painting inoculating Carroll, later died from self-experimentation related to yellow fever. The 1939 painting was presented to the Walter Reed Army Institute of Research in 1954.

PESTILENCE: DEATH OF THE FIRST BORN: This painting was created by William Blake (1757–1827) around 1805 with pen and watercolor over graphite pencil. The image depicts a haunting ghost-blue male figure above colorless weeping figures. The painting is in the collection of the Museum of Fine Arts, Boston.

VIRGINIA WOOLF: WOMAN, INTERRUPTED

The life of Virginia Woolf (1882–1941) was marked by interruptions, usually in the form of convalescences, as she suffered from bipolar disorder. Nevertheless, she was able to write *Mrs. Dalloway* (1925), *To The Lighthouse* (1927), *A Room of One's Own* (1929), and other books, in addition to extensive correspondence. Woolf drowned herself on March 28, 1941, in the River Ouse near her home in Sussex, England.

EXCERPT FROM THE DIARY OF VIRGINIA WOOLF, JUNE 22, 1928

Friday 22 June

So far I wrote & was interrupted—always interrupted ... am now off to Ruislip with Pinker to wed her, & it is

THE SISTERS 8

According to the three creators of *The Sisters 8*, theirs is the only children's book series created by an entire family. Written by Lauren Baratz-Logsted, with husband Greg Logsted and daughter Jackie Logsted, *The Sisters 8* is a magical collection of tales about eight sisters with eight cats, eight gifts, and eight special talents. But these girls have lost their parents. Their mother was on her way back from the kitchen with drinks, and their father was on his way back from the woodshed, when—poof!—they mysteriously disappeared. The stories take readers on exciting adventures in a current-day setting as the girls, determined to live on their own, try to learn whether their parents are dead or alive.

THE POWER OF OCTUPLETS IN POP CULTURE

While there are currently only two sets of octuplets alive in America, there's been at least two TV shows about families of eight children. The number eight has generated fascination and notoriety in pop culture, religion, science, and mathematics. What about *The Sisters 8*? Is there a special meaning to their number? "The number eight was originally a total random thing for us!" said Lauren Baratz-Logsted. She added that in December 2006 her family was trapped in Colorado by a blizzard that closed down the airport. Her daughter, Jackie, was six at the time. With time on their hands, Baratz-Logsted asked Jackie what kind of book she'd like to read. Being an only child, Jackie said she'd like to read a book about sisters. When her mother asked her how many, she said eight. Then they decided it would be fun if the octuplets were born on August 8, 2000, meaning they'd turn eight on 8/8/08.

FLANNERY O'CONNOR: A SENSE OF PLACE

It's said that when Southern writer Flannery O'Connor (1925–1964) was six years old, she taught a chicken to walk backward. But that's not her claim to fame. She is most famous for two novels, *Wise Blood* (1952) and *The Violent Bear It Away* (1960), and the short story collections *A Good Man is Hard to Find* (1955) and *Everything That Rises Must Converge* (1965). Afflicted with lupus, she spent her last years on her family farm, Andalusia, in Milledgeville, Georgia, where she raised peafowl and continued to write. Her childhood home in Savannah, Georgia, has been renovated; details can be found online at www.flanneryoconnorhome.org. The home offers tours and also operates as a literary center.

FLANNERY O'CONNOR LETTER TO BRAINARD AND FRANCIS CHENEY, DECEMBER 15, 1953

Dear Lon and Fanny,

My mother thinks I was mighty smart to get out of that blizzard when I did. Mrs. Stevens came over this morning and informed us that it was six inches of snow in Nashville Tennessee at nine o'clock last night. She looked as if she had just got back from there. She always tells us every morning what the weather is in different parts of the country, giving exact time and location.

I had a lovely time as you must know. We hope the next thing will be your stopping with us here, but all I can assemble in the way of guests is Mrs. Stevens. She always shows up when we have company anyway—with some unnecessary message—so as to get a look at them.

The trip back was very rough and punctuated by a little boy across the aisle from me who lifted his head from his paper cup every now and then to say in a hoarse voice, "Can't we go back on da twain?"

I'm enclosing that story and always welcome any suggestions on how I could improve it. Merry Christmas.

Flannery

W.B. YEATS: POOR SPELLER WINS NOBEL PRIZE

Some of the greatest writers have been notoriously poor spellers and possibly dyslexic. The great Irish poet W.B. Yeats (1865–1939) received the Nobel Prize in literature—not too shabby for someone who attended formal school for only two years and never applied to a university. That should be enough inspiration for aspiring writers who have trouble reading, spelling, or both.

W.B. YEATS LETTER TO LADY GERALD WELLESLEY, JULY 8, 1935

Dear Lady Gerald,

May I bring my daughter with me to Penns in the Rocks on August 14 or thereabouts? I go on to Masefield and she to the Shakespeare festival at Stratford on Avon. She has two passions, painting and the stage—she has made a modern stage with electric light, etc. At six or seven she was an artistic prodigy but is now just an ordinary talented art student. I shall know nothing of her in another three years. Tick-tick—one hears the infernal machine ticking. How long may we stay? Would a week be too long? Please say if it would. I expect to be in England about three weeks.

In October I go to Mallorca. My various doctors advise a winter in a warm climate. I had thought of going to India but that fell through so I told my Indian monk, Purohit Swami, that we would go to some warm place for two months and that while there I would put this translation of the Upanishads into good English. My doctors have spread those two months into four. I had meant to write poetry all the rest of the time but I doubt if my Oxford Book on Modern Poetry will let me. I have a longing to escape into a new theme—I am tired of my little personal poetry, your 'Matrix' has given me a glimpse of what I want.

I know I must be spelling abomidably—my daughter has beaten me in two games of crocket—I am tired of correcting proof sheets.

I will write a better letter if I can and without waiting for your reply to this.

Yrs. ever,
W.B. Yeats

LORD BYRON: "I LOVE YOU" FAN MAIL

In 2008, the U.K. *Independent* discussed some rather racy unpublished letters that the poet Lord Byron (1788–1824) received between 1812 and 1814. The article claimed that the author of *Don Juan* (1819–1824) was not the reluctant hero, as many scholars have thought. In fact, the article revealed, many women wrote Byron letters laced with sexual undertones and inquiries about trysts, asking that their letters be burned to protect their reputations. Apparently Byron kept the letters as trophies.

EXCERPT FROM LORD BYRON LETTER TO JOHN CAM HOBHOUSE, OCTOBER 12, 1821

America is a Model of force and freedom & moderation—with all the coarseness and rudeness of its people.

RANDOM DON JUANS IN THE ARTS

THE SHIPWRECK OF DON JUAN: In the Musée de Louvre, Paris, you'll find this 1840 painting by French

Romantic painter Eugène Delacroix (1798–1863). The subject, taken from Byron's 1819 poem *Don Juan*, is a boat crowded with shipwreck survivors.

DON JUAN DEMARCO: This 1994 film stars Johnny Depp in the role of Don Juan. Also stars Marlon Brando. The film is about a man who presents himself as Don Juan and a doctor who must cure him of his belief of being the greatest lover in the world.

THE TRICKSTER OF SEVILLE AND THE STONE GUEST: Some scholars believe that this 1630 play by Tirso de Molina is the earliest known depiction of Don Juan. Molina was an ordained priest who spent his life in a monastery.

DON GIOVANNI: Wolfgang Amadeus Mozart's famous 1787 opera is considered one of the greatest representations of the legend of Don Juan. A screen version was filmed in 1979. It's one of the most performed operas in North America.

THE LITTLE CAVALIER DON JUAN: French postimpressionist painter Henri Rousseau (1844–1910) was ridiculed in youth but became a self-taught genius. His playful painting shows Don Juan standing in a room with a dog and was created around 1877.

DON JUAN TENORIO: This 1884 play by José Zorrilla is an intensified Romantic interpretation of the Don Juan story. Zorrilla once started a newspaper that was shut down by government agents.

DON JUAN IN HELL: The 1903 play *Man and Superman* by George Bernard Shaw features a third-act dream sequence that is often performed on its own as *Don Juan in Hell.* The dream sequence is a philosophical debate between Don Juan and the Devil.

GEORGE ORWELL: IT'S ALL IN A NAME

Authors' pen names usually have a harmless quality, occasionally an exotic one. Samuel Langhorne Clemens became Mark Twain; Charles Dodgson became Lewis Carroll; Pearl Gray became Zane Grey; and Daniel Handler transformed into Lemony Snicket, to name a few. The pen name George Orwell (1903–1950), sounds ominous to our ears thanks to two books that have been disturbing readers for decades: *Animal Farm* (1945) and *1984* (1949). The term "Orwellian," which is itself creepy, relates to the totalitarian future as described in Orwell's anti-utopian novel *1984.* Sadly, the author's real name, Eric Arthur Blair, lacks the mysterious luster of his pen name.

GEORGE ORWELL LETTER TO T.S. ELIOT, JUNE. 28, 1944

Dear Eliot,

This MS [Animal Farm] has been blitzed which accounts for my delay in delivering it and its slightly crumpled condition, but it is not damaged in any way.

I wonder if you could be kind enough to let me have Messrs Fabers' decision fairly soon. If they are interested in seeing more of my work, I could let you have the facts about my existing contract with Gollancz, which is not an onerous one nor likely to last long.

If you read this MS yourself you will see its meaning which is not an acceptable one at this moment, but I could not agree to make any alterations except a small one at the end which I intended making anyway. Cape or the MOI, I am not certain which from the wording of this letter, made the imbecile suggestion that some other animal than pigs might be made to represent the Bolsheviks. I could not of course make any changes to that description.

Yours sincerely
Geo. Orwell

CAMPUS SCANDALS: *THE PROFESSORS' WIVES' CLUB*

Do a Google search for campus scandals and you'll find all kinds of shenanigans involving university officials, students, and more, from the Ivy League to the California state universities. Although Joanne Rendell's *The Professors' Wives' Club* (2008) is fiction, some might find that her book captures a microcosm of the scandalous life at universities. Her novel pits the seemingly powerless professor's wives against the dean, who in his little fiefdom has incredible power. Rendell, herself a professor's wife, said she wanted to show that when a dean makes a decision, it goes beyond the faculty—it affects anyone affiliated with the school. "I think it's this mystery of the ivory tower, and the professors who inhabit it, which makes the university so compelling." Her book speaks not just to university communities but women everywhere.

D.H. LAWRENCE: SON OF THE WORKING CLASS

English author D.H. Lawrence (1885–1930) was the fourth son of a barely literate miner. The working class provided raw material for the works of Lawrence, who grew up in the coalmining town of Eastwood, in Nottinghamshire. His novel *Sons and Lovers* (1913) is acknowledged as a vivid portrayal of working-class realities. Lawrence is also known for his novels *The Rainbow* (1915) and *Lady Chatterley's Lover* (1928). An expatriate who rarely returned to England, Lawrence called his voluntary exile his "savage pilgrimage."

EXCERPT FROM D.H. LAWRENCE LETTER TO MARTIN SECKER, DECEMBER 3, 1928

Dear Secker

Long since I've written—but nothing new in the world. We left that island—too uncomfortable. It's pretty and very pleasant here, nice little hotel for 40 frs. But of course, dull—a bit like Spotorno. We've had sunshine all the time, and are sheltered when the cold wind blows. It seems to suit me pretty well and the French here are very nice in their way, so self-sufficient and free. It's about 10 miles from Toulon.

I wanted to go to Tuscany and finish the Etruscan essays, but am a bit scared of tombs in winter. Orioli though worries me a bit—I don't hear from him, he doesn't send out Lady C. when she's ordered—I'm afraid he's really ill. Afraid I shall have to go to Florence and see to things. I don't really want to. We want to go to Spain—it's not very far. Have you heard of the pirated editions of Lady C.—apparently two out in America—and a man bought a copy in London for 30.—I suppose it was bound to happen, especially over there ...

OSCAR WILDE: SEXUAL DEVIANT

One of the most successful playwrights of the Victorian Era was Oscar Wilde (1854–1900). His play *The Importance of Being Earnest*, which debuted in 1895 at London's St. James Theatre, has been the basis for several movies. With respect to his sexual orientation, Wilde said he belonged to a culture of male love inspired by the Greek paederastic tradition of relationships between adolescent boys and adult men. In *The Secret Life of Oscar Wilde* (2003), Neil McKenna wrote that the literary great first kissed a boy at 16. Although he was immensely popular in social and literary circles, he was imprisoned for two years in 1895 after reputed relations with blackmailers, cross-dressers, homosexual brothels, and male prostitutes. The charge was gross indecency—but not "buggery," the term for sodomy at that time.

OSCAR WILDE LETTER TO MRS. GEORGE LEWIS, JANUARY 15, 1882

My dear Mrs Lewis, I am sure you have been pleased at my success! The hall had an audience larger and more wonderful than even Dickens had. I was recalled and applauded and am now treated like the Royal Boy. I have several "Harry Tyrwhitts" as secretaries. One writes my autographs all day for my admirers, the other receives the flowers that are left really every ten minutes. A third whose hair resembles mine is obliged to send off locks of his own hair to the myriad maidens of the city, and so is rapidly becoming bald.

I stand at the top of the reception rooms when I go out, and for two hours they defile past for introduction. I bow graciously and sometimes honour them with a royal observation, which appears next day in all the newspapers. When I go to the theatre the manager bows me in with lighted candles and the audience rise. Yesterday I had to leave by a private door, the mob was so great. Loving virtuous obscurity as much as I do, you can judge how much I dislike the lionizing, which is worse than that given to Sarah Bernhardt I hear. For this, and indeed for nearly all my successes, I have to thank your husband. Pray give Mr Lewis my most affectionate remembrances, also to the Grange, and believe me, very sincerely yours

OSCAR WILDE

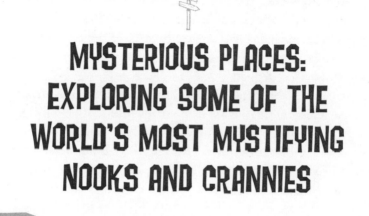

MYSTERIOUS PLACES: EXPLORING SOME OF THE WORLD'S MOST MYSTIFYING NOOKS AND CRANNIES

T here are some places in the world that have a truly weird effect on you. They make you want to know more. If you're like me, you search every bit of trivia related to such locales. Maybe you're lurking in a strange jungle fort or a creepy cemetery. Maybe there's some local lore that makes your skin crawl. You explore because you are a tourist in your own life. You explore because you are drawn to finding all possible meaning in your destination. Your mind spins as you dig for answers. Unfortunately, the answers we seek about certain places are not usually found in tourist guides. "Mysterious Places" is like a kiosk of information for you to read while standing in a place of utter mystery.

In this chapter you'll find such stories as "Nabutautau, Udre Udre's Grave, and the Cannibal Islands." We've all heard of cannibalism as a bizarre abnormal behavior practiced by a few cultures. But has cannibalism truly disappeared as a cultural norm? Follow along as I explore some of Fiji's man-eating mysteries. In "Hell Town at the End of the World" you'll take a tour of remote towns and roads in northeastern Ohio. Local lore about toxic zombies and the legend of a giant python are the fodder of many spooky tales. In the American Southwest, there are stories of ghost-filled tunnels beneath the famous Las Vegas welcome sign. I'll take you on a brief exploration of the flash-flood zones below the city in "Ghosts Beneath the Famous Las Vegas Welcome Sign."

"Mothman, the Curse of Point Pleasant, and Baby Mothman" explores the strange legends of Point Pleasant, West Virginia. If you've never heard of Mothman, the Silver Bridge collapse, or Chief Cornstalk's curse, then you might be booking a flight to Point Pleasant after reading what I have to say about the area's strange sightings and oddly connected events. Other mysterious places in the chapter include a bone-filled ossuary in Vienna, possible Chinese tunnels in Central California, and a strange pyramid built around a pyramid that is believed to be an astronomical clock.

NABUTAUTAU, UDRE UDRE'S GRAVE, AND THE CANNIBAL ISLANDS: EMBARRASS YOUR ENEMIES BY EATING THEM

When you get hungry, do you think of your enemies? What about cultures that once ate their rivals—are they still thinking of boiled humans as snacks? On the Fiji Islands in the South Pacific, the idea of embarrassing your enemies by eating them was once a cultural norm, and there is some question about whether cannibalism has really ceased to exist there. The practice of eating rival warriors and unsuspecting missionaries supposedly ended on the outermost islands more than 60 years ago. But then again, all of Fiji was once known as the Cannibal Islands, and old habits are hard to break.

A North American businesswoman touring the remote Fiji

island of Rotuma in 2000 claimed to have heard an old female islander whisper a dark secret about an ancient eating habit that was supposedly dead and buried. She heard the 80-year-old woman, who was washing clothes and hanging them outside to dry, say that a man who had raped a girl was eaten by villagers. "At first I didn't believe her," the tourist said. "I thought maybe they were the rantings of an old woman. But as she spoke I knew she was revealing a secret."

The businesswoman, who was one of very few North Americans on Rotuma at the time, said that what scared her was how sweet, shy, and very normal the old woman looked, while seeming to condone the act. Asked what she felt about the idea of people eating each other, the tourist said, "I was horrified and sickened by it."

Yet cannibalism hasn't always been culturally sickening to the people of Rotuma, which lies several hundred miles north of the main islands. The mysterious island was first contacted by Europeans in 1791. Missionaries followed in the decades since then and were equally disgusted by Rotuman eating habits. During their exploration of the islands and their culture, they learned the Rotuman word for spirit: *'atua.* Literally translated, *'atua* means "dead person, spirit, ghost." Rotumans say *'atua* in reference to a person killed in warfare or defeated in a wrestling match.

A BAKER COOKED IN AN OVEN?

Thoughts of modern-day cannibalism make some local villagers shudder. On Fiji's main island of Viti Levu, Nabutautau villagers believe their tribe encountered poverty as a result of cooking and eating a missionary in the hillsides in 1867. In 2003, the villagers tried to make amends with the family of Reverend Thomas Baker, whom their relatives had cooked in an earthen oven 136 years earlier. The villagers offered cows, woven mats, and whale teeth to the missionary's descendants. In 1993, the same village took Baker's old boots, which cannibals had once tried to cook and eat, and offered them to the Methodist Church of Fiji. The church apparently didn't respond kindly to the gesture.

The first road ever built to that bad-luck village was cut by a logging company in 2003. Find the road to Nabutautau and you just may find a path to destiny. Tours to the village—only for the fittest—are offered for just a few U.S. dollars. Sightseers are shown the very spot on a grass-covered hillside where Baker was killed and eaten.

CANNIBAL TABLE MANNERS AND ETIQUETTE

On Viti Levu, tourists can stop by any novelty shop and pick up a replica cannibal fork. They're creepy looking, almost like bug mandibles. Forks that have actually been used are supposed to be strictly museum artifacts, unless you talk to that little old lady on the outer island of Rotuma, who spilled her dark secret to the businesswoman. You'll know the forks when you see them. They come in all shapes and sizes—small forks for eating eyes and brains, larger forks are for nibbling on the fleshy parts. Interested parties can even purchase such novelties online. Try Jack's of Fiji in the city of Nadi, Viti Levu, for a black-painted ceremonial tourist fork (www.jacksfiji.com).

While on Veti Levu, outside of Nadi, tourists can look for King's Road as it turns into Vaileka. There lies the grave of Udre Udre, who is reported to have been the most celebrated cannibal the Fiji Islands have ever known. He is rumored to have found his victims so tasty he would eat them to the last bite, consuming every fleshy part of the body. Count the stones around his grave—there are nearly 900. Each one represents a body the tribal chieftain is believed to have eaten.

OBSESSIVE BITE: All of Fiji was once known as the Cannibal Islands.

TWENTY-FIVE RANDOM CANNIBAL ODDITIES

100,000-YEAR-OLD NEANDERTHALS: In the Moula-Guercy cave in southeastern France anthropologists found that Neanderthals didn't just butcher their game to get at the fatty marrow. They also did the same to each other.

PREHISTORIC SMORGASBORD: New criteria for identifying marks on human fossils helped archaeologists determine that man has been dining on his own kind for quite a long time.

ANASAZI POO: Apparently, 1,000 years ago, the Anasazi Indians in the Americas were chowing down on each other. Human myoglobins have been found in fossilized turds.

CHINESE FAMINE: During a severe famine in China in the years 1876–1879, locals were known to have killed and eaten each other in order to survive.

AZTEC CEREMONIES: Human hearts and good leg meat were often eaten ritually at the elite level. Don't worry, the lower classes got their fair share too.

DOG-HEADED MAN-EATERS: In 1552, Hans Staden found himself shipwrecked among the Tupinamba people on the remote coast of Brazil. He thought he was among a fabled tribe of dog-headed man-eaters.

But no, it was just a local tribe of cannibals who hated the Spanish and Portuguese for their cruelties. His shipmates were all eaten.

WALLED CITY OF SONG: They weren't singing love songs outside this Chinese city in 594 B.C. Surrounded by the army of Chu, citizens ate each other's children as well as the dead.

PUT IT ON ICE: In the 9th century, a Persian trader reported that human flesh was sold openly in Tang Dynasty markets.

CHINESE MEDICINALS: A 16th-century book titled *Bencao Ganmu* reportedly describes the medicinal benefits of eating human flesh.

POWERS OF THE DEAD: The 2005 documentary *Feeding the Dead* shed light on a secretive 1000-year-old Hindu sect whose holy men took bodies from the Ganges River and ate them.

ETHNIC JOKES: A New Zealand Maori elder once joked that he was European. "You are what you eat," he said.

REASON TO DIET: If you eat someone and experience a sudden loss of coordination, dementia, or paralysis, you likely have a prion disease that's affecting your brain cells.

SIX-MONTH FEAST: In April 2009, it was reported that two Russian brothers attempted to cover up the murder of a third brother by eating his body over a period of six months. Referring to the bare-bones skeleton that was dug up from their yard, they said, "Yes, we decided to eat Rafis."

TRY A BITE: One of the torture techniques practiced by the Native Americans of Canada and New York was forcing a prisoner to swallow pieces of his own flesh.

CAPTIVES COOKED: According to a Jesuit priest, the eating of captives by Iroquois Indians was considered a religious duty.

SIEGE OF LENINGRAD: During the 847-day German siege of this Russian city that began in 1941, many inhabitants were known to resort to cannibalism in order to survive.

CONGO PYGMIES EATEN: In 2003, it was reported that marauding rebels massacred and ate the sexual organs of Pygmies in the dense forests of the Congo. Further atrocities were reported in 2007.

ALBINOS IN FEAR: Albino Africans were butchered by the dozens in 2008 in Tanzania because their body parts supposedly brought good luck when eaten.

BEAUTY TIPS: In 2007, it was reported that people in China were eating infant corpses and fetuses as a part of beautification rituals. In Guangdong, body parts are considered a highly sought-after delicacy and are purchased from hospitals.

SAILED THE OCEAN BLUE: Christopher Columbus was said to have encountered cannibals in the West Indies during his expeditions.

FORMS OF CANNIBALISM: Exocannibalism is consumption of humans of another culture, while endocannibalism is eating those within one's own culture.

NOT FLOWER CHILDREN: Tribes in Papua New Guinea are said to have performed cannibalism into the 1960s. Many people suffered from a brain disease related to eating human brains.

FAMOUS CANNIBALS: In the winter of 1846–1847, members of the Donner Party, traveling to California across the snowy Sierras, resorted to cannibalism to prevent themselves from starving to death. Out of 89 travelers, 46 survived.

ANDES PLANE DISASTER: In 1972, 16 out of a group of 45 passengers survived for 77 days after a plane crash in the Andes mountains by eating their dead.

THE LEOPARD MEN: In ancient Egypt the leopard was esteemed as divine. For centuries, a West African cult known as "the leopard men," mostly in Nigeria and Sierra Leone, killed humans by slashing and mauling them with steel claws and knives. During gruesome ceremonies they would drink the blood and eat the flesh of their victims. Members of the cult were hung in 1948.

SINGING SAND DUNES OF THE MOJAVE DESERT

There's a place in California's Mojave Desert that stands more than 600 feet tall and sings. It's not an opera singer or an outcast rock star. It's quite large at 45 square miles, and it's what's called a dune field. Hike to the top of the Kelso Dunes and slide down slowly. You'll hear her low operatic voice. She'll boom. Her low-frequency rumble can be both heard and felt. Some call such places "booming dunes" or "singing sands." There are similar phenomena at California's Eureka Dunes, Nevada's Sand Mountain, and as far away as the Namib Desert in Africa.

It wasn't revealed until recently where the singing sand in the Mojave Desert originated. Geologists said that five times in recent eons, rivers and lakes in the area went dry, sending wind-swept sandy beds of quartz and feldspar into the 25,000-year-old Kelso Dunes. But the singing is timeless. It depends on the dryness of the sand's unique minerals mixing with the moisture of any given day, and the friction caused by rubbing against the surface of the sand.

Less than 10 miles north stands the Mojave National Preserve Visitor's Center, a place rich in untold stories in a ghost town called Kelso where trains still rumble through. A large train depot in Mission Revival style was built here, in the middle of California's Mojave Desert, in 1923. This grand Spanish clubhouse, filled with the ghosts of travelers, was closed as a depot in 1962. The rest of its functions ceased operation in 1985. When the Union Pacific sought to tear the depot down, it was rescued and eventually transformed into one of the grandest and most beautiful visitor's centers anywhere in America. Far removed from society, it seems more like the imaginary Tatooine of *Star Wars*, where the Jedi recluse Obi Wan might hide out in a distant rocky canyon. In reality, the depot operated for decades with its quaint little restaurant for hungry travelers, boarding rooms, billiard room, and library. You can still eat at the old lunch counter, the same place where thousands of travelers passed like desert shadows. The depot stands in what some people might think of as a spiritless landscape, midway between Interstate 40 and Interstate 15. But of course it's not spiritless if you sing with the nearby dunes.

RANDOM NOTES ON SAND

A MAN AND HIS SAND: Rob Holman of Oregon State University has collected more than 1,000 types of sand from around the world.

WHITE SAND: Found in tropical and subtropical coastal areas, white sand consists of eroded limestone and may contain organic material, coral, and shell fragments.

BIOGENIC SAND: These organic sands are composed of the remnants of living organisms and are among the most interesting to sand collectors.

PRECIPITATED SAND: Some sands come from evaporated bodies of salt-rich water. Death Valley borax and sand from the Great Salt Lake come from such types of mineral rich deposits.

ARKOSE SAND: Usually contains lots of feldspar and comes from the weathering of granite.

BLACK SAND: Can include magnetite, volcanic basalt, and obsidian. Punaluʻu Black Sand Beach on the Big Island of Hawaii was formed from the meeting of hot lava and seawater.

DRY QUICKSAND: Sand with its density reduced by air pockets or from having been blown into the air and then settling. Indiana Jones gets caught in dry quicksand in *Indiana Jones and the Kingdom of the Crystal Skull*.

QUICKSAND: Sand found near rivers, lakes, and marshes that's lubricated with water and so cannot support significant weight.

IRON SAND: Sunlight can cause this dark-gray or blackish sand with high concentrations of iron to burn skin. It is mined and used to create steel in New Zealand.

OBSESSIVE BITE: Kelso, the ghost town where the train depot sits, is a town built on a coincidence. Three men once put their names into a hat and John Kelso's name was pulled out. The town was named after him, as were the nearby Kelso Dunes. It's unknown if he ever went sliding down them.

HELL TOWN AT THE END OF THE WORLD

The fog rolls in along the Ohio and Erie Canal in northeastern Ohio, where for mile upon mile of its remains, snapping turtles lounge among duckweed-covered logs. That's enough for some urban dwellers to get spooked. The braver sort who love to explore ghost stories, whether real or legendary, might want to find their way to an area in the Cuyahoga Valley collectively known as Hell Town. There they will hear rumors of mutants and toxic-filled barrels, Satan worshippers, a ghoulish cemetery on an Indian mound, a road called the End of the World, and a python legend big enough for a yearly festival.

Hell Town is not really one locale but an area of small communities, towns, and rural roads all nestled among the canal's dilapidated remains of mills and rock quarries. It winds parallel to the Cuyahoga River and cuts through sites of ancient Native American Mound Builder culture. Once rich with bustling industry, the Hell Town area, part of Boston Township, has since been partially taken over by eminent domain. You can still find abandoned houses in what is now a giant government park. That area, near Boston Mills Ski Resort, brings its share of ghost hunters.

LAKE ERIE MONSTER

Also known as South Bay Bessie and Lemmy, this rumored North American Nessie creature was first sighted in Lake Erie in 1817. An American Hockey League team, the Lake Erie Monsters, is even named after it.

AT "THE END OF THE WORLD"

Autumn Johnston grew up in Boston Township in the 1970s and early 1980s. In 2009, she worked as general manager at Fishers Café and Pub, a popular restaurant in the area. Once, while horseback riding in the 1980s, she saw deer skins hanging in the trees, though shooting deer in the park is illegal. It could have been the Satanists. A popular legend has it that Satanists come into the area and commit animal mutilations. One of the local churches is also rumored to be a Satanist church, with an upside-down cross. As for the End of the World, that's a road some people also call Top of the World. Ghost websites list the road as a popular attraction for the unnerving feeling people get when making the trek. Johnston admitted she helped bolster the myths by playing tricks on ghost hunters. She and some friends placed logs behind the tires of parked cars, and they would also tailgate cars to try to scare people off. Other locals hid in trees to scare midnight revelers coming to the cemetery in Boston Township, a place rumored to have a ghost that sits on a bench. Johnston's grandfather was once the Boston Mills Cemetery caretaker, as was his father before him. She said her father once worked there years ago too. She added that most of her family is buried on the cemetery hill that is an actual Indian mound.

BURIAL MOUNDS WITH MYSTICAL ENERGY

Over the years, people have occasionally sneaked onto the cemetery mound: ghost hunters, paranormal thrill seekers, and worshippers of the ancient, mystical, and mysterious Mound Builder culture. A woman whose family builds the round nomadic tents called yurts said she would sneak onto the ancient burial ground where many of the area's early white settlers lay buried, including many children who likely died from sicknesses like whooping cough in the 1700s. The woman claimed the mound's energy and mystical power is akin to that of crystal skulls, affecting the body in strange ways. Artifacts including human bones have been found at the site by archaeologists and even locals. The son of one of the cemetery caretakers found a skull in the mid-1900s. Could it have been that of a Mound Builder? Park rangers said the mound was excavated. They also said there were other mounds hidden nearby whose locations aren't disclosed to the public but are the sites of archaeological digs. Yet, for all the cemetery's weirdness, the real haunt may be the house next door to the cemetery: a little boy once drowned in the river behind the house. In the backyard there's even an Indian mound.

SERPENT MOUND

A quarter of a mile long and 20 feet wide, this ancient Mound Builder structure to the gods found in Ohio looks like a gargantuan spermatozoa.

TOXIC MUTANTS OF HELL TOWN

It's no great mystery that many factories and mills once thrived along the Ohio and Erie Canal in northeastern Ohio. Of course, the canal these days lies in ruin. Stories of mutants living in the woods close to the canal and of an old butane factory chemical spill have also been the topic of local legend. Locals suggest that homes were built on the butane factory grounds. In the 1970s and 1980s, the swampy area in question was fenced off and many No Trespassing signs were placed on the houses. Fifty-gallon barrels were stacked around yards. Government workers could be seen coming and going. Locals say they simply don't know what the government workers were doing; it has been the topic of great local conversation. While it's a local legend that toxic zombies come out of the area to haunt, people living on Hines Hill Road, near the toxic zone, have actually been diagnosed with a rare disorder that causes muscle tremors and loss of muscle control.

THE PENINSULA PYTHON LEGEND

The history of Hell Town goes back many years. The story of the Peninsula Python is about a giant snake rumored to have escaped a circus train in 1944. The *Atlantic Monthly* reported tales in which locals said they saw a 15- to 18-foot python creeping through yards near the train tracks that border the Cuyahoga River and the Ohio and Erie Canal. At the time, people were afraid their children might get eaten. A posse was even assembled to try to find the giant snake.

Peninsula is a quaint town near Akron, Ohio, set on rolling streets and surrounded by beautiful woodlands. Tourists flock there by the thousands each summer to ride bikes and walk along the old canal towpath. The town is touristy and attracts sightseers and outdoor enthusiasts. But the snake legend keeps people returning year after year.

The Peninsula Library even has a mural depicting the surrounding landscape that some say symbolizes the escaped snake. The mural was designed for the Peninsula Library and Historical Society by artist Honoré Guilbeau in 1964 and resembles an aerial view of the Cuyahoga River Valley. According to the library's website, the mural covers the heart of the Peninsula Python legend. Many see the river in the mural as a symbol of the monster snake.

There's even a festival celebrating the Peninsula python. On July 19, 2008, Peninsula rekindled the legend with a parade and people dressed in snake costumes. Snake sculptures six feet tall were built and decorated, while a giant snake resembling a Chinese dragon was carried down State Route 303 by 17 people. Fishers Café and Pub, also on Route 303, had a giant fisherman snake and also celebrated with python hot dogs and snake-bite drinks. Given all the fanfare, it's strange that some say the entire story is a hoax. Peninsula Python Day presents a panel of storytellers claiming to have witnessed the events back in 1944.

TWENTY-FIVE RANDOM MOSTLY PYTHON TALES

PET PANIC: In 2009, the Melendez family's 18-foot-long pet python coiled itself around their three-year-old son. The parents stabbed the snake more than a dozen times before it let go of the child. Both parents were arrested. The snake was euthanized.

SNAKE INVADERS: Burmese pythons are an invasive species in south Florida because pet owners have released the creatures into the open. Wildlife managers say the snakes can grow to over 20 feet long. The sole job of some animal control officials is to catch these invading cat- and dog-eaters.

SNUGGLE TIME: According to Snopes.com, an Internet hoax in 2007 created a panic when stories began to appear about pet pythons snuggling closely against their owners and starving themselves in preparation for a mutinous human meal.

TASER THAT SNAKE!: WPXI news reported that police were called to a scene in Fayette County, Pennsylvania, where a man had his hand caught in the mouth of an albino python. Officers used a Taser on the snake to get it to let go.

EXPLODING PYTHON: In 2005, a python was reported to have exploded after trying to swallow a six-foot-long alligator in Everglades National Park.

DOG VS. SERPENT: Janice McNaughton claimed that her dog, Mona, got into a fight with a python living at the Othan Sports Club in Kent, England. The dog emerged from the battle with one eye mostly gouged out.

TWO HEADS ARE BETTER THAN ONE: A two-headed carpet python born in Kansas and shown to the public at the World Aquarium in St. Louis in 2007 is expected to live for 25 years and grow up to 12 feet long.

FLUSHED AWAY: A woman in a Dutch hotel had quite the surprise when she found a Burmese python in the toilet. Apparently the snake had escaped from animal smugglers in a nearby room and got into the hotel drainage system.

WE'LL CALL HIM FLUFFY: The Columbus Zoo paid $35,000 in 2008 for its 24-foot-long pet python, Fluffy, which is as thick as a telephone pole.

FOUR-STORY BUILDING: In Indonesia a 49-foot-long reticulated python was captured in 2003. It took 65 men and the blessing of a tribal leader to snare the beast. The animal eats about four dogs per month and when stretched out is as long as a four-story building is tall.

MICROCHIP SERPENTS: As of January 1, 2008, Florida pet owners are required to get a permit and a microchip for their pet pythons.

LARGEST SNAKE SKELETON: Cornell University Museum claims to have the largest snake skeleton in the world, that of a 22-foot-long reticulated python. Originally, the snake was 26 feet long when killed in the mountains of the Philippine Island of Luzon. It was found in 1915 after U.S. Army officers sitting by a campfire shot the snake out of a tree. They laid the snake across some anthills, and a few days later there was nothing left but 1,000 bones.

DOG GONE: A Cairns, Australia, family got rid of their python in 2008 after it swallowed the family dog. Around the same time, another Cairns man took a video on his rural property of a wild python eating a wallaby.

CARELESS STUDENT ZOOKEEPER: In 2008, a university biology student in Caracas, Venezuela, broke park rules at a zoo and entered a cage holding a python. He was found crushed to death. Zoo officials said the student underestimated the snake's instinct.

TSUNAMI RESCUE—FACT OR FICTION? In 2004 during a tsunami in Indonesia, a Norwegian clothing vendor named Riza was helping two nine-year-old twin sisters when they all grabbed on to a giant python swimming past. The snake was reported to have taken them to shallow waters.

TURKEY BINGE: An African rock python was reported to have got itself stuck in a Miami turkey pen after bingeing on the feathered creatures in 2005. The snake was so fat that when it was pulled out it puked up a turkey. Just a few days before, another python was captured outside a Miami Gardens home after eating the homeowner's Siamese cat, Frances.

COP VS. PYTHON: In 2008, an Oregon pet store owner called a police officer a hero after he helped wrestle the woman free of a snake. She didn't want the officer to stab the snake, because the beast was worth 850 dollars.

A LOVE STORY: A seven-year-old boy and a 16-foot-long snake in Cambodia are reported to have a special bond and have been sleeping together since the boy was an infant in a cradle.

EL DIABLO: A Virginia Beach woman was killed in 2008 by her pet python after trying to give it medication. The snake's name was Diablo, which means "devil" in Spanish.

HEAD-EATER: In Uhldingen, Germany, with one lunge, a python was able to completely cover a zookeeper's face with its mouth. The woman survived the 2008 attack and was treated for bites and shock.

YEAR OF THE FAKE SNAKE: In 2000, a Salon.com article claimed fake python skin patterns were in fashion. Their intricate designs covered everything—pants, shoes, dresses, blouses, belts, and jackets. The article claimed such "walking snakes" were the result of feminist spirituality movements reaching mainstream fashion.

SNAKE GOBBLES BOY: In 2002, in South Africa, an 18-foot-long African rock python reportedly was the first of its species to not just kill a human, but devour one. Several boys hid in nearby mango trees as their 10-year-old friend was eaten. No trace of the child was ever found.

TITANOBOA: Considered the all-time titan of boas, this giant 43-foot-long prehistoric South American constrictor had a three-foot-wide body and could eat crocodiles for breakfast, lunch, and dinner. Fossil remains were reported to have been found in northern Colombia in 2009.

MAN BITES SNAKE: In 2001, a South African man fought off a 10-foot python that had wrapped itself around the poor fellow by not just punching and kicking the beast—he also bit the snake behind its head.

PYTHON, THE EARTH-DRAGON: Python, the earth-dragon of Delphi in Greek mythology, protected the center of the earth, which was represented by a stone. In some Greek myths, Apollo slays Python at the oracle of Gaea in Delphi. In others, Apollo kills the serpent in order to claim the oracle for himself.

GHOSTS BENEATH THE FAMOUS LAS VEGAS WELCOME SIGN

Not many people realize there are over 400 miles of tunnels beneath Las Vegas. These storm drains that crisscross the city are home to many subterranean dwellers. Close to one of the tunnel openings is the famous "Welcome to Fabulous Las Vegas Nevada" sign. The sign appears in many Hollywood films, television commercials, and tourist photos and is the gateway to an oasis of gambling and strip club dreams. There, in 2004, explorer-journalist Matthew O'Brien began one of his many journeys beneath Las Vegas. A pioneer of the underworld, O'Brien discovered a dangerous network of storm washes, sewers, and dismal camps where people lived below ground, yet worked topside, sometimes on the Strip. "I thought it was interesting that as you walk into this tunnel you can see the sign, as if you're entering the real Las Vegas," O'Brien revealed in his book *Beneath the Neon: Life and Death in the Tunnels of Las Vegas*.

MAN ON THE CHAISE LOUNGE

Not far inside the tunnel that originates near the Las Vegas welcome sign, a variation of a line from Milton's *Paradise Lost* is spray-painted on a dark wall: "Aghast the Devil Stood ... and Felt How Awful Good It Is." Nearby, a man named David, whom O'Brien encountered sitting in the dark on a chaise lounge, was living a lonely life. David told O'Brien that he had lived in the drain about three months. He said he didn't like it down in the tunnels because of flash floods. "It doesn't have to be raining down here for it to kill you. It can be raining fifteen miles away in the mountains, and it'll come down in the wash," he said.

But the area by the Las Vegas sign where David lived is peculiar. O'Brien carefully recorded David's thoughts about the place: "It gets very dank down here. And it gets real dark. Two guys died in this tunnel, and sometimes I hear footsteps at two or three in the morning. I shine my flashlight down there, but nobody's coming." David told O'Brien that he asked another tunnel dweller why he heard footsteps and was told the story about the two men. He said another man had seen the two ghosts in a nearby tunnel.

O'Brien said that a lot of people he has talked to in the tunnels have a ghost story. They mention friends or people they knew who drowned in the tunnels or were murdered, and they say they can still see them or hear them late at night. "Indeed, you see and hear some strange things down there," O'Brien said. "Most of it can be explained by the lighting, acoustics, and things going on aboveground. Some of it, however, isn't as easy to explain."

STRANGE ART BENEATH CAESARS PALACE

O'Brien explored many of the more than 400 miles of tunnels in the subterranean depths of Las Vegas. He followed the paths of floodwaters and of a psycho killer and found many denizens who call the underworld beneath the neon home. He said that since writing the book he has gone back into the channels to see the strange art or to help the homeless people who live there. He escorts friends and journalists into a subterranean tunnel known as the art gallery, which lies under Caesars Palace. It's a place of graffiti-covered walls filled with strange writings.

When asked what was the most interesting or overwhelming discovery he had made in the tunnels under Las Vegas, O'Brien said it was that people were actually living in them. He said the flood channels can fill with water at a foot per minute when it's raining hard. "It's quite a contrast to the world above in the hotel-casinos and the Las Vegas we usually see on TV and in films," O'Brien said.

RANDOM LAS VEGAS HAUNTS

PARANORMAL SIN CITY: Haunted Las Vegas Tours says there are more than 21 places where paranormal activity has been documented in Las Vegas.

MOTEL OF DEATH: On March 22, 1999, actor David Strickland of the TV show *Suddenly, Susan* hung himself with a bedsheet at the Oasis Motel in downtown Las Vegas.

"BUGSY" SIEGEL: Guests lounging by the pool at the Flamingo Hotel & Casino or visiting its garden late at night report seeing his ghost. Siegel, however, was murdered in Los Angeles.

TUPAC SHAKUR: The rapper-actor died on Friday the 13th, 1996, after being gunned down on Flamingo Road. There are reports that his ghost walks in the area late at night and on the balcony of his home.

REDD FOXX: The 1970s star of *Sanford and Son* died of a heart attack on October 11, 1991. Several buyers of his home have claimed it is haunted by a ghost that pulls pranks.

LIBERACE: People report that a ghost can be seen staring into the windows at Carluccio's Tivoli Gardens restaurant, which the famous pianist once owned. Liberace died of AIDS on February 4, 1987. Explaining his weight loss associated with the disease, his manager claimed that the pianist had simply been on a watermelon diet.

ELVIS PRESLEY: The King's ghost has reportedly been seen in a white-sequined suit by stagehands at the Las Vegas Hilton. His ghost has also allegedly been seen on the hotel's top floor, in the basement, and in a freight elevator he once used to avoid fans.

PERSONAL REPORT: BAKERSFIELD'S MYSTERIOUS CHINESE TUNNEL ENTRANCE

Bakersfield, California, is a city with two urban legends: The Lords of Bakersfield and Chinese Tunnels. In my fiction novel *Lords* I dug into the psychological nature of the creepy Lords of Bakersfield mythos of the late 1970s. The legend is that prominent gay men, including a police commissioner and the publisher of the *Bakersfield Californian*, preyed on young boys, sometimes with murderous aims. The book is based on newspaper articles, interviews, and the area's rich seedy history, which dates back to the 1800s. I've explored the other local urban legend too—that Chinese people dug tunnels beneath the city's downtown area. But the Chinese tunnel legend has been somewhat elusive. That's because if there are secret tunnels, people don't really talk about them.

TUNNELING INTO SECRETS

With the Lords of Bakersfield, there are plenty of people who will tell stories. (Whether they're true or not, that's another discussion.) Not so for stories about the Chinese tunnels. Around 2008, in a room that was a mix of 1970s architecture and Chinese décor, I sat at a table with the old Chinese owner of a restaurant named Bill Lee's Bamboo Chopsticks. We were in a conversation about tunnels, and he denied that there had ever been any beneath the city. Never mind that some were being excavated in nearby Fresno. This, while some historians claimed that the dual Chinatowns in central Bakersfield were at one time the largest of their kind west of the Mississippi.

The restaurant owner said, "How would they [the Chinese] have had time to build tunnels? After a long day's work?" He added, "What was there was interconnected basements." He claimed that basements connected apartments that once existed along 18th Street in downtown Bakersfield. Other sources, including a university historian and treasure hunters, have long suggested there were tunnels as well as cellars. One historian said the tunnels radiated outward from beneath an old Land Company building like spokes on a tire. It could be that the local Chinese population is simply being hush-hush about the tunnels. Perhaps they want to save the embarrassment of being associated with the opium smoking, gambling, and prostitution that went on throughout the early 1900s, as described in newspaper accounts of tunnel raids during that period.

SEARCHING BLIND ALLEYS

I led an exploration into some of the basements beneath downtown Bakersfield buildings, hoping to find a tunnel entrance. On that brief journey I was accompanied by Jay Jones of Fox 5 San Diego and an ABC23 cameraman. Unfortunately, though a local mortician claimed he had been in tunnels that had archways scrawled with Chinese lettering, all we could find was cement-covered brick walls. A cover-up? Had the tunnels been closed off?

As a journalist, I could have written a story about basements. But I was after a tunnel story, not a basement story. There just wasn't enough information. Other leads have come up empty. And it never fails—every time someone says they know someone who can get into the tunnels, the lead turns cold. It doesn't help that there's also rumored to be an old Chinese laundry downtown that has three levels of basements. One underground Chinese legend at a time, please.

> **OBSESSIVE BITE:** The first Chinese people in the vicinity of Bakersfield were poverty-stricken migrants from southern China who worked in quartz mines.

THE OSSUARY AT STEPHANSDOM

People's instinct when walking into a place like the Stephansdom in Vienna, Austria, would likely be to look up, not down. That's because when people think of Gothic cathedrals from the 12th century, they don't necessarily consider what might lurk beneath them. Yet below this famous cathedral in the heart of Vienna are crypts jammed with bone-filled pits in what's called an ossuary.

The giant front door of Stephansdom, called the Riesentor, used to have a relic of the ice age hanging above it. The bone of a mastodon had been placed above the door as a sign of past giants that once walked the earth. A strange symbol of the ancients, that bone was perhaps more symbolic of tens of thousands of bones filling the church crypts. Typically, one had to be royalty or pay to be buried within a cathedral crypt. Beneath Stephansdom there are chambers still being used to this day for burial purposes. There's also what's called a ducal crypt for royal bones interred there. More than 70 containers are filled with the hearts, viscera, and bodies of dozens of members of the Habsburg dynasty. And in a darker part of the crypt lie the jumbled bones of more than 11,000 people. In some sections coffins deteriorate, and bones and skulls are stacked as neatly as cordwood.

BUBONIC PLAGUE AND THE STRANGE BONE GUIDE

In 1735, a wave of bubonic plague ravaged Vienna, necessitating a mass burial for the wealthy and paupers alike. Authorities of the time decided to dig massive pits in the crypts of Stephansdom, where bodies were thrown onto massive piles. When the smell of rotting bodies began wafting into the church, prisoners were sent on a hellish mission into the catacombs to scrape the flesh off the bones, many of which were stacked in organized piles. Imagining the gore in such dark, damp, torchlit rooms is unfathomable to most, though tourists continue to visit the dark chambers.

A tourist who recently took a tour of the bone pits of the Stephansdom said she had a very strange feeling in the ossuary. In the cold, lantern-lit catacombs she saw a giant pit filled with a hodge-podge of human bones. The tour guide looked like a messy academic in a rumpled blazer and spoke in a booming voice with a crazy accent that was a cross between Inspector Clouseau and JarJar Binks. The tourist doesn't know why, but she took the tour twice, and it was the same guy both times. Wanting to take some snapshots through the window of one of the bone-filled rooms, she lagged behind the group. She suddenly got a strange feeling—a whispering presence that she could only liken to the tens of thousands of tortured souls cast into the church pits, somehow still present there beneath the cathedral. There were reports that the catacomb entrance seemed hidden away from tourists. A peek at the Stephansdom website (www.stephansdom.at) offers very little about its ossuary, so you should go and explore it on your own to find out what's really there.

OBSESSIVE BITE: Speaking of buildings and bones, in the Czech Republic capital of Prague you can visit the Bone Church, otherwise known as Sedlec, which is decorated with human bones transformed into chalices, chandeliers, coats of arms, and strange art by a woodcarver named Frantisek Rint. Centuries ago, in 1511, a half-blind monk built six giant pyramids of bones in the church, all created using the parts of 40,000 to 70,000 people. In 1278, prior to the building of the church, Abbot Henry visited Jerusalem. He returned with ashes from Golgotha that he spread over Sedlec's ancient cemetery, making it one of the most coveted resting places in all of Bohemia.

COLORADO STUPA AND THE TEMPLE THAT DOESN'T LIKE GIRLS

Stupas were originally simple mud or clay burial mounds. Before the Buddha reached a state of parinirvana he asked that he be buried inside a group of 10 stupas. Over centuries, stupa burial mounds evolved into temples that honored the living and celebrated an awakening of the minds of Buddhist followers. Each stupa is rich in metaphoric shape symbolic of the Buddha, who is crowned and sitting in meditation on a lion throne. The first great stupa to Buddhist teachings in the United States was built at the Shambhala Mountain Center at Red Feather Lakes in northern Colorado in 1988 and consecrated in 2001. The 108-foot-tall stupa is built of concrete developed to last a thousand years. The number 108 is sacred in Buddhism, representing the 108 temptations a person must overcome to reach enlightenment. Buddhist temples often have 108 steps. The Colorado stupa was blessed by the Dalai Lama. It is filled with Buddhist symbols and mysterious carvings. It stands near mountaintops and steep cliffs and is meant to feed off the energy of those surrounding landforms.

Behind the Stupa are trails leading to a smaller Japanese temple. Colorado writer Erika Rae was visiting a friend who had attended a camp behind the stupa. She told Rae the little Japanese temple was not very well known and had a strange dislike of certain people. The friend warned Rae that the goddess of the temple didn't like girls. Not believing her friend, Rae paid a visit to the temple with two girlfriends, taking care to bow as they passed through a series of gateposts. "So we were going up this path. My Filipino friend walked up ahead. My other friend was next to the temple when one of the gates suddenly slammed shut," Rae said. It was daytime and there was no breeze. She said the temple must not like females, because the heavy log gate couldn't have moved by itself.

OBSESSIVE BITE: An unusual feature of the 108-foot-tall Colorado stupa is that it isn't sealed like most Buddhist monuments. The Hall of the Buddha on the first level is open to the public.

MOTHMAN, THE CURSE OF POINT PLEASANT, AND BABY MOTHMAN

In recent years people have reported sighting giant birds soaring over Texas and China, angels gliding across the river Thames, and giant mothlike creatures off the islands of Hong Kong. But nothing comes close to the Mothman legend of Point Pleasant, West Virginia, a place some believe is cursed ground.

Sightings of the legendary Mothman creature began occurring near Point Pleasant in 1966. One of the earliest known sightings, possibly the first, was in the town of Clendenin. A group of men digging a grave claimed that a creature that looked like a brown human being with wings suddenly lifted off from nearby treetops and flew directly over them.

THE SIGHTING THAT SPOOKED A TOWN

November 15, 1966, marks one of the most startling sightings of the creature, one that got people scared that some kind of winged manlike creature was in their midst. It happened when two couples driving near the Point Pleasant fairgrounds decided to park at an abandoned World War II TNT factory that some later called "the birdhouse." The area around the factory contained a few hundred acres of woods, manmade ponds, an animal refuge, domes for storage of weapons materials, and underground tunnels. News reports said the couples saw something strange as they were driving by the site. Brenda Knight, whose brother-in-law was in the vehicle, said the reality was a little different. Knight described the TNT area as an environmentally unsafe, swampy wasteland of abandoned government buildings used by down-and-out kids and teenagers. The TNT factory itself, since torn down, was a huge three- or four-story red-brick building overgrown with foliage and ivy. Knight said the car wasn't driving past the birdhouse; it was already parked. "Two couples were going to make out in this toxic swamp," she said.

The couples reported seeing red eyes peering at them through the darkness. They got out of their car and saw a creature shaped like a man, but bigger, close to seven feet tall, with wings folded against its back. Sensing that the creature might be dangerous, the foursome jumped in their car and sped off. The creature was reported to have chased them at speeds of 100 mph, all while staring in their window. "It could hover and fly over them. They drove directly to a police station," Knight said. The couples spoke with a deputy who thought their story was credible.

NEWELL PARTRIDGE SEES RED EYES

The website PrairieGhost.com claims that Newell Partridge, a building contractor from Salem, West Virginia, 90 miles from Point Pleasant, also saw a strange creature on the same night the couples were chased. At around 10:30 P.M., Partridge had been watching television when the screen went dark and a strange pattern appeared on it. Partridge then heard whining noises, and his hunting dog, Bandit, started howling and making a commotion. When Partridge went outside, he saw the dog looking toward a hay barn that stood about 150 yards away.

Partridge described the whining noises as like the wheezing of a generator winding up. Others have described hearing similar eerie sounds, even shrieking, during Mothman sightings. Curious, Partridge shined a flashlight toward the barn. He discovered two red orbs or eyes that looked like bicycle reflectors staring at him. According to the report, Partridge fled back to his house and called his dog in. But the dog ignored him and chased after the creature. Partridge grabbed a gun but was too afraid to go back outside. He slept with the weapon propped against his bed. His dog, Bandit, was gone the next day.

One of the men in the two couples who said they saw Mothman that same night reported seeing a large dead dog while fleeing the creature. The dog was gone when they went back to look for it. Partridge read about the sightings in the newspaper two days later and immediately thought of his missing dog, Bandit. In telling the story, PrairieGhost.com cited books by early researchers of the supposed sightings and people associated with UFO-related research and possible hoaxes in the area, such as Gray Barker, Loren Coleman, Jerome Clark, and John Keel (author of *The Mothman Prophecies*).

MUTANT BIRD FROM A TOXIC SWAMP?

But what was it the couples and Partridge saw? A batman? An illusion? Something supernatural? The mysterious creature wasn't known as Mothman upon its first sighting—it was given that name by an Ohio newspaper copyeditor who may have thought the name Batman was overused and didn't like the associations of Birdman. "We all thought it was a mutant sandhill crane because of the toxins in the swamp," Knight said. Like many families in the Point Pleasant area, Knight's family worked for the U.S. Defense Department, which used the area to store radioactive components and weapons materials. "That's why we all lived there," Knight said. "The government would transport all these explosives, weapons, and plutonium there."

Knight pointed out, as do Internet reports, that because of the U.S. government's poor understanding of toxins in weapons and raw materials, "when they stocked the TNT in the swamp, the Defense Department decided to dump all this TNT in the ground. It wouldn't go away. The whole area became environmentally unsafe, and people knew that." Knight said the knowledge that the environment was ruined led people who lived in the area to suspect that the creature could be some kind of mutant bird.

The Point Pleasant Depot, which Knight described as a futuristic compound, with its armaments and plutonium, is a well-known U.S. materials stockpiling area. It was where Knight's parents worked, met, and fell in love. She thought it was strange that her parents worked with radioactive material. "My parents were in charge of the disposition of plutonium from World War II. They were really young people with great responsibility. But that was their job."

According to a U.S. Defense news wire, stockpiles of material were assembled at Point Pleasant Depot in the 1940s and 1950s to decrease dependence on foreign sources of certain raw goods in the event of a national emergency or catastrophe. Ferrochrome, one of 42 commodities remaining in the inventory, was once hand-stacked into 40-foot-high piles of ore; 75,000 tons of it was hoarded at the facility. The giant stacks were broken down into smaller piles in 2005.

OBSESSIVE BITE: Sandhill cranes have a wingspan of more than six feet and are known to eat their young.

BUG-EYED MIB: WHO WERE THEY?

By the end of 1967, there had been around 100 credible reports of Mothman sightings. Some thought that Point Pleasant was haunted by the mysterious creature and eventually began to wonder whether it was an alien entity or some kind of strange curse.

The sightings suddenly began to include mysterious men

in black, some with bulging eyes, seen hanging around Point Pleasant. People claimed to see not only see Mothman, but strange lights in the sky, some of them around the TNT area. Even the town's newspaper reporter, Mary Hyde, who covered Mothman stories for the Athens, Ohio, *Messenger*, reported to have run-ins with strange men in black.

In UFO lore, MIB aren't comedic good guys like those portrayed by Tommy Lee Jones and Will Smith in the *Men in Black* films and in series like *The X Files*, but mysterious beak-nosed suit-wearing men driving around in strange cars, eager to make threats. Yet some UFO experts claim that the MIB seen around Point Pleasant were part of an elaborate hoax perpetrated by the very people who create UFO lore. Either way, the strange sightings of the MIB around Point Pleasant, as well as the creepings of UFO lore expert John Keel and UFO prankster Gray Barker, both in the area researching the Mothman events, add to the mystery. Barker and Keel, some believe, would benefit from raising the local panic level. Both were writing books and building popularity as experts on UFOs and urban legends, the very tales they might help create.

BRIDGE COLLAPSE THAT SHOCKED A NATION

Whether the Mothman story is a real event, a supernatural occurrence, part of an elaborate hoax, or some kind of government conspiracy, the recorded sightings tapered off after a horrific tragedy occurred just 10 days before Christmas 1967 in Point Pleasant. On December 15, just as many people were getting off work and were on their way home or running Christmas errands, the aluminum-painted 1,800-foot Silver Bridge, which spanned a portion of the 2,235-foot distance across the Ohio River from Point Pleasant, West Virginia, to Kanauga, Ohio, collapsed. According to reports, 46 people died and nine others were seriously injured. Thirty-one cars, along with the bridge, fell into the icy waters of the Ohio River. Only 44 bodies were eventually recovered.

One man said he heard what sounded like a shotgun volley before the roadway on the bridge tilted in what was described as "surreal slow motion, spilling sparks from a parted power cable into the dusk and ... vehicles onto the weedgrown riverbank and into the 6 mph current beneath." One witness said, "The bridge just keeled over, starting slowly on the Ohio side and then folding like a deck of cards to the West Virginia side."

The *West Virginia Quarterly* in 2001 cited the eyebars that supported the bridge as the culprit. It reported some people saying they heard a sonic boom before the collapse, but according to the *Quarterly*, that wasn't plausible because it would have caused building damage. But if sonic booms routinely caused building damage, there would be widespread evidence of damage from modern jet aircraft.

One man recalled in 2007 that the eyebars were swinging terribly that night, like hands clapping. He wasn't on the bridge when it collapsed, but he had been on it earlier, and he suffered nightmares for years. The Huntington, West Virginia, *Herald-Dispatch* reported in 2007 that it took a long time after the disaster for Christmas to feel like Christmas again for many people in the area.

TWENTY-FIVE RANDOM BRIDGE COLLAPSES

STIRLING BRIDGE: In September 1297, the Stirling Bridge in Scotland is said to have collapsed during a battle between English forces and those of William Wallace and Andrew Moray. The collapse may have been assisted by those defending the bridge.

RIALTO BRIDGE: In 1444, during the wedding of the Duke of Ferrara in Venice, the Rialto Bridge is said to have collapsed under the weight of too many spectators.

YARMOUTH BRIDGE: In May 1845, 79 people drowned after the Yarmouth Bridge in England collapsed from the shifting weight of people on the bridge watching as a circus clown floated downriver in a barrel pulled by geese.

TAY RAIL BRIDGE: A locomotive gained the nickname "The Diver" and was used for more than 20 years after plunging into a Scottish river in December 1879 from the collapse of the Tay Rail Bridge. At least 60 people died. Can you say "ghost train"?

MUNCHENSTEIN RAIL DISASTER: In 1891, a faulty wrought-iron truss caused a train to fall through the center of this bridge in Munchenstein, Switzerland, killing 71.

PONT DE QUÉBEC BRIDGE: In August 1907, the Pont de Québec Bridge, which crosses the lower Saint Lawrence River between the cities of Québec and Lévis, collapsed under its own weight during construction, killing 74 people. In 1916, the same bridge killed another 11 people while the central span was being hoisted into place.

SETA RIVER RAILROAD BRIDGE: A typhoon striking Otsu, Japan, in 1934 wiped out the Seta River Railroad Bridge, killing 11 people and wounding more than 200.

APPOMATTOX RIVER DRAWBRIDGE: In December 1935, a bus drove across the Appomattox River Drawbridge in Virginia while it was open. More than two dozen died.

HONEYMOON BRIDGE: This bridge at Niagara Falls was pushed off its foundations by an ice jam in January 1938. Luckily, no one died. The bridge was eventually replaced by the Rainbow Bridge.

GALLOPING GERTIE: The real name of this aerodynamically-flawed structure in Washington state was the Tacoma Narrows Bridge. A dog was killed when the bridge partially fell in November 1940.

CHESAPEAKE CITY BRIDGE: In July 1942, the tanker ship *Franz Klasen* slammed into the drawbridge supports of the Chesapeake City Bridge in Maryland, causing the structure to fall apart.

LUDENDORFF BRIDGE: This bridge across the Rhine River in Remagen, Germany, collapsed in March 1945 due to a previous battle. The bridge had been under constant artillery assault in several battles between Allied and German forces to control the Western Front. It collapsed 10 days after its capture by U.S. forces as 28 Army engineers were working to strengthen the structure. All of them perished, and 93 others were injured. At one point during the fighting over the bridge, 11 V-2 rockets were fired at it from 120 miles away.

FOOTBRIDGE AT HARROW & WEALDSTONE STATION: This pedestrian footbridge in England was struck by at least one train and collapsed during an accident in October 1952. At least 112 people died.

TANGIWAI RAILWAY BRIDGE: A New Zealand volcano spewed a wall of mud called a lahar that damaged the Tangiwai Railway Bridge minutes before a passenger train passed onto it in 1953. More than 150 people died in the ensuing train wreck.

SIDNEY LANIER BRIDGE: The freighter *African Neptune* knocked out several spans of the Sidney Lanier Bridge in Brunswick, Georgia, in November 1972. Ten people died in the tragedy.

14TH STREET BRIDGE: Air Florida flight 90 struck the 14th Street Bridge spanning the Potomac River between Arlington, Virginia, and Washington, D.C., in January 1982. The plane smashed into the bridge on takeoff, killing 78 people on the plane and four on the bridge, which was destroyed.

AMARUBE RAILROAD BRIDGE: An out-of-service train in Japan crashed into a fish-processing factory after winds collapsed the Amarube Railroad Bridge in 1986. The train conductor and several factory workers died.

KAPELL BRIDGE: More than 70 of 111 famous paintings burned in August 1993 on what was the oldest wooden bridge in Europe, after a cigarette caught the structure on fire. The Kapell Bridge in Lucerne was one of Switzerland's most-photographed attractions.

CSXT BIG BAYOU CANOT RAIL BRIDGE: In 1993, near Mobile, Alabama, a barge towboat struck part of the CSXT Big Bayou Canot Rail Bridge in the fog, knocking the railroad tracks on the bridge out of alignment. Minutes later, Amtrak's Sunset Limited crossed the bridge and derailed, crashing into the water and killing 47 people.

ESCHEDE, GERMANY: More than 100 people died after the axle of a high-speed train broke, causing the train to crash into a bridge pillar, which then collapsed back onto the train in Eschede, Germany, in 1998.

RAFIGANJ RAIL BRIDGE: In 2002, terrorists sabotaged India's Rafiganj Rail Bridge, causing 130 people to die when the luxury train the Rajdhani Express fell off the 300-foot-high bridge into the Dhave River. The train was heading for New Delhi.

KINZUA BRIDGE: A tornado blasting through Kinzua Bridge State Park, Pennsylvania, in July 2003 smashed this historic steel rail bridge.

MINNEAPOLIS I-35W BRIDGE: In August 2007 the Interstate 35W bridge in Minneapolis collapsed under the weight of bumper-to-bumper traffic. More than a dozen people died.

HARP ROAD BRIDGE: A truck hauling an excavator

caused the Harp Road Bridge in Oakville, Washington, to collapse in August 2007. Residents had to make a 23-mile detour afterward.

KASHMIR, INDIA: A bridge crossing the icy Jhelum River, under construction in Indian-controlled Kashmir in the Himalayas, collapsed in November 2008. At least 23 workers were feared dead. A report on Indian bridges claimed they often fall because of shoddy craftsmanship and little regard for safety.

HAUNTING OF THE SILVER BRIDGE

Robert Rimmey, who lives three miles outside Point Pleasant, was 28 years old when he saw the bridge fall and helped rescue a pregnant woman. "I can remember it just like it was yesterday," Rimmey said to the Huntington (W.V.) *Herald-Dispatch*. He said he lost his friend Doc Sanders, a local cab driver who was in the middle of the bridge when it fell.

Charlene Lawson was the pregnant woman Rimmey helped rescue. She told the same newspaper that when the bridge started shaking she threw her car into reverse, but the car stalled and the bridge broke off in front of her. "It's been 40 years, and if a bridge is loaded with cars, I stay way back," she said. "A lot of times, I just get off of it. I just can't cross. Any bridge, it's the same thing."

During the rescue efforts, legends emerged about what divers encountered when they entered the frigid waters of the Ohio River to recover bodies. Catfish the size of cars were reported, and the divers were reluctant to work in the spooky waters. Could there also have been toxic-made monsters lurking in the Ohio River as well as a toxic bird creature?

Some people claim there are paranormal ties between the

Silver Bridge collapse and Mothman. Internet lore suggests that Mothman-type creatures have been seen prior to other disasters as well, including 9/11 and a bridge collapse in Feng-huang, China, in 2007 that killed at least 47 people. A blogger writing about the Chinese bridge collapse stated that the legend of the *fêng huang*—a mythological Chinese bird akin to the phoenix—dates back 7,000 years. According to the *Washington Post*, reporting on the Chinese bridge collapse was banned and reporters were beaten and chased from the area.

STRANGE HAPPENINGS TO THOSE WHO SAW MOTHMAN

Some say that people who have ties to Mothman are part of its curse. Cryptozoologist Loren Coleman compiled a Mothman death list, last updated in 2005, that numbers 84 deaths he believes are tied to Mothman. The list includes victims of the Silver Bridge disaster, cryptozoologists, UFO story writers, and people associated with the film *The Mothman Prophecies* (2002), starring Richard Gere. Could the death list actually be much larger, and what is this so-called curse?

OBSESSIVE BITE: A number of individuals associated with the film *The Mothman Prophecies* (2002) died within a few years of the film's release:

JESSICA KAPLAN, 24: Film crewperson died in a plane that crashed into a Los Angeles apartment on June 6, 2003.

TED DEMME, 38: Died on January 13, 2002, in a charity basketball game. A filmmaker and friend of Mark Pellington, producer of *Yo! MTV Raps*. Pellington went on to direct *The Mothman Prophecies*.

TED TANNENBAUM, 68: Died of cancer on March 7, 2002. He was the film's executive producer.

ALAN BATES, 69: Died on December 27, 2003. He played Alexander Leek in the film.

BETTY JANE MULLIGAN, 82: Died in March 2004. She was an extra in the film.

JENNIFER BARRETT-PELLINGTON, 42: Died on August 3, 2004, after an illness. She was the wife of director Mark Pellington.

MARTIN BECKER, 49: Died on August 13, 2004. He was a special-effects coordinator who lent assistance to the film.

CHIEF CORNSTALK CURSES POINT PLEASANT

Many believe the Point Pleasant area has more than its share of strangeness because a Shawnee chief named Cornstalk may have cursed the area in his dying breaths after he was viciously shot in 1777 while trying to warn Colonials about the conspiring British.

According to the West Virginia Division of Culture and History, Cornstalk was not always friendly toward European settlers. He is said to have led many raids against white settlements after becoming a chieftain in 1763. Born in 1735, he became king of the Northern Confederacy of Indian Tribes, ruling over all the Shawnees, Delawares, Mingoes, Wyandottes, and Cayugas.

In a 1774 battle that some in West Virginia consider the first battle of the American Revolution, Cornstalk led 1,100 braves against Colonial troops at Point Pleasant, but was defeated. The Mothman Museum claims that the battle was related to the

War for Independence because the British were inciting warfare between Native Americans and Colonials to divert attention from the infectious idea of independence.

After losing the battle, Cornstalk pursued a path of peace with Colonials. In 1777, he, along with two companions, went to Point Pleasant to warn Colonials of British attempts to get Indian tribes to wage war against the colonies. Colonials, fearing an imminent Indian attack, captured Cornstalk and his men, imprisoning them at Fort Randolph. One month later, Cornstalk's son, Ellinipsico, came to visit. While he was at the fort, a soldier was killed nearby and another was injured by hostile natives. Angry soldiers rushed into Cornstalk's quarters, and after a brief pause during which Cornstalk calmly faced the angry soldiers, he was reportedly shot a dozen times. Cornstalk's son and two companions were also killed. According to the Mothman Museum, as Cornstalk died, he cursed the land for 200 years. The museum also points out that Cornstalk's curse may have simply been a fictitious plot element in a Point Pleasant play performed in the early 1900s.

OBSESSIVE BITE: President's Curse: There is no known evidence for the claim that Tenskatawa, a medicine man and half-brother of the Shawnee chief Tecumseh, put a 20-year curse on William Henry Harrison and all the presidents following him. While the curse might not be real, it held true all the way through the presidency of JFK. Astrologers believe there are planetary signs for why the curse was broken.

1840: William Henry Harrison—Died of pneumonia one month after inauguration.

1860: Abraham Lincoln—Assassinated by John Wilkes Booth in 1865.

1880: James Garfield—Shot in the back in July 1881.

1900: William McKinley—Shot in 1901.

1920: Warren G. Harding—Heart attack in 1923.

1940: Franklin D. Roosevelt—Cerebral hemorrhage in 1945.

1960: John F. Kennedy—Assassinated by Lee Harvey Oswald in 1963.

1980: Ronald Reagan survived the curse by an inch when a bullet narrowly missed his heart in an assassination attempt in 1981.

COULD CHIEF CORNSTALK BE MOTHMAN?

Strangely, Cornstalk's curse on the land, if it is real, also seemed to affect his rather restless resting place. After being buried at Fort Randolph, his remains were unearthed in 1840 and moved to the grounds of the Mason County Courthouse. When a decision was made to destroy the old courthouse in 1954, what was left of Cornstalk—three teeth and 15 bone fragments—was dug up, placed in a box, and sealed in the center of a four-ton stone monument. Whether Cornstalk's bones will ever again be moved remains to be seen. The question of what happened to most of his bones remains a mystery too. Could it be that Cornstalk himself was the Mothman? Could he have transformed into some sort of interdimensional creature warning of curses and imminent danger, as when he tried to warn the Colonials on the eve of his death?

In another movie-related twist to the Mothman legend, Doug TenNapel, who has worked in television, film, children's books, and comic books and is the creator of *Earthworm Jim*, *Gear*, *Creature Tech*, and other works, in 2002 mysteriously ceased production on his own Mothman film, which he had been working on since the 1990s. According to reports, at least one person related to that film died.

SERPENT OF LIGHT AT KUKULCAN PYRAMID

While modern people may be spooked by strange birdlike entities, the myths, legends, and ghost stories of the ancients are replete with tales of serpents and dragons. At the ancient capital of the Maya known as Chichén Itzá, located on the Yucatán Peninsula in Mexico, tens of thousands of people were sacrificed to forestall the end of the world. Many of those people were killed atop the Kukulcan Pyramid, which twice a year is visited by a serpent of light.

The serpent of light is a snake that, in the form of dancing triangles of sunlight, appears to slither its way down the Kukulcan Pyramid twice each year, at the spring and fall equinox (March 20 and September 21). The pyramid, also called El Castillo (Kukulkan-Quetzalcoatl) or the temple of the Feathered Serpent God, is square at the base, approximately 75 feet tall, and has nine steps. The structure has four 91-foot-long staircases that together total 364 steps. Add the top platform as the final step and you have 365, the number of days in a year. The pyramid was built around A.D. 800.

Kukulcan was also believed to have taken human form as a man. "The Kukulcan was described as a tall Caucasian man with long flowing hair, deep blue eyes, and came from the sea," said writer Steve Alten. Alten, who has worked with the History Channel on the documentary *2012: Doomsday Prophecy*, used his research on the Kukulcan Pyramid for his fiction trilogy, *Domain*. "The first white men didn't come until 500 years until after his [Kukulcan's] passing," Alten said, citing later explorations by Spanish conquistadors in the region. He also noted that Mayans elongated the skulls of their children to mimic the shape of Kukulcan's mysteriously shaped head.

PYRAMID INSIDE A PYRAMID

Alten visited the Kukulcan Pyramid for research around 1998 and again around 2005. He said the pyramid we see today was actually built over a smaller pyramid, but people can no longer climb Kukulcan's stairs, or enter the inner pyramid. Alten described the inside of Kukulcan as a dank, dark place:

> It's like walking through a dark corridor of limestone. The walls are sweating. It's slippery. The corridor ascends up a tight stairwell. I was trying just to not break my neck in there because the Mayans were small people and I have size-12 shoes. The crawlspace between the two pyramids is a sort of antechamber. Inside, there's a figure of a jade jaguar behind steel bars that the Mayans worship.

ANCIENT CLOCK OF THE STARS

Actually a precision clock, the pyramid was built for astronomical purposes. At the vernal equinox (March 20) and the autumnal equinox (September 21), sunlight bathes the western balustrade of the pyramid's main stairway for a brief time in the afternoon. Seven isosceles triangles then form the body of a 37-yard-long serpent that creeps downward until it joins the huge serpent's head carved in stone at the bottom of the stairway. (A quick YouTube search will reveal the entire brief phenomenon to curious searchers.) The pyramid is said to be the symbol of a sun-Pleiades-zenith conjunction. The serpent of dancing light that can be seen slithering along its edge twice a year is a reminder of the serpent-god constellation and the sun's zenith, which together are fixed directly over the pyramid at those times.

"One of the wilder things was going up the pyramid itself," Alten said. The climb up the steps is exhausting and is like climbing a six-story building. There are no guard rails, which could be why people aren't allowed onto the pyramid anymore. Alten said that in the 8th and 9th centuries thousands marched up the pyramid and were sacrificed, just as the film *Apocalypto* depicts. "There's a little chamber on top and you can see the stone is still stained in blood," he said. In his 2006 film *Apocalypto* Mel Gibson used a cast of Mayan descent, and the dialogue is spoken entirely in the Yucatec Maya language.

"SNAKE DAY" AND THE 72-YEAR WINDOW
The World Mysteries website claims that the serpent of light will only be visible during a 72-year window from 1976 to 2048. Directly at the midpoint of that window of time is the year 2012, which is when the Great Cycle of the Mayan calendar ends. On May 20, 2012, the passage of the sun's zenith and the Pleiades constellation will be joined by a solar eclipse. That date will be known as "snake day." Regarding the possibility of an apocalypse in 2012, Alten said he thinks it will be a time of great change that could go either way—it may result in destruction or in renewal. As a writer, he believes the "glass is half empty" aspect of the calamity makes for great reading. Of the Mayans, Alten said, "They're an enigma and a paradox. A people who could come up with all these astronomical findings, yet they couldn't master the wheel." He likened their achievement to mastering Beethoven on the piano but not being able to play "Chopsticks."

OBSESSIVE BITE: Writer Steve Alten has visited Kukulcan twice. He is the author of *The Shell Game*, in which
he claims the world is on the verge of running out of oil.
Although the book sold 30,000 copies, Alten said it was
blacklisted and shut down by mainstream media.

PERSONAL REPORT: BLUE HOLE OASIS, NEW MEXICO

Break down in northern New Mexico in a battered old car and
you just might see a mysterious oasis called Blue Hole where
divers lurk, along with the ghost of a Spanish conquistador who
once may have stopped there for water.

CORONADO AND THE CITY OF GOLD

Searching for Cíbola—the fabled city of gold—in the 1540s,
Spanish conquistador Francisco Vázquez de Coronado passed
through the region of northern New Mexico where the Blue Hole
is located. He crossed the Pecos River on his way to what's now
modern-day Wichita, Kansas. Thinking of Coronado, one of the
earliest European explorers in the region, gives the millions-of-
years-old desert even more of a timeless quality—imagine a man
in a suit of armor, followed by an entourage of more than a
thousand soldiers, natives, and slaves, marching up the dusty
highway toward you.

UNCOVERING BLUE HOLE

Just before you get to the Blue Hole on Interstate 40 there used
to be a colorful billboard advertising the spot. It might still
be there. The sign's bold letters and comic book images read:
"NATURAL," "GREAT FOR SCUBA DIVING AND FUN
FOR THE WHOLE FAMILY," "COME TO THE MYSTE-
RIOUS BLUE HOLE IN SANTA ROSA," "WORLD FAMOUS
GOLDFISH AND DIVING," "SIXTY-FIVE DEGREES AND

EIGHTY-SEVEN FEET DEEP, ONE OF NEW MEXICO'S GREAT NATURAL WONDERS."

The billboard poked above the worn New Mexican countryside near some clumps of weather-beaten houses. It was not far from the towering rise of Tucumcari Mountain—an old Comanche lookout looming 4,999 feet above sea level, where the myth of Tucumcari originates. That's where the Apache warrior Tocom supposedly died while fighting for his Indian princess, Kari. At Tocom's death, Kari killed his victor and then hopelessly stabbed herself, taking her own life. The name originated with her father, an Apache chief, who touchingly cried "Tocom-Kari!" before ending his own life in despair.

Around one side of Park Lake in Santa Rosa, New Mexico, there is a gate onto a dusty road. If you pass the gate and walk a little farther, you will come to a very large hole filled with crystal-clear blue water in the middle of the desert. Cliff walls rise above it, and there is a ledge from which you can jump straight down into the deep, crystalline waters. Scuba divers swim beneath the surface.

MYSTERIOUS CAVES OF THE DEEP

The oasis is a limestone sinkhole fueled by an underground spring. It is shaped like a bell, or a soda bottle, 130 feet in diameter at its largest and 80 feet in diameter at its smallest. The water at Blue Hole is somewhere between 61 and 64 degrees Fahrenheit. The water runs off into nearby Park Lake at an astounding rate. People drive hours to dive at Blue Hole.

The entrances to caves in the depths of Blue Hole are now sealed off, as divers in the 1970s got lost in miles of underwater tunnels that some say stretch as far away as Texas. A mysterious oasis? For sure. The water is far clearer than in nearby Park Lake or the muddy waves of Santa Rosa Lake, built in 1982 to trap the waters of the Pecos River. The *Washington Post* reported in 2006 that toys lie wedged in cracks at the bottom of Blue Hole. Leaves cover the bottom. And after a weekend of dipping into its mysterious waters, divers can usually recognize by name all the fat goldfish that live there. Perhaps this oasis, so strangely cold for the desert, was the reason Coronado stopped in this area. Maybe it wasn't the Pecos River at all, but the mysterious spring waters that fill Blue Hole.

> **OBSESSIVE BITE:** When the author's car broke down in Santa Rosa, New Mexico, in 1996, the mechanic who repaired it drove him to the oasis as a surprise. He said, "If you walk past the lake [Park Lake], you'll find the entrance to something wonderful."

THE CHILL OF EDGAR ALLEN POE'S GRAVE

On a midnight walk in Baltimore you might find yourself in shadowy streets, with hissing manhole covers and people passing in the night. You may not realize that the burial place of one of America's most popular authors of the macabre is nearby, at Westminster Hall. The grave of Edgar Allan Poe, author of such 19th-century American classics as *The Fall of the House of Usher* and *The Cask of Amontillado*, is marked by a ghost-white square marble tombstone. An artistic rendering of Poe's face is carved into the marker. On a ledge surrounding the gravestone people often leave dried flowers—and trinkets. During a recent outing to the site, it was reported that coins, a plastic sun face, and even orange Tic Tacs were left on the grave. Adding to the mystery surrounding, an unknown visitor affectionately referred to as the "Poe Toaster" has paid homage to Poe's grave every year since 1949 with red roses and a bottle of cognac. Poe died in 1849 under suspicious circumstances. He was found delirious and wearing another man's clothes.

A footpath leads from Poe's tombstone around the side of the church, where you will find one grave marker that has been featured in *Ripley's Believe It or Not*: a grave on four pillars that sags as if sadly defying gravity. Below the church is a crypt containing more bodies. The surrounding grounds harbor many tombstones, including one enclosed by a low fence. On one visit, a man saw that on that grave rested a broken portion of a tombstone, and on top of that, a tattered Bible held in place by a brick. Yet Poe's grave is the most mysterious. It imparts a peculiar chill to those who touch it.

RANDOM CEMETERIES FOR YOU TO HAUNT

CEMETERY HIGH: When students look out the windows at Lakes Community High School in Lake Villa, Illinois, they don't just see a football field. Home Oak Cemetery shares the same corner as the high school. Apparently, students walk through the cemetery to get to school.

REAPPEARING CEMETERIES: According to the *Washington Post*, long-lost plantation and farm cemeteries in rural areas are creating headaches for builders. As a result, cemeteries are becoming commonplace amid parking lots and suburban developments in the American South.

MOVIE THEATER GRAVE: In New Brunswick, New Jersey, Mary Ellis's grave has monopolized a parking space for the better part of the 20th century. Once situated outside a flea market, her grave now rests alone in the Loew's Theater parking lot.

PÈRE LACHAISE CEMETERY, PARIS: Here you can find the graves of writer Oscar Wilde, French philosopher Peter Abelard, and even rock star Jim Morrison. People say that even on a gorgeous sunny day there is an eerie sea of gray sculptures to behold. It is said Chopin's grave is always decorated with red roses.

WADI AS-SALAAM: Considered the largest cemetery in the Muslim world, with as many as two million Shiite Muslims buried there, Wadi as-Salaam was the site of a 36-hour graveyard battle between U.S. forces and the Iraqi Mahdi Army in August 2004. Soldiers crept through the cemetery as bats flew out of crypts and graves opened beneath their feet. Militia fighters hid underground and overhead. "It was like New Orleans meets Baghdad," a soldier said to the *Washington Post*.

CITIES OF THE DEAD: Cemeteries in New Orleans, Louisiana, consist of aboveground vaults collectively called "cities of the dead." The dead are buried aboveground because the water table is so high that coffins pop from the ground during wet weather or float if graves are dug too deep. Visit St. Louis cemeteries 1, 2, and 3 near the French Quarter.

SLEEPY HOLLOW CEMETERY: Washington Irving, author of *The Legend of Sleepy Hollow*, about a headless horseman, is buried in this famous and beautiful cemetery up the Hudson River from New York. Irving once wrote a letter saying that it would be a blunder if the cemetery wasn't named after the Sleepy

Hollow Church. Others had wanted to name the cemetery "Tarrytown," after the nearby community.

CHACO CANYON COSMIC RELATIONSHIPS

Major buildings of the Native American Chacoan culture in New Mexico that were built between 900 and 1130 have been found to refer to solar and lunar cosmology in their orientation, internal geometry, and geographic interrelationships with sun and moon cycles.

THE FLAGSTAFF CRATER

A hole in the ground 50 stories deep near Flagstaff, Arizona, is the mysterious home of—nothing. Boring deep into the crater yielded no meteorite.

DEVIL'S HOLE CAVE

In Arkansas there's the opposite of a tall tale—a tale of the deep. Some say that in a cave 200 feet below ground north of Fayetteville, Arkansas, lives a gowrow: a giant man-eating lizard.

WINCHESTER MYSTERY HOUSE

In San Jose, California, Sarah Winchester built a home with 10,000 windows. The tale gets really creepy when you learn there are ghostly reasons for her building 160 rooms, 47 fireplaces, and more. She even had a secret séance room.

THE WHITE HOUSE

It's been rumored that 1600 Pennsylvania Avenue is haunted. Once, while visiting, the Queen of the Netherlands said she saw the ghost of Abraham Lincoln, who knocked on her door.

BIBLIOGRAPHY

BOOKS

Anderson, Fred, and Cayton, Andrew. *The Dominion of War.* New York: Viking, 2005.

Anderson, Mark Cronlund. *Cowboy Imperialism and Hollywood Film.* New York: Peter Lang, 2007.

Benshoff, Harry M. *Queer Images: A History of Gay and Lesbian Film in America.* Lanham, Md.: Rowman & Littlefield, 2006.

Beran, Michael Knox. *Jefferson's Demons: Portrait of a Restless Mind.* New York: Free Press, 2003.

Boulton, James T. *The Letters of D.H. Lawrence.* New York: Cambridge University Press, 1979.

Bowling, Kenneth R. *The Creation of Washington, D.C.: The Idea and Location of The American Capital.* Fairfax, Va.: George Mason University Press, 1991.

Boyd, William Harland. *The Chinese of Kern County, 1857–1960.* Bakersfield, Calif.: Kern County Historical Society, 2002.

Breuer, Hans. *Columbus was Chinese: Discoveries and Inventions in the Far East*. New York: Herder and Herder, 1972.

Brockman, John. *The Greatest Inventions of the Past 2,000 Years*. New York: Simon & Schuster, 2000.

Brown, David E. *Inventing Modern America: From the Microwave to the Mouse*. Cambridge, Mass.: MIT Press, 2002.

Burrage, Henry S., ed. *Early English and French Voyages: 1534–1608*. New York: C. Scribner's Sons, 1906.

Crowther, J.G. *Discoveries and Inventions of the 20th Century*. London: Routledge & K. Paul, 1966.

Demos, John. *Entertaining Satan*. Oxford, U.K.: Oxford University Press, 1983.

Eaton, Margaret. *Innovation in Medical Technology: Ethical Issues and Challenges*. Baltimore: Johns Hopkins University Press, 2007.

Eckert, Allan W. *A Sorrow in our Heart: the Life of Tecumseh*. New York: Konecky & Konecky, 1992

Federal Writers' Project. *The American Slave: A Composite Autobiography: Georgia Narratives*. Westport, Conn.: Greenwood Pub. Co., 1972.

Fitzgerald, Sally, ed. *The Habit of Being: Letters of Flannery O'Connor*. New York: Farrar, Straus, Giroux, 1979.

Fuson, Robert H. *The Log of Christopher Columbus*. Camden, Me.: International Marine Pub. Co., 1987.

Glynn, Ian. *The Life and Death of Smallpox*. New York: Cambridge University Press, 2004.

Habakkuk, H. J. *American and British Technology in the Nineteenth Century*. Cambridge, U.K.: University Press, 1962.

Hamilton, Alexander. *Alexander Hamilton: Writings*. New York: Library of America, 2001.

Hart-Davis, Rupert, ed. *Selected letters of Oscar Wilde*. New York: Oxford University Press, 1979.

Joyce, James. *Letters.* New York: Viking Press, 1957-[66].

Juster, Susan. *Doomsayers.* Philadelphia: University of Pennsylvania Press, 2003.

Karlen, Arno. *Napoleon's Glands and Other Ventures in Biohistory.* Boston: Little, Brown, 1984.

Kelly, John, ed. *The Collected Letters of W.B. Yeats.* New York: Oxford University Press, 1986.

Kerouac, Jack. *On The Road: The Original Scroll.* New York: Viking, 2007.

Krebs, Robert E., and Krebs, Carolyn A., eds. *Groundbreaking Scientific Experiments, Inventions, and Discoveries of the Ancient World.* Westport, Conn.: Greenwood Press, 2003.

Labor, Earle, Leitz, Robert C., and Shepard, I. Milo, eds. *The Letters of Jack London.* Stanford, Calif.: Stanford University Press, 1988.

Marchand, Leslie A., ed. *Lord Byron: Selected Letters and Journals.* Cambridge, Mass.: Belknap Press of Harvard University Press, 1982.

Miller, Edwin Haviland. *Selected Letters of Walt Whitman.* Iowa City: University of Iowa Press, 1990.

Miller, Richard G., and Weigley, Russell F., eds. *The Federal City: 1783–1800.* New York: W.W. Norton and Co., 1982.

Myerson, Joel, and Shealy, Daniel, eds. *The Selected Letters of Louisa May Alcott.* Boston: Little, Brown, 1987.

Naipaul, V.S. *Between Father and Son: Family Letters.* New York: Alfred Knopf, 2000.

Nicolson, Nigel, and Banks, Joanne Trautmann, eds. *The Letters of Virginia Woolf.* New York: Harcourt Brace Jovanovich, 1975–80.

O'Brien, Matthew. *Beneath the Neon: Life and Death in the Tunnels of Las Vegas.* Las Vegas, Nev.: Huntington Press, 2007

Orwell, Sonia, and Angus, Ian, eds. *The Collected Essays,*

Journalism, and Letters of George Orwell. New York: Harcourt, Brace & World, 1968.

President's Commission on the Assassination of President Kennedy [Warren Commission]. *Investigation of the Assassination of President John F. Kennedy: Hearings Before the President's Commission on the Assassination of President Kennedy.* Washington, D.C.: U.S. G.P.O., 1964.

Rollins, Peter C., and O'Connor, John E., eds. *Why We Fought: America's Wars in Film and History.* Lexington, KY: University Press of Kentucky, 2008.

Skinner, Kiron K., Anderson, Annelise, and Anderson, Martin, eds. *Reagan: A Life in Letters.* New York: Free Press, 2003.

Stuhlmann, Gunther, ed. *A Literate Passion: Letters of Anaïs Nin and Henry Miller, 1932–1953.* San Diego: Harcourt Brace Jovanovich, 1987.

Szczeklik, Andrzej. *Catharsis: On the Art of Medicine.* Chicago: University of Chicago Press, 2005.

Thompson, Kristin. *The Frodo Franchise: The Lord of the Rings and Modern Hollywood.* Berkeley, Calif.: University of California Press, 2007

Thorpe, Charles. *The Tragic Intellect.* Chicago: University of Chicago Press, 2006.

Tolkien, Christopher, and Carpenter, Humphrey, eds. *The Letters of J.R.R. Tolkien.* Boston: Houghton Mifflin, 1981.

Twohig, Dorothy, ed. *The Papers of George Washington.* Charlottesville, Va.: University Press of Virginia, 1998.

Usher, Abbot. *A History of Mechanical Inventions.* Cambridge, Mass.: Harvard University Press, 1954.

Ventura, Varla. *The Book of the Bizarre: Freaky Facts and Strange Stories.* San Francisco: Weiser Books, 2008.

Vermes, Geza. *The Complete Dead Sea Scrolls In English.* New York: Allen Lane/Penguin Press, 1997.

Wade, B.F. *Report of the Joint Committee on the Conduct of the War*. Washington, D.C.: Government Print Office, 1865.

Williams, Trevor I. *A History of Invention: From Stone Axes to Silicon Chips*. New York: Checkmark Books, 2000.

Woodward, W. Elliot, ed. *Records of Salem Witchcraft*. Salem, Mass.: Higginson Book Company, 1998.

Zinn, Howard. *A Power Governments Cannot Suppress*. San Francisco: City Lights, 2007.

ONLINE SOURCES

ABC23, Bakersfield, Calif. (www.turnto23.com)

ABC News (http://abcnews.go.com)

Age, The (Australia) (www.theage.com.au)

Alice in Wonderland Syndrome (http://aiws.info)

Amazon.com

American Hauntings (www.prairieghost.com)

American Society for Microbiology (http://newsarchive.asm.org/may01/topic5.asp)

American University (www.american.edu)

Anaïs Nin (www.anaisnin.com)

Andy Colvin (www.andycolvin.com)

Architect of the Capitol (www.aoc.gov)

Associated Content (www.associatedcontent.com)

Australia Travel Blog (http://blog.oztralia.tv)

Bakotopia Magazine (www.bakotopia.com)

BBC News (http://news.bbc.co.uk)

Best Job in the World (www. islandreefjob.com)

Biology News Net (www.biologynews.net)

Blennerhassett Island Curse (http://www.wvghosts.com/stories/story-The_Curse_Of_The_Blennerhassetts-145.php)

Blennerhassett Island State Park (www.blennerhassettislandstatepark.com)

BNET (http://findarticles.com)

Bristol Robotics Laboratories (www.brl.ac.uk)

British Journal of Psychiatry (http://bjp.rcpsych.org)

Buzzle.com

Cambridge University Spaceflight (www.800.cam.ac.uk/page/26/cu-spaceflight.htm)

CBC News (Canada) (www.cbc.ca)

Celebrity Diseases Blog (www.celebritydisease.blogspot.com)

Chicago Sun-Times (www.suntimes.com)

Chicago Tribune (www.chicagotribune.com)

Chinese Medicine News (http://chinesemedicinenews.com)

Christian Science Monitor (www.csmonitor.com)

CNN (www.CNN.com)

Cobworks.com

Daily Mail (U.K.) (www.dailymail.co.uk)

Daily Record (U.K.) (www.dailyrecord.co.uk)

Daily Stab (www.dailystab.com)

Discover Magazine (www.discovermagazine.com)

Discovery Channel (http://dsc.discovery.com)

Doug TenNapel (http://tennapel.nomoretangerines.com)

Face News (Bakersfield, Calif.) (www.facenews.org)

FijiLive (www.fijilive.com)

Filmreference.com

FishLore.com

Flannery O'Connor Childhood Home Foundation (www. flanneryoconnorhome.org)

Fox News (www.foxnews.com)

Free Patents Online: All the Inventions of Mankind (www. freepatentsonline.com)

GameSpot (www.gamespot.com)

GlobalSecurity.org (www.globalsecurity.org)

GoldCoast (www.goldcoast.com.au)

Google (www.google.com)

Grave Mappers (www.gravemappers.blogspot.com)

Green Building Elements (http://greenbuildingelements.com)

Guardian (U.K.) (www.guardian.co.uk)

Hanson Robotics (www.hansonrobotics.com)

Harper's Magazine (www.harpers.org)

Haunted Ohio: Helltown (www.prairieghosts.com)

Hello Kitty Hell (www.kittyhell.com)

Herald-Dispatch (Huntington, W.V.) (www.herald-dispatch.com)

Independent (U.K.) (www.independent.co.uk)

Internet Movie Database (www.imdb.com)

In the News (U.K.) (www.inthenews.co.uk)

IPWatchdog (www.ipwatchdog.com)

Irish Independent News & Media (www.independent.ie)

ITN Headline News (U.K.) (www.itn.co.uk)

Jack's of Fiji (www.jacksfiji.com)

James Joyce and Disease (http://www.racgp.org.au/afp/200808/200808kaplan.pdf)

Japan Times Online (www.japantimes.co.jp)

Jedi Church (www.jedichurch.org)

Jediism Way (www.thejediismway.org)

Jedi Sanctuary (www.jedisanctuary.org)

Job Profiles: Your Guide to Careers and Education (www.jobprofiles.org)

Kern County Pirate Guild (www.myspace.com/piratesofthecountykern)

Kosmix.com

Kungfucinema.com

Lawrence Livermore National Laboratory (www.llnl.gov)

LifeScript (www.lifescript.com/Life/Timeout/Chill/6_Famous_Paintings_of_Women_That_You_Should_Know)

Live Science (www.livescience.com)

Los Angeles Times (www.latimes.com)

Louisa May Alcott's Orchard House (www.louisamayalcott.
org)

Matthew Shaer (http://mattshaer.tumblr.com)

Mirror (U.K.) (mirror.co.uk)

Modern Mechanix: Yesterday's Tomorrow Today (http://blog.
modernmechanix.com)

Morgellons Research Foundation (www.morgellons.org)

Mothman Death List (www.lorencoleman.com)

Mothman Museum (www.mothmanmuseum.com)

MTV (www.mtv.com)

NASA (www.nasa.gov)

National Center for Biotechnology Information (www.ncbi.nlm.
nih.gov)

National Geographic (www.nationalgeographic.com)

National Space Biomedical Research Institute (www.nsbri.org)

National Spasmodic Dysphonia Association (www.dysphonia.
org)

National University of Singapore (www.nus.edu.sg)

NCBuy.com

New York Social Diary (www.nysocialdiary.com)

New York Times (www.nytimes.com)

New Zealand Herald (www.nzherald.co.nz)

Nobel Prize (http://nobelprize.org)

Plain Dealer (Cleveland, Ohio) (www.cleveland.com/plain-
dealer)

Pravda (http://english.pravda.ru)

Reel Ninja (http://reelninja.com)

Retail Week (www.retail-week.com)

Riddles in Stone: The Secret Architecture of Washington, D.C.
(Video: www.cuttingedge.org)

Rob Ossian's Pirate's Cove (www.thepirateking.com)
Rotten Tomatoes (www.rottentomatoes.com)
Salon.com
San Francisco Magazine (www.sanfranmag.com)
Sanrio (www.sanrio.com)
Santa Rosa: the City of Natural Lakes (www.santarosanm.org)
Science Daily (www.sciencedaily.com)
Scientific American (www.sciam.com)
Scientific Electronic Library Online (scielo.br)
Shambhala Mountain Center (www.shambhalamountain.org)
Sleepy Hollow Cemetery (http://sleepyhollowcemetery.org)
Snopes.com
Softpedia (www.softpedia.com)
Son of the South (sonofthesouth.net)
Stephansdom Ossuary (www.stephansdom.at)
Sun (U.K.) (www.thesun.co.uk)
Sydney Morning Herald (www.smh.com.au)
Telegraph (U.K.) (www.telegraph.co.uk)
Temple of the Jedi Order (www.templeofthejediorder.org)
The Nervous Breakdown (www.thenervousbreakdown.com)
Timeout Beijing (www.timeout.com/cn/en/beijing)
Times Online (U.K.) (www.timesonline.co.uk)
Today's Woman Writing Community (www.todays-woman.net)
Tolkien Society (www.tolkiensociety.org)
Toronto Star (www.thestar.com)
Travelers Notebook (http://thetravelersnotebook.com)
UC San Diego (http://orpheus.ucsd.edu)
University of Utah (www.utah.edu)
USA Today (www.usatoday.com)
U.S. News & World Report (www.usnews.com)
Virginia Quarterly Review (www.vqronline.org)
Washington City Paper (www.washingtoncitypaper.com)

Washington Post (www.washingtonpost.com)

WebExhibits.org

West Virginia Division of Culture and History (www.wvculture. org)

Wikipedia: The Free Encyclopedia (wikipedia.org)

Wizrocklopedia (http://wizrocklopedia.com)

World-Mysteries.com

Yahoo News (www.news.yahoo.com)

Yourdailyfact.blogspot.com

YourZombiePlan.com

YouTube (www.youtube.com)

INTERVIEWS

Alexander, Brad. Sr. VP/Pre-Visualization Director, Halon Entertainment. 2009.

Alten, Steve. Novelist. 2009.

Baratz-Logsted, Lauren. Novelist. 2009.

Bartl, Kevin. VP, Communications, Bakersfield Condors ECHL Ice Hockey. 2009.

Bell, Chris. Wastewater operator. 2009.

Blau, Jessica Anya. Novelist. 2009.

Businesswoman. Fiji tourist. 2009.

Carroll, Melinda. Blogger/cover model. 2009.

Colvin, Andy. Photographer, writer, videographer. 2009.

Del Rio, Candy. Burlesque performer. 2009.

Gordon, Maria. Former tarot card reader. 2009.

Heatherwick, Julia. Artist. 2009.

Hemsley, Rik. Sufferer from Alice in Wonderland syndrome. 2009.

Johnston, Autumn. Restaurant manager. 2009.

Knight, Brenda. Writer, editor. 2009.

Mauldin, Aaron. Pawnbroker. 2009

Moore, Emily. KERO News anchor. 2009.

Noble, Fergus. Cambridge University Spaceflight. 2009.

O'Brien, Matthew. Writer, explorer. 2009.

Rae, Erika. Writer. 2009.

Rendell, Joanne. Novelist. 2009.

Saberon, Melody. Advice columnist. 2009

Shaer, Matthew. *Christian Science Monitor* journalist. 2009.

Webster, Matt. Former poop shoveler. 2009.

ACKNOWLEDGMENTS

It's never too late to thank someone. Let me begin.

Brenda Knight called me a spider shaman and provided me opportunity. She answered all my questions about the little things, and we all know those add up. Mark Rhynsburger not only knows how to cook up a good woolly mammoth joke, he challenged me to great depths. Felice Newman, publisher extraordinaire, for believing in weird trivia books. Brad Listi's foreword could have been fifty pages. He's the kind of writer who is like fuel: read him, meet him, see him, and you walk away like you just consumed a six-pack of Monster drinks. His storytelling is a slap in the face because the world needs it. Any related sugar crash just makes you want more.

The Tuesdays are a faraway group of writers in Fresno, California whom I am always with in spirit. The best supporting cast any aspiring writer could need are the group's Bonnie Hearn Hill and Hazel Dixon-Cooper. They wave magic wands and I continue to be mesmerized by their encouragement, direction, and matchmaking.

CSU Bakersfield continues to be the library that I love. Its books inspire. People are like that too: Melody Saberon, Melinda Carroll, Jordan Belardes, Landen Belardes, Matt Munoz (who understands the art of promotion). Thanks to the Irresponsibles, who are mostly just TheNervousBreakdown.com writers in disguise.

ABOUT THE AUTHOR

Historian Nick Belardes turned into a TV/online journalist over-night after blogging his way to success. His articles and essays have since appeared on the homepage of CNN.com and other news sites across America. The founding editor of Face News, an online news and nonfiction site, he also runs a nonfiction writing group. Nick is the author of the first original literary novel on Twitter, *Small Places*, and you can follow his daily rants there: twitter.com/nickbelardes. Nick toils away on this blog, "Weird Stories, Random Obsessions" at www.nickbelardes.com. He lives in Bakersfield, CA.